HIDDEN
MIRTH

THE GRACE BEHIND THE GOODNESS

HIDDEN MIRTH

THE GRACE BEHIND THE GOODNESS

JEFFREY A. MACKEY

Pleasant Word

Pleasant Word (a division of WinePress Publishing, PO Box 428, Enumclaw, WA 98022) functions only as book publisher. As such, the ultimate design, content, editorial accuracy, and views expressed or implied in this work are those of the author.

Unless otherwise noted, all Scriptures are taken from the Holy Bible, New International Version, Copyright © 1973, 1978, 1984 by the International Bible Society. Used by permission of Zondervan Publishing House. The "NIV" and "New International Version" trademarks are registered in the United States Patent and Trademark Office by International Bible Society.

Scripture references marked KJV are taken from the King James Version of the Bible.

Scripture references marked NASB are taken from the New American Standard Bible, © 1960, 1963, 1968, 1971, 1972, 1973, 1975, 1977 by The Lockman Foundation. Used by permission.

ISBN 1-4141-0590-8
Library of Congress Catalog Card Number: 2005908590

DEDICATION

I dedicate this little volume to my sisters and brothers in Christ who have trusted me with their congregations while they have been on sabbatical or holiday. Knowing I am blissfully happy as a college dean and professor, they know I am not looking to take their job! I am always honored to minister to another congregation (or a repeat assignment) and I am always delighted to know that someone else is pastor! And so, to the Rev'ds Victor Austin, James Heron, Douglas Holmes, Joan Jackson, Thomas Miller, Frank Walner, and Roberto Felicie I dedicate my efforts.

Thank you dear friends for the privileges you afford me to celebrate the mass and preach the Word. May continued blessings attend your ways.

A special thanks to the personnel of Blackfriar Books in Woodstock, New York for their interest in seeing these sermons in print. They have carried the cost of this venture.

And you would not be holding this work if two dedicated proofreaders had not scanned the manuscript several times, Mrs. Maxine Moore, of Trinity Episcopal School for Ministry, and my wife LaVonne. Thank you, good ladies!

TABLE OF CONTENTS

INTRODUCTION

Since July of 1999 I have been privileged to travel up and down the Hudson River Valley of New York State supplying at the altar and preaching for Episcopal priests as they vacation, take study leave, are on sabbatical, or do any number of other things demanded of a parish priest.

I have met the most incredible people. I have enjoyed ministry in some of the loveliest churches in America, and I have had the distinct privilege of preaching the Scriptures to these wonderfully willing-to-listen people. I am a preacher who happens to be a priest. I trained to be a preacher, and I have spent my entire adult ministry of thirty years, preaching. I have been convinced that preaching is a noble calling, modeled by none other than our Savior Himself, and certainly by apostolic and patristic saints as well.

Fifteen years ago when I was in the process of training candidates for ordination in the Christian & Missionary Alliance, the denomination I then served, I was assigned the task of working with candidates to sharpen their preaching skills. To begin the book I wrote at that time, I quoted from a long-time friend of mine, Dr. James Montgomery Boice. His words are as apropos today as when they were written decades ago:

"Over the years I have developed a number of concerns for which I am nearly always ready to go on crusade. One is the place of scholarship in preaching. We have a pernicious doctrine in contemporary evangelicalism- I do not hesitate to call it that- which says that if a minister is average in his skills and intelligence, he should take an average church. If he is above average, he should take a larger church. If he is really exceptional-if he is keen about books and simply revels in the background, content, and application of the Word of God-he should teach in a seminary. Ugh! I am convinced that those with the very best minds and training belong in the pulpit, and that the pulpit will never have the power it once had (and ought to have) until this happens."

I found a moving and wonderful ordination hymn some years ago. This, too, celebrates the wonder and richness of the act of preaching. It may be sung to the tune *REGENT SQUARE* or to *HYFRYDOL.*

Grant us, Lord, the joy of preaching
All the truths Thou dost impart.

That Thy precepts may be planted
In the depths of every heart.
Alleluia, Alleluia, Savior of the World Thou art.

Grant us, Lord, the joy of teaching
Faith and hope and Christian love.
While Thy Holy Spirit's favor
Rests upon us, from above.
Alleluia, Alleluia, May we ever faithful be.

Grant us, Lord, the joy of healing
All the hurts of humankind.
May we, in Thy glorious Gospel,
Holiness and wholeness find.
Alleluia, Alleluia, Love with heart, and soul, and mind.

As Thy martyrs and Apostles
Witnessed in the days of yore.
May we spread salvation's story
Unto earth's remotest shore.
Alleluia, Alleluia, Serving Thee, whom we adore.

I must also share that these written versions of the homilies are from the preaching notes I use. I do not like to be read to, nor to read to others, so I preach eye-to-eye and I preach to the people entrusted to my care. Therefore I do not possess manuscripts of what I say. The written version is therefore much shorter than the generally 15 – 17 minute sermons I preach, and they cannot carry the passion and the emotion of the spoken word.

Phillips Brooks the famous Episcopalian preacher defined preaching as "Truth through personality." I have held to this for over thirty years, and when that personality is absent (as in the printed page) something of the preaching is lost as well.

The motivation for this series of annual sermons is: first, to honor the churches I am invited to serve; second, to record the gist of the sermons preached since many ask for the outlines; and, finally, to record some of the wonderful poetry and quotations I am led to use. Many are helped by this, and I am forever grateful that I took a Doctor of Ministry degree in a field called "Poetry as Ministry." It has not failed me.

Peace to you as you are confronted with the word of God and my feeble attempts at expounding it.

—Jeffrey Allen Mackey+
Pentecost 2005

The author has taken every avenue to find the source of quotes and poems. Where these have been found, they are listed with gratitude. Should a reference not be included, the author is anxious to hear of its source so it may be added in subsequent volumes. All quotations from the Bible are the author's own translations.

CHAPTER 1
THE FIRST SUNDAY
OF ADVENT

St. Gregory's Church, Woodstock, New York
Isaiah 2:1-5; Psalm 122; Romans 13:8-14
Matthew 24:37-44

We enter the Advent season this morning. We are challenged by church history to look back to an Incarnation event of 2,000 years ago, while looking forward to an eschatological event sometime in the future of time. The season is designed to make us mature; to change us; to develop our Christian lives-to *make us*, in other words.

Isaiah's familiar prophecy we read is one of visionary inclusiveness as "all nations will flow" to the mountain of the God of Israel. And the prophecy captures our need for and the provision of *an extensive perspective.* We are to come and "walk in the light of the Lord." Walking in the light is vastly different than fumbling in the dark or groping in the dusk. Walking in the light is not necessarily seeing the light itself, but seeing everything else more clearly because of the light. The Old Testament prophet would have spoken of insight as a gift of God for those who would see more than the surface.

Contemporary Christianity is very surface-oriented. "What you see is what you get," has become a confession of goodness in the religious sphere. When, in actuality, the Christian faith seems to say what you get is far beyond and far deeper than what you see.

William Blake captured this when he wrote of the five senses (taste, sight, smell, hearing, touch) as the "dim windows of the soul," and challenged us to see with more than our eyes, for seeing only with the eyes may lead us into error and falsehood. Blake's words:

> Life's dim windows of the soul,
>> Distort the world from pole to pole.
> And goad us to believe a lie
>> When we see with, not through the eye.

God's intent is for us to see through the eye with the vision of the conscience. And Isaiah aptly agrees, "Come, let us walk in the light of the Lord." Walking in the light of the Lord opens doors otherwise shut and enlightens paths otherwise disguised.

Possibly the hymn-writer captures the rewards of such walking when we sing

> Walk in the light, so shalt thou know
>> That fellowship of love
> His Spirit only can bestow,
>> Who reigns in light above.

Walk in the light! And thou shalt find
    Thy heart made truly His.
Who dwells in cloudless light enshrined
    In whom no darkness is.

Walk in the light! And thou shalt own
    Thy darkness passed away,
Because that light hath on thee shown
    In which is perfect day.

Walk in the light! And thine shall be
    A path, though thorny, bright:
For God by grace shall dwell with thee
    And God Himself is light!
              —Bernard Barton 1784-1849

Perhaps C. S. Lewis sums up this lesson best with the insightful words, "I believe in Christianity as I believe that the sun has risen not only because I see it but because by it I see everything else."

Paul in Romans deals with the "putting on of Christ" as in the putting on of new clothes. You remove the old and replace them with something new. In the Christian case, it is the *explicit façade of Christ Himself.* There is so much of the other which is removed (hence Advent points backward) and so much to put on (and hence Advent points ahead).

In *The Voyage of the Dawn Treader,* C. S. Lewis tells this story:

"'Well, exactly the same thing happened again, and I thought to myself, oh dear, how many skins have I got to take off? ... So I scratched away for the third time and got off a third skin, just like the two others, And stepped out of it. But as soon as I looked at myself in the water, it had been no good.

'Then the lion said, You will have to let me undress you....

'The very first tear he made went so deep that I thought it had gone right into my heart. And when he began pulling the skin off, it hurt worse than I've ever felt...And there it was lying on the grass: only so much thicker and darker, and more knobbly looking than the others had been....'After a bit the lion took me out and dressed me... in new clothes – the same I've got on now, as a matter of fact.'"

The explicit putting on is done for us as God removes the former things and clothes us with himself for these latter days.

The Gospel is profound. It has been used to beat people over the head with "second coming" fear and fantasy, and yet its lessons are simple and meaningful if we will pause before these words of Christ Jesus. So much is written about this eschatological coming of Christ, that we fail to realize that the Word became flesh – we have become so very adept at making it words again!

Jesus never says speak or listen for the end is coming, but rather watch. God is working a cosmic drama out which can only be discerned by vision. It is the challenge to an *expectant hope*. Watch. Just watch. Watch for the otherwise hidden hand of God; for the purposeful good things that come forth from bad things; for the providence which parades as coincidence; for the personal touch to all things which appear so inorganic. Watch for when we don't expect, then will the Christ appear.

One writer says, "We like to fit and manage life rather than to wait for it to unfold. When Buddha asked a question similar to the one Jesus asked: 'who do people say that I am?' his disciples all gave reasons… 'Oh you're this,' or 'Oh you're that…' The Buddha replied, 'I am awake.' To be awake is to be vigilant and active."

So men and women, here we are on the threshold of Advent. And I am reminded of Robert Lewis Stevenson, growing up in Scotland at the turn of the century. Each night in his small village he would look out onto the streets below as the lamplighter would move from pole to pole to illumine the dark walkways. He remembered saying to his mother, "Look mother, there is a man down there who punched holes in the darkness."

And this Advent we are called to punch holes in the darkness for the light of Christ to be cast in long bright beams across the human landscape. And as our collect of the days so poignantly says, "Give us grace to cast away the works of darkness, and to put on the armor of light." Amen!

CHAPTER 2
THE SECOND
SUNDAY OF ADVENT

St. Gregory's Church, Woodstock, New York
Isaiah 11:1-10; Psalm 72; Romans 15:4-13
Matthew 3:1-12

Peering into the mists of gray
That shroud the surface of the bay,
Nothing I see except a veil
Of fog surrounding every sail.
Then suddenly against the cape
A vast and silent form takes shape,
A great ship lies against the shore
Where nothing has appeared before.

Who sees the truth must often gaze
Into a fog for many days;
It may seem very sure to him
Nothing is theré but mist-clouds dim.
Then, suddenly, his eyes will see
A shape where nothing used to be.
Discoveries are missed each day
By men who turn too soon away

—Clarence Edward Flynn

Advent is a time of staring into the fog-both the fog of the long past and the Pauline "dark glass" of the future. It is no mistake that we are brought back to the original incarnation each year and no mistake, for sure, that we are reminded again and again that there is a dramatic doctrine still to find its actual outworking in the Eschaton of God.

The great Oxford writer, Dorothy Sayers aptly concluded that the "doctrine is the drama," which is really sought by humanity. And Advent reminds us of Biblical doctrine which is as dramatic as drama gets.

One contemporary writer humorously puts it this way, "If the three wise men were three wise women, they would have planned their route, asked directions, arrived on time, brought practical gifts, and there would be peace on earth!" But we are stuck with wise men, smelly stables, a crying baby, a virgin mother, and a most perplexed step-father. And these are the facts, folk. And they bring us to the questions of truthful doctrine.

Isaiah draws us to the question of how shall this righteousness conquer and reign in light of the reality of our fallen-ness? For those who will know the slaughter of the innocents, the massive Crusades, the Inquisition, the Holocaust, World Wars, contemporary terrorism, and on and on-how can this be rectified? Can wrongs be righted and right be rewarded? And the

Prophet assured us that it is an established reality that will unfold.

Paul sees in this incarnate Christ the oneness of humanity. There is now no Jew or Greek; and calls all to "let all the peoples praise him!" And there will be joy and peace in believing – not all the answers – but an honoring of all the questions – an acknowledgment of the fog. We are challenged to recognize that the actual must never overcome the divinely intended. Advent tells us God's will, will be done!

And this is the marvelous Gospel record of the flea-bag John the Baptizer, who comes proclaiming the greatness of the Lamb of God who takes away the sins of the world. And the one to whom he points looks like a common Galilean – not a messianic deliverer. The one who will baptize you with the Holy Spirit and with fire looks like a commoner to me! He is shrouded in a fog.

Is it possible that this one, this Jesus Bar Mary is exactly who he says he was because he appeared the way he did? Could the humble shroud of the barn and the birth merely call us to look longer to see clearly?

I have been unable to shake the lessons of two contemporary poems relating to seeing Jesus Christ, the incarnate second person of the Holy Trinity more clearly. The first is by John David Burton. You have heard me quote him before – he was one time Poet-in-Residence at Princeton University. He writes,

He leaves the house, neglecting to close the door,
Thus blows in the wintry wind to chill the others.
They call to Him in irritation, "Damn it, Jesus!
Close the door! Were you born in a barn?"

He comes back in to give reply to their scolding.
"As a matter of fact I *was*, born in a barn, that
is. My folks had gone to Bethlehem at tax time.
Joseph was of David's clan, thus paid tax in the City
of David. Mary was well along in carrying unborn
me, but taxes had to be paid on time in Rome.
There was not a room to be had, but a kind desk clerk
said there was room in the barn out back,
so Mary and Joseph bedded down there, on the
hay
they say, her water broke and there I was, bawling,
squirming, groping for a nipple in the night.
Since you ask, yes, I was born in a barn."

Churchmen these days seldom ask about the barn.
They ask about the Building Fund for a new
sanctuary
to replace what looks like a useful worship place,
but which churchmen say is liturgically incorrect.
A new and nobler room for worship, churchmen say
will make for grander preaching and more moving
of
The Spirit.

Churchmen ask about the budget for next year
and
will there be money for salary raises for senior
clergy at least and new vestments all around.
All the while, the poor of earth go by, homeless
in the winter street. At the Hyatt Regency there
is no room. Where I live in Kentucky fine barns are
built to shelter horses and to dry tobacco.
Not many barns are open to the poor these days.

I wonder whether Jesus hangs around the Church
waiting for someone to ask, "Were you born in a
barn?"
If we give Him time to answer, will He say
"Why yes, I was. Do you know the meaning of
that?"
They asked Him once, in irritation, "Jesus Christ,
were you born in a barn?"
Churchmen these days seldom ask about the barn.

The barn is a fog which shrouds Jesus and we are
called to look long to see clear.

And the second contemporary challenge is addressed to Mother Mary, and its questions too, call us
to a long Advent look…

Mary did you know,
That your baby boy would one day walk on water?
Mary did you know,

That your baby boy would save our sons and
daughters?
Did you know
That your baby boy has come to make us new?
That this child you deliver
Will soon deliver you?
Mary did you know,
That your baby boy will give new sight to the
blind man?
Mary did you know,
That your baby boy would calm a sea with his
hand?
Did you know,
That your baby boy has walked where angels trod?
And when you kiss your little baby
You've kissed the face of God?

Mary did you know,
That your baby boy is Lord of all creations?
Mary did you know,
That your baby boy would one day rule the
nations?
Did you know,
That your baby boy was heaven's perfect Lamb?
And the child you are holding
Is the great "I Am?"

Mark Lowrey

"Who sees a truth must often gaze
Into a fog for many days…"

May we give ourselves to intensive gazing into the fog of divine paradox and come forth with a clearer view of the dramatic doctrine of the Incarnate Jesus, the coming King. Amen!

CHAPTER 3
THE FOURTH
SUNDAY OF ADVENT

St. John's Episcopal Church, Kingston, New York
Isaiah 7:10-17; Psalm 24; Romans 1:1-7 & Matthew 1:18-25

King Ahaz and God have a discussion. It is recorded by prophet Isaiah in our text of the morning. The outcome of the give and take is that God will cause a virgin to conceive as a sign of God's own faithfulness, and the record of the fulfillment of the promise is in the Gospel record of the morning. The orthodox doctrines of 2,000 years of church history have celebrated the virgin conception and birth of Jesus of Nazareth, Christ (or God) incarnate. So powerfully was this believed that Mary was called the *Theotokos* or the "God-bearer," thus protecting the belief in the deity of Jesus Christ.

But let's leave some of this heavy theology this morning and see the conversation between Ahaz, King of Judah, and God. Ahaz is not the kind of person you would want as King. He had sacrificed his first-born child to the god Molech and had also mixed his Hebrew worship with the worship of the Canaanite fer-

31

tility rites. He was into some of those sexual worship styles. He was a religious pervert – far from a faithful Jew.

To get Ahaz's attention, God directs him to ask for a sign to prove that God is who he says he is; and, with a false humility and a hypocritical piety, Ahaz responds that he doesn't want to test God. In actuality he was admitting that he didn't really believe in the God of the Hebrew people – at best Ahaz's god was a distant deistic figure who was irrelevant to the historic matters at hand.

The give and take is captivating. One sees God as saying "Go ahead, ask me something – anything – and have I got something to show you." It is a divine taunt – God is ribbing Ahaz, playing the stronger partner, teasing him with full intent of surprising him with the response. God's playfulness will be matched by His production.

Ahaz will have none of it, and in a superficial piety dismisses God with a false spiritual humility. "I will not put the Lord to the test." Why not Ahaz, everyone else in history has – why be different? You know you want to! Give it up, Ahaz – ask what God directs. In his not wanting to put God to the test, he fails the first and major requirement of God for ongoing relationship, and that is obedience. The goodness of God in grace invites the faithfulness of humanity in loving obedience. Ahaz won't play God's celestial, historic game.

God's response is, well, as God's response always is, "I'll do it myself." And God breaks a number of established rules.

First, God reveals what He plans to do in quite complete detail. "A virgin shall conceive and bear a son and shall call him Emmanuel." God doesn't usually give us sure clear leading. Often the leading of God is clouded, calling for faith in the fog and obedience in obtuseness. But God, in playing the game with Ahaz shows him exactly what the plan entails. God gets the last laugh.

Second, God breaks rule number two, virgins don't conceive. It is as if God needs a sex education class. After all, Lord, you made them male and female with all the working parts – do we really need to tell you how it works? Virgins are, well, virgins.

My favorite poet, John David Burton has captured this in a wonderful way in a poem entitled "Prenatal":

And God said,
"Spirit go! Go to My chosen, Mary, and get her
with Child."

And Spirit said,
"Who? Me? You never asked this of Me before.
It is not the sort of thing I am good at nor
do I like. I have no time for women, busy as
I am with the universe.
Intercourse will interrupt My important Life

and work, plus the resulting obligations.
Send someone else. You have angels by the score
who never lift a hand to help, just praising
You the livelong day. You and I are much too
close for Me to leave Our Heaven for earth."

And God said,
"Your intimacy with Me is the reason, can't You
see, for You to go.
You cannot stay close to Me and stand afar off
from people, not even a village girl.
You will have some help. Joseph will stand in
for You, to feed and change the Child, teach
Him the carpenter's trade. But for the Grand
Conception, I want You there."

And Spirit said,
"But what will people say? You know how they
talk!"

And God said,
"Let them talk."

And Spirit said,
"All right, if that is the way You want it.
Still I do not like it.
To have Me beget a Child seems a shoddy way
for You to break in on history and the world."

And God said,
"It is My way. Spirit, go!"

Then there is the third breaking of the rules. In the eighth century before Christ, you could not predict the gender of a child. It just can't happen. And God tells Ahaz, "she will bear a Son." Impossible. Unheard of. It just doesn't happen, and God breaks the rules.

Finally, and as we all know, God just doesn't become human. Emmanuel is an impossibility. There is just no such thing as an incarnation – God in the flesh is God who ceases to be God. And God laughs at His plan, and puts it into effect anyway. And 70 years later John would write in his Gospel, "And the Word became flesh and dwelt among us." The breaking of the rules results in the salvation of the world.

Is this God toying with Ahaz? Yes, yes, a thousand times yes. For when we say God can't do something, it is precisely when God does something. It is the foundation of the Christmas miracle and mirth.

Years ago a priest by the name of David Edman served in Stone Ridge. His wee book *A Bit of Christmas Whimsy* begins with a few wonderful statements – they are truths which will cause us Christmas laughter right from the heart of God:

"Have you ever considered the whimsy involved in that very first Christmas gift of all? I mean, specifically, the manner in which it was given. Not that the gift itself was entirely whimsical. It was, more or less, what we'd always needed.

But the wrapping of it! Mere wood and straw. It was as though the fragility of the thing had something to do with it, truth being exceedingly fragile. Yet surprising wouldn't you say? A deceptive bit of packaging for such a lavish gift. And the surroundings! All that braying and mooing. Even cackling. I wouldn't be surprised. And that amoniacal barnyard odor. And the rustics barging in. And the sounds of revelry from next door.

Really, the entire episode was engineered in a most whimsical manner. So much so, that one is led to suspect a sort of divine humor behind it all.

A surprising idea, perhaps. And more surprising still when one considers that, if this be so, there remains the possibility of a fundamental merriment under everything that exists – everything, everything, everything.

One could even suppose that the molecules dance to some cosmic gigue, that the chromosomes form a garland about some quintessential joy, and that beyond the rim of space there abides an eternal good laughter which promises…that all will be well….

Count upon it, say those who know more about these things than I, Christmastide is the time when heaven forces its joy upon us. Not directly, to be sure. But in a roundabout fashion, through an unconscionable assortment of pranks and wiles….

[There is] that very Christmas whimsy which I personally find myself too timid to believe and too terrified to deny."

Men and women – Christmas will follow this fourth Sunday of Advent and will bring with it the terror and the joy of believing that God has visited us – and we'll never be the same. Amen!

CHAPTER 4

FIRST SUNDAY AFTER CHRISTMAS

St. John's Episcopal Church, Cornwall, New York
Isaiah 61:10-62:3; Psalm 147; Galatians 3:23-25; 4:4-7
John 1:1-18

It was a year ago today that in an ice storm a small number of us huddled in the chancel to worship and hear a few words spoken on the Gospel record of the day. We return on this First Sunday After Christmas to the texts which remind us of the human emphasis of the divine incarnation. That it was all of God's doing cannot be questioned. That it was and is all for human benefit is unparalleled in any religious system or teaching in the world.

The human condition is addressed by God-become- man in Jesus of Nazareth-for "His name shall be called 'Jesus,' for he shall save his people from their sins..." And again, "God so loved the world that He gave His only begotten son that whosoever believes in Him shall not perish but have everlasting life." And then in the Epistle record of the day we are reminded by Paul that this Incarnate One was "born of a woman to redeem those under the law…" God's doing, human benefit. [This certainly fits the human desire to get something for nothing].

And so we turn to the metaphors of need and provision in the lections of the day. First, we've been invited to a celebration for which we are not properly clothed. Prophetically foundational for the parable of Jesus regarding the marriage supper, we are told that the natural dressing is inadequate for the celebration for which we are invited. Note that we are therefore to be clothed with garments of salvation and robes of righteousness. They are new clothes – with a divine origin and provision.

In his book *The Voyage of the Dawn Treader,* C. S. Lewis has his major character speak in the presence of the lion, the Christ figure:

"'Well, exactly the same thing happened again. And I thought to myself, oh dear, how many skins have I got to take off?…So I scratched away for the third time and got off a third skin, just like the two others, and stepped out of it. But as soon as looked at myself in the water I knew it had been no good.

'Then the lion said, You will have to let me undress you….

'The very first tear he made was so deep that I thought it had gone right to my heart. And when he began pulling the skin off, it hurt worse than anything I've ever felt….And there it was lying on the grass: only ever so much thicker and darker and more knobbly looking than the others had been....

'After a bit the lion took me out and dressed me.... in new clothes—the same I've got on now, as a matter of fact.'" The old clothes are gone – we are dressed by God in the clothing which is provided by heaven. When I was a child in Sunday school, we used to sing "Oh the best thing in my life, I ever did do, was to take off the old clothes and put on the new." The theology of the song was a bit Pelagian, but the concept of being clothed in righteousness is as Biblical as it can be and it is a metaphor for what Christ has done for us.

Then in the Epistle we find that we have been called to a family into which we have not been born, and therefore we are granted adoption. God's covenants of the old dispensation were through Israel, and his new covenant grafts us in and adopts us into a family through which he had been accomplishing his purpose for thousands of years. And there are such wonderful blessings to the adopted – a few moments of meditation could bring many to mind.

I am reminded of a little Protestant elementary school boy who after a number of years was adopted by Catholic parents in Ireland. Students at his new school would taunt him and harass him for being adopted, and he would run home crying many afternoons.

One day though, he boldly came through the door laughing at the top of his lungs. His father inquired as to the source of his good humor, and the little chap replied, "I finally told all those other boys that since they were born into their families, their parents had to love them. But since I was adopted, I was chosen by you to be loved." The wonderful benefits of being adopted into the family of God are evident.

Finally, we've been called to a relationship with God from whom we have been estranged, and therefore we are visited by that God Himself. The celebration of today, and yes, these twelve days, is that the second person of the Holy Trinity took on flesh [carne as in chili *con carne*] and became incarnate.

Commenting on Galatians 4:4 Dr. John Daivd Burton, one-time Poet-in-Residence at Princeton writes,

> God, we have found You out, learned You could not do on Your Own what You wanted done above all else, to let Yourself be seen in a Form so fair that human eyes would look again, again, and yet, again, to let Your Voice be heard in a voice so clear that – above all sounds of hate –human ears would listen, listen for the love.

> All of this You wanted, and You could not do it on You Own, unable – earthworm like – to reproduce Yourself with Yourself alone. Even You, the Lord of Life, cannot do it on Your Own.

For You to be made Flesh, a peasant girl is needed, a girl quite like all the women ever born to bear daughters and sons, to nurse them in the night, watch them grow, then let them go to a world which often slays the children.

You, O Lord, cannot come among us except as You are birthed as we are birthed, "of a woman made." You, Who rounded the earth in the hollow of Your Hand, could not come to earth except as You were willing to round the belly, swell the womb of a peasant girl.

All year long the preacher's word tells of God, high and holy and lifted up, apart from us. The Christmas word is "God Plus Mary Equals Jesus."

Theological lessons, yes. But infinitely more than this – metaphors of God's doings for us. For us – that is the wonderfully Christmas gift we are called to receive. For we have been clothed, adopted, and visited. All we ever need has been provided.

A. B. Simpson, the founder of the school at which I teach simply stated it this way one Christmas, "In the heart of man a cry; in the heart of God, supply." Amen!

CHAPTER 5
THE FIRST SUNDAY
AFTER THE EPIPHANY

Holy Cross Episcopal Church, Kingston, New York
Isaiah 42:1-9; Psalm 89:1-29; Acts of the Apostles 10:34-38
Matthew 3:13-17

During Christmas we might often hear the question, "What do you give to someone who has everything?" It is legitimate in our day of gross materialism where we are defined by what we have. I am always particularly taken by the Lexus commercials where wives, husbands, and college-age daughters are given brand new cars for Christmas – a parent or spouse can go and spend $40,000.00 without anyone else in the family knowing about it. Maybe I live on a different level than this. But just what do you give to someone who has everything? That is the Christmas question.

There is an Epiphany question which is quite different than this but takes the same form. What do you give to a God who gives everything? And Epiphany calls us to ask that question of Jesus Christ. According to Scripture God, in Christ, gives everything. Without our being recipients, we have nothing. Everything we have as Christians has been given to us. And so the question becomes hauntingly inviting on this first Sunday after the Epiphany.

Note the words of Jesus in the Gospel record of the day. Speaking of his own baptism by John he says, "It is necessary for us to fulfill all righteousness...." Jesus is indicating that his act of being baptized fulfills the demands of righteousness.

On the basis of this, let us look at the three texts of the morning. First Isaiah's prophecy is telling in that over and over and over again we are told that "He will..., He will,...He will..." do thus and so. This is a Messianic prophecy concerning Jesus who will do what needs to be done. Jesus Christ of Nazareth will do what the human race needs to have done for it. This flies in the face of our human and national tendency to do it ourselves. It is a declaration of the grace of God – a statement that God gives everything you and I need.

Spiritually the church of 2,000 years has successfully made us guiltily fearful that we have not done enough for God and the church. While touting grace the church has pushed a works righteousness. Jesus' own words at his baptism make plain that we cannot fulfill righteousness – he already has. The prophet proclaims it!

Then in the Acts passage of the day we are told that "God shows no partiality...," and that Jesus is "Lord of all." There is no one outside the effects of the work of Christ. But this, too, is discomforting to those of us who have been taught that we are right and all others wrong.

This is the scandal of God's grace. Graham Johnston in *Preaching to a Postmodern World* writes, "Salvation based on one's good works is sensible. Grace, like life, is messy." God's doing it all and Jesus Christ being Lord of all is theologically imprecise and ethically frustrating. If indeed all of this is true, then to whom do I compare myself to come out looking better than they?

And this leads us back to the Gospel of the day. Jesus plainly says, "This is necessary for us to fulfill all righteousness." What if all righteousness is already fulfilled and we are merely called to own it? I am freed from having to produce, measure up, be perfect, and on and on. The fear of failure is gone, and the introspective guilt and unworthy feelings are dispensed with.

Graham Johnston again addresses this. "To understand just how the absence of grace impacts people's perception of the church, the following is a list of 'religious abuses' according to baby boomers:

- Obsessive praying, talking about God, quoting Scripture
- Thinking the world and our physical bodies are evil
- Refusing to think, doubt, or question
- Excessive judgmental attitudes
- Isolation from others

- Unrealistic fears, guilt, remorse, and shame
- Thinking only in terms of black and white – simplistic thinking
- Excessive fasting and compulsive overeating
- Belief that sex is 'dirty'
- Cries for help: physical and mental breakdown
- Attitudes that conflict with science, hospitals, and schools"

What Johnston is saying is that the world looks at the church as caught up with striving for something it cannot existentially produce.

The Epiphany message is that grace is present to free us from having to reform anyone including ourselves – that all of this is in the hands of One who has successfully met all the demands and kept all the rules for us.

What exactly are the implications? Simply these: what God demands of you Jesus did for you. The life we now live, we live in gratitude for grace. [Oh there is the risk that some Christians will go and live like hell – but they are God's problem and not ours – Our only concern is that our lives be lives of gratitude]. For what can you give to a God who gives everything? Yourself-only yourself. Amen!

CHAPTER 6
THE THIRD SUNDAY AFTER THE EPIPHANY SEPTUAGESIMA

St. Paul's Episcopal Church, Chester, New York
St. David's Episcopal Church, Highland Mills, New York
Amos 3:1-8; Psalm 139; I Corinthians 1:10-17
Matthew 4:12-23

There is a certain ease in following Jesus Christ. Oh, yes, the church has often made it rigorous and strenuous, and challenging, and hard. And there are those things which demand our commitment and dedication if we are to be faithful and appreciative of the grace imparted to us. But alongside of these demands of grace, there is the ease of grace – that all that is left to be done is for our "Amen!" to be joined to God's "Follow me."

It is noteworthy in the Gospel record of the morning, that in the two calls to follow – the would-be disciples, follow. This is it. Matthew, a brilliant tax collector – learned in the languages and cultures of his day makes no effort to embellish the story with discussion, argument, or coercion – probably for the simple reason that there was none.

The riveting nature of this Galilean rabbi or teacher is enough for these rambunctious fishermen to leave their nets to their companions, family and co-workers, and merely follow. It is enough.

Elsewhere we are told that Jesus tells would-be disciples who fished for fish that they would henceforth fish for men [sic] or for persons as we would say.

Let's take note of several applicable matters which will challenge and comfort our own faith.

First, Jesus speaks to Jewish believing fishermen with the simple words, "Follow me." There is nothing of condemnation, nothing of invitation to radical repentance, nothing of hell-fire and brimstone. It is a simple follow me. This is the epitome of the faithful walk – it is a following of Christ. Conversion is conversion – necessary and of great importance. But following is following, and is a simple beginning. It is putting one foot in front of the other and going where Jesus goes.

The places we follow are many and varied. There are the dusty roads of Palestine, the busy streets of Jerusalem, there is the house of Mary and Martha, there is the company of publicans and sinners, there is the encounter with prostitutes and with tax collectors – and all we are given to do is to follow.

Assignments may, and probably will follow later, but they will fall into place if the call to follow is heeded. The fundamentalists would dictate methodologies; revivalists would postulate pathways; pietists would post all kinds of moral strategies, but Jesus says, "Follow me."

A nineteenth century cleric in New York City, Albert B. Simpson wrote this delightful gospel song:

O how easy it is to be saved;
 If to Jesus you only would come.
He is waiting to welcome you just as you are,
 And there's nothing to do but to come.

He has said He'll in no wise cast out
 The soul that to Jesus will come;
Only come at His word and His promise believe,
 For there's nothing to do but to come.

Do not struggle for feeling or faith,
 There is nothing to do but to come;
He is willing to fill you with all you require
 From the moment to Jesus you come.

Such a simple little chorus with eternal implications. "Follow me," the simplicity of the invitation.

Secondly we find that this is a call. The sons of Zebedee, Matthew tells us, receive from Jesus a "call." So often this is interpreted as some mystical and deep vision of call to holy orders, or missionary work, or sacrifice. No the words "Follow me" are, simply, a call.

Therefore each of us has Christ's call upon us – it is to follow. They leave their nets (their proverbial baggage) and they follow.

Philip Yancey, writing about Mahatma Gandhi gives us insight at this juncture:

"Gandhi found that the process of spending less money and acquiring fewer possessions simplified his life and gave him inner peace….Reading that account, I recall with a pang that when I moved from Chicago to Colorado the movers calculated my household belongings to weigh twelve thousand pounds. Even subtracting the six thousand pounds of books, that leaves three tons of material accumulation! And with all this baggage, do I have a life measurably richer than Mahatma Gandhi?"

Certainly I am not advocating this ascetical removal of ourselves from the stuff of the world – but Jesus is stiffly calling us to remove the stuff of the world from our final valuations. In comparison to following Jesus – nothing measures up.

Finally, we see that they do indeed follow. There appears to be that simple satisfaction in following this Jew from Nazareth. This is the reflection of the ease of following Jesus. Oh, yes, the world may have a problem with our Christianity – the world always has trouble with another person's conscious, serious faith. So be it.

But for you and me, there is the simple satisfaction, I am following Jesus.

The great G. K. Chesterton in his book *Orthodoxy* writes this captivating definition of following Jesus. Stating that we are "born upside down," he writes:

"The skeptic may truly be said to be topsy-turvy; for his feet are dancing upwards in idle ecstasies while his brain is in the abyss. To the modern man the heavens are actually below the earth. The explanation is simple; he is standing on his head; which is a very weak pedestal to stand on. But when he has found his feet again, he knows it. Christianity satisfies suddenly and perfectly man's ancestral instinct for being right way up; satisfies it supremely in this; that by its creed joy becomes something gigantic and sadness something special and small. The vault above us is not deaf because the universe is an idiot; the silence is not the heartless silence of an endless and aimless world. Rather the silence around us is a small and pitiful stillness like the prompt stillness of a sick-room. We are perhaps permitted tragedy as a sort of merciful comedy: because the frantic energy of divine things would knock us down like a drunken farce. We can take our own tears more lightly than we could take the tremendous levities of the angels. So we sit perhaps in a starry chamber of silence, while the laughter of the heavens is too loud for us to hear.

"Joy, which was the small publicity of the pagan is the gigantic secret of the Christian…"

"Christianity satisfies suddenly," are Chesterton's words. These fishermen who follow are satisfied. It is, kind of, that simple.

Several weeks ago I preached in another parish and word got back to me that a certain person was blessed by the sermon. Her words were something like this, "So often I go home from church feeling guilty. Today I went home feeling valued and forgiven."

Have we missed the bliss of following Jesus while we have wallowed in the church-induced guilt of working our way to that which is a gift? Good Lord, deliver us! Amen!

CHAPTER 7
THE FOURTH SUNDAY AFTER THE EPIPHANY SEXAGESIMA

St. Paul's Episcopal Church, Chester, New York
St. David's Episcopal Church, Highland Mills, New York
Micah 6:1-8; Psalm 37; I Corinthians 1:18-31
Matthew 5:1-12

Epiphany is that period in the church calendar when we celebrate the revelation of Jesus Christ, the uncovering of truth, the opening up of the things of God for view. The texts appointed for this Lord's Day reveal to us the wonders of grace [an often misunderstood word] and blessing [a word, in the West, at least, which is always misunderstood]. These are the two poles upon which today's epiphanies turn.

Often we think of grace as only "unmerited favor." But this doesn't always fit the context in which we are reading. Grace appears to be a satisfaction of all we long for; a fulfillment of all we seek; a provision of all we need; and an enabling for all we must do. It is a large and comforting doctrine – an encouragement, particularly to those of us who are convinced that we can't really do it all on our own. Grace is the ability to grasp truth and make it applicable in our lives. Somehow it is that quality which empowers us to do all God requires as God requires. It is the given fulfillment of the task at hand for the believer.

Micah records God's question to Samaria and Jerusalem which in essence is "What more can I, God, do than I have already done for your benefit?" The interrogations are all summed up in this essence. God rehearses their history, their heritage, and their hope; and reminds them that the hope is becoming dim due to its inexorable ties with their history and heritage, which are being forfeited in their willful blindness to the blessings from God.

The sacrificial system, good for its intent, becomes blinding when it becomes a substitute for a life of belief. It is interesting that the Hebrew language does not have a word for "faith," but always employs a form of "faithfulness," when referring to one's faith in God. The closing lines of Micah's prophetic pericope here give us the parameters of the life of faith. They are to know that God defines the good; God reveals the requirements: ours is to be a people of justice, kindness, and humility. And of course each of these could be unpacked with divine challenge, human obedience, and personal and global application.

[Just as an aside, isn't it interesting to note that Paul, in Galatians 5, lists the fruits of the Holy Spirit in the believer's life, and they appear strangely similar to Micah's list: "The fruit of the Spirit is love, joy, peace, gentleness, meekness, kindness, longsuffering, against such there is no law."]

We are led on to the writing of Paul in I Corinthians where we are confronted with the truth that Christ is omni-competent for the needs of humanity. Not only are we recipients of grace, we are related to the one who graces us. "He is the source of your life in Christ Jesus, whom God has made our wisdom, our righteousness, our sanctification, and our redemption...therefore boast in the Lord." These appear as big theological words, but the essence of the text is immensely practical. Paul is affirming that what we can't know by mere intellectual rationalism, God grants through the gift of Jesus Christ as our wisdom; what we can't drum up as a badge of righteousness that meets all divine standards, God gives us the righteousness of Jesus Christ; when we cannot quite live out the perfectly sanctified and holy life, it means that Christ has already lived that life for us; and it means that when I can't possibly fathom that I am redeemed, I am.

This is a potent word from Paul who so often focused on no one but himself. Here he gives Jesus Christ his due – Jesus is, as one writer put it, "perfect everything." This is no God of human construction. We'd make it harder (or simpler as the case may be). We all like works religions because we can appear better than others. (This is a recurring theme this Epiphany).

C. S. Lewis wrote in *Mere Christianity,* "If Christianity were something we were making up, of course we could make it easier. But it is not. We cannot compete, in simplicity, with people who are inventing religions. How could we? We are dealing with Fact. Of course anyone can be simple if he has no facts to bother about." The facts are – whatever we need he provides. This is grace.

The second major look for our Epiphany lesson is the word "blessing," and it is used repeatedly in the Gospel text of the morning. No doubt a part of a much repeated lesson in Jesus' preaching, the "Beatitudes" as they have come to be known are also often misunderstood. We think (because the church has falsely taught us to think) that to be blessed means to be happy. Read that into the context. How many mourners are happy? How many persecuted are happy? How many are reviled with all kinds of evil spoken against them who are happy? It simply doesn't work.

So what does Jesus mean? (We do not have time here to do the immense word-study I have done on "bless," but from the root words in Hebrew and Greek, I believe the word "bless" means "to make God-conscious.") So let's use this definition. God-conscious are those who are poor in spirit, for theirs is the kingdom of heaven….Okay, we're on a roll. God conscious are those who are meek for they will inherit the earth…We can go on and on. When I am blessed, regardless of the feelings, the things, the outcomes, I am conscious of God in the given situation.

There are few things in life I am willing to go on crusade for, but the true meaning of blessing is one. And the essential reason is that in Western Christianity where we have wealth, power, prestige, and comfort, we think these are blessings, and often they are the precise things that curse us rather than bless us. They remove our vision from God and leave us with only the wealth, power, prestige, or comfort while God is veiled.

The examples of true blessing abound and many could be cited for our case. But let us think for a moment of a pastor I met in Bombay, India in 1985. He pastored a church of hundreds in this large Hindu city, and was so anxious to host forty of us who were on a tour of his country. When he found out I, too, was a pastor, he was anxious to show me his library. I, too, was anxious. Libraries are my hobby and since my own library then had about 7,000 volumes and now has about 32,000. I followed him into the second room of his two room flat where he and his wife and family lived, and where church met on Sundays. There he proudly displayed his seven volumes of Biblical and theological works. He said, "God has blessed me with this library."

The sight of this caused me great conviction, for I knew the immensity of my own collection at home. Tearfully, I rejoiced with him, knowing that his living in such simple blessing, could bless me and refocus my own ownership of my library.

Grace and blessing - they will get at us when we least expect.

John David Burton captures this with insightful poetic form:

Watch the way you watch for grace and blessing
        Spring up in surprise when least you expect.
Those who have are found without and those with
        nothing Or less, may have the most of all.

When God's things we just cannot do – when
        believing
Is the farthest thing from all our minds,
Just then grace comes shining through with all the
        Effort we have sought – and more.

When we have amassed and added to that mass
        and
Know that we are secure for what we have or hold
Then, just then we meet the one who has so very
        much
The less, and knows of God in conscious way.

Deliver us, then Lord from the presumption that
        it is
In having that we are blessed or that in
Getting that we are graced in some special way.
Deliver us to grace and blessing. Amen.

CHAPTER 8
THE FEAST OF
ST. TITUS, BISHOP
AND CONFESSOR

Nyack College Chapel/Bethel Gospel Assembly
Church, Harlem, New York City
Psalm 122

I t is often wise to begin with a disclaimer. You have chosen me, I did not choose you. I am an appointed preacher, not the one who asked for this job tonight. I am reminded of an interview someone once had with the great Dr. David Martin Lloyd-Jones, Senior Minister of Westminster Chapel, Buckingham Gate, London. They were building up the good doctor and saying things of him he would never say of himself, when the reporter asked how he got his great confidence in the pulpit.

Lloyd-Jones answered, "Sir, each Sunday as I leave the vestry room and follow the long, narrow corridor toward the pulpit steps, I am reminded of the Scripture, "As a lamb, led to the slaughter…" The good doctor's confidence was only in the Lord. And I, too, this evening ask that you pray with me as we take a wee look at Psalm 122.

"Let the words of my mouth, and the meditations of our hearts, be acceptable in your sight, O Lord, our strength and our Redeemer. Amen!"

Since we are two campuses gathered tonight, I am reminded of a story. A chap is out of work an inordinate amount of time. After many, many months, he sees an ad in the newspaper for a position at the local zoo. He follows up and is hired. It appears that their gorilla had died and a group of school children were coming to visit the zoo and they particularly wanted to see the gorilla. His job was to dress as a gorilla and play the part well so that the school children would have no idea he was not the real thing.

All went well. And yet about four o'clock in the afternoon he began to feel a bit queasy after eating all the bananas thrown to him through the day. So to get away, he climbed up into a tree and promptly fell asleep.

Soon he turned over, and as he did, he fell from the tree, right into the lion's cage. The lion was eyeing him up, and the man (dressed as a gorilla) started to scream. "Let me out – get me out of here before the lion kills me." The lion crept closer and closer until he was right next to the gorilla (I mean the man). The screams were louder than ever when the fellow heard the lion say, "Shut-up buddy before you get us both fired!

The moral of the story is that before you scream to get out of a situation, find out if you are the only one there. These two were in it together. And that is the theme of Psalm 122.

"Jerusalem is built as a city
That is at unity with itself;"

The original purpose of this Psalm was praise. And the praise was only successful when those singing it made it a declaration of truth. This unity was not something left to the devises of the worshippers – to somehow make Jerusalem united. It was rather a responsorial Psalm of truth-"Jerusalem is…at unity with itself." It was a celebration of the oneness of Zion, the City of God.

It was St. Augustine who brought to our attention the diametrical opposition of the cities of God and the city of man [sic]. The city of God is united; the city of man is divided; the city of God is a city of integrity; the city of man is a city of disintegration; the city of God is a city of brothers and sisters; the city of man is a city of strangers.

It is as if Augustine was saying that if we are not part of that existent unity, we are part of the divisive diversity.

Someone has aptly said, "To live above with saints we love, Oh say, that will be glory. But to live below with saints we know, well, that's another story!"

Simply put, men and women, we are called to manifest the unity of the city of God. This "Song of Ascent" is a creedal declaration that God's city is one.

As believers at an institution of higher learning, you and I are challenged to live out that unity in the midst of our educational endeavors. Ours happens to be on multiple campuses. We are to be about working out our place as this educational institution in the city of God. "Our feet are standing in Zion's gate," to quote the Psalmist.

To look at these facts, we must face the truth that legally, ethically, and morally, we are one institution under the laws of New York State. Hardly something to put in a sermon – hardly something for which the preacher would hear an "Amen." But this is the indivisible legal unity of Nyack College in the calling of God.

Secondly, we are systemically (or in the senior administration) one school-one president, one treasurer. These are the two corporate officers who administer what we benefit from.

But there is a third sense in which we are one-that is, we serve one Lord. We recognize God's declaration that we are one in Christ. The gifts of the Spirit that you and I possess are for the use in one body. The unity is necessary if the praise is to be worthy. To endeavor to praise from divisiveness is to forfeit the praise as unworthy of its object. We are members of the body of

Christ, called to Nyack College with a mission which few institutions like us share. We are called by one Lord to be one school in two locations with two clientele for two intermediate ends and one ultimate purpose: the glory of God. Therefore when tonight's service was announced, "I was glad when they said unto me, let us go to the house of the Lord."

There are some strong and true matters which we must therefore confront. First, as members of one another in Christ, we must will the blessing and success of the other. Benign neglect is no substitute for willful prayer. Either I want you to be blessed in Nyack or Manhattan, or I am disobedient to the promptings of Holy Spirit. This is the foundation of the Christian unity which is actual.

We either participate in the unity of Christianity or we exist outside its umbrella of blessing. Either I see you as a brother or sister in Christ for whom Jesus died and for whom God has wonderful plans, or I am a pathetic, selfish prig who supposes I know more than Jesus himself who prayed in John 17 that we all be one as He and the Father are one.

A second reality is that God does not only have a limited amount of blessing. For Nyack, Rockland to succeed does not mean that Nyack, Manhattan must suffer or vice versa. If God is who we claim him to be, there is bountiful blessing for both locations to succeed and flourish. Unity demands that I allow God to bless you as well as me.

The implications, my brothers and sisters, are vast. Oh, yes, there are divisions or diversities we must sustain- there are different locations, different clientele, different faculty. There will need to be contextually defined differences in curriculum and methodologies of planning and calendar creation. But these are systemic not essential.

Our oneness is not ancillary to the work God has called us to do – it is deeply organic. Our place in the city of God necessitates that we recognize and celebrate that we are one in Christ – not only individually, but as a Christian institution. There is no place for the pride-induced supposed superiority which on occasion spills out into word and action. I will succeed, I will be blessed, as I pray for and long for your success and blessing. Then, with the Psalmist, we can, as the tribes of the Lord, go up to the house of God, "to praise the Name of the Lord."

From our school have gone multiplied thousands into the world for the sake of Christ. If time permitted, I would share stories of those I know from each location. I would show you pictures of ministerial and secular success. It would be these that would be the best illustration to the sermon.

But I am reminded of a story of former President Jimmy Carter, Menachem Begin, and Anwar Sadat at the Camp David Peace Talks. This is the story.

It seems that after days of deliberation, the talks grew to a standstill. Nothing was moving. The mediator, President Carter did not know where to turn on this, so bid both Middle Eastern gentlemen "Goodnight." All went to their own rooms for the night. By morning, one of the two men, who had so opposed one another that occasionally at Camp David they would not meet face to face, came out of his cottage with pictures of his children. He had glanced at them the night before and knew that peace must come for their generation. Soon all three men were sharing portraits of their families together. It was this gesture of the portraits of loved ones that brought the peace accords to the table.

It is interesting that when we focus on others – not on ourselves, we tend to be more peaceful and peace oriented. We can have an accord when the portraits are shared around.

Boy have I got portraits for you. And when you see them, I believe you and I will want to get at the peace process as soon as possible. Amen!

CHAPTER 9

THE LAST SUNDAY
AFTER THE EPIPHANY
QUINQUAGESIMA

St. Paul's Episcopal Church, Chester, New York
St. David's Episcopal Church, Highland Mills, New York
Exodus 24:12-18; Psalm 99; Philippians 3:7-14
Matthew 17:1-9

Jesus clearly conveyed to his followers that they who see him, see the Father. There is a direct correlation between the understanding of the Incarnate One and the One who sent him. It is insightful, revelatory, health-giving, and faith-enlivening to see Jesus as the fullness of the revelation of God. "In him dwelt the fullness of the Godhead bodily," the Scriptures assure us.

This has to be settled before we make any attempt to relate the Scriptures of the day to one another. It is only in the unifying person of Jesus that these make sense together. Just a few short weeks ago we celebrated the historic mighty act of God's becoming human in the Incarnation. Canon Michael Green of Great Britain writes, ""he absolutely became our contemporary; God became man for 30 years or so in order to bring us to a new dimension of life, through knowing him...."

And as we today end our celebration of the Epiphany of this Incarnate one, I believe our texts are a fitting summary of the revelation. Mind you, never a full understanding but one in outline – one which allows us to grasp the essentials of the revelation of God in Christ Jesus.

Beginning with the Gospel account, it is insightful to note that Jesus and those who place their faith in him:

- Transcend human time limitations; Jesus, the timeless one, with Peter, James, and John, hold conversation with Moses and Elijah. There is something essentially powerful to this timeless truth: "For the believer, life is changed, not ended" as the burial office mass asserts.
- Manifest that he is more than mere mortal; Jesus Christ is the Son of God – previously acclaimed by John the Baptist; reaffirmed on the Mount of Transfiguration. Either he is who he says he is or he is a fraud. C. S. Lewis leads us to accept that Jesus is either liar, lunatic, or Lord of all.
- Decline the permanent mountain-top residence; Peter's desire to the contrary, Jesus clearly wants to return to the dusty roads of Palestine and the busy streets of Jerusalem to accomplish his work. There is no place for Christ apart from those he comes to seek and to save.
- Remain the sole focus of devotion; though much has happened, Jesus remains the central character. This

is powerfully instructive for those who would follow Christ —though there is a Christian worldview of everything, there is a Christian worldview of nothing if it is not Christian. The church may not-cannot-retreat from this.

Following the Gospel, we see the Exodus passage centering on the giving of the law. This, too, is fulfilled in Jesus, who, in his own words "came not to destroy the law, but to fulfill it." There is a meeting of the demands of God by Jesus. Men and women, the implications of this are vast – he has met the Law's demands to the fullest. Epiphany says to us that what we cannot do has been done.

Finally, the Epistle reading draws the net, so to speak, with its Christo-centricity. There is an exclusivity to the ultimate claims of Christ on our lives. We don't surrender our humanity in light of his claims, we regain it. Paul presses on to embrace all of the truth claims and relationships available through Christ and has the audacity to claim to be the possession of Christ.

Such audacity is completely in keeping with the call of God on our lives. It is no mistake that Matthew writes in the record of the Transfiguration, "Jesus took with him Peter, James, and John...." Jesus takes us with him.

It makes the Christian focus, not fanatical, but relational. I can take my focus off incidentals and place it on the essentials. One poet put it this way:

71

Once it was the blessing; now it is the Lord;
Once it was the feeling; now it is his Word.
Once the gift I wanted, now the Giver own.
Once I sought for healing, now Himself alone.

Once 'twas painful trying, now 'tis perfect trust;
Once a half salvation, now the uttermost.
Once 'twas ceaseless holding, now God holds me
    fast;
Once 'twas constant drifting, now my anchor's
    cast.

Once 'twas busy planning, now 'tis trustful prayer;
Once 'twas anxious caring, now He has the care.
Once 'twas what I wanted, now what Jesus says.
Once was constant asking, now is ceaseless praise.

Once it was my working, His it hence shall be,
Once I tried to use him, now he uses me.
Once the power I wanted, now the Mighty One;
Once for self I labored, now for Him alone.

Albert B. Simpson

The implications are obvious. Epiphany's central focus is Jesus Christ of Nazareth – true God and true man – incarnate of the virgin Mary his mother. Come to earth for you and for me. We are the beneficiaries of this momentous act of God.

And, oh, the quote from Canon Michael Green at the beginning goes on – allow me to quote it again with its final sentence. "The absolute became our contemporary; God became man for 30 years or so, in order to bring us to a new dimension of life through knowing him. But how can we demonstrate so staggering a claim? How can we bring it home to others [and thus be an Epiphany for them]? The answer is, by witness."

The Epiphany blessing at the end of each mass says, "May Christ the Son of God be manifest in you, that your lives may be a light to the world...." I pray this for you, and for me, my brothers and sisters in Christ. Amen!

CHAPTER 10
THE SECOND
SUNDAY IN LENT

St. John's Episcopal Church, Kingston, New York
Genesis 12:1-8; Psalm 33:12-22; Romans 4:1-17
John 3:1-17

To leave a country as Abraham does in our Old Testament lesson, and to travel to a destiny yet undisclosed, certainly calls for the singularity of vision. The story of Lot's family's deliverance from Sodom reinforces the singularity of vision when Lot's wife turns to look back and is turned into a pillar of salt. Watch where you are going, for you will inevitably go where you are watching.

A little boy in Sunday School one Sunday morning is told the story of Lot's wife turning to look back and being turned into this salt pillar. "That's nothin'," said the little chap, "my mom was driving down the road and when she turned to look back she turned into a telephone pole."

Watch where you are going for you will inevitably go where you are watching. And this is the central focus of Lent, that Jesus Christ becomes our lens through which we see life. It necessitates our being drawn closer to the Christ life – to make the spiritual as real as the physical, and allow the spiritual to permeate all of life. This is the essence of Jesus' directive to Nicodemus that he "must be born again."

Known as the doctrine of the new birth, this is often seen out of relationship with Jesus who is its focus – and so we must make every attempt at restoring it to its place in our view through the Jesus lens.

First, from whence we have Jesus must be seen. This is the one "come from God," in Nicodemus' own testimony. That truth settles why we reason from Jesus to God and not vice versa. "He who has seen me has seen the Father," says Jesus. We have Jesus because Jesus Christ comes from God. We celebrated this in our incarnational celebrations of Christmas just two short months ago. And this fact of Jesus Christ's origin leads us to understand why one cannot come into contact with Jesus and not be effected.

The story is told of a French Bishop preaching in a large venue. He told the story of three teenagers who had come into some money and had decided to spend it in a night of drunken, wild revelry. That evening the three teens did everything money could buy – drugs, alcohol, women, gambling. It was a night of unbridled lust and its fulfillment. As they were staggering along the sidewalk at sunrise, they passed a church.

Two of the three teens began to chide the third that he needed to go into the church for confession. They told him that if he would go into the church, make the confession and do whatever the priest directed him to do for penance, that they would give him the remainder of the money which was significant.

The boy took the bet. Into the confessional he went and began to spew forth every sordid detail of the previous evening. The priest heard snickering from the pews and saw the other two teens listening in on the confession. Immediately he knew what was going on.

The priest listed patiently and then responded. "If you wish to be absolved from all your sin, leave the confessional, walk down the center isle of the church, kneel in front of the crucifix, look intently into the eyes of the Savior and say, "Lord Jesus Christ, I know everything you did for me on Calvary; everything you did for the salvation of my soul, and frankly I don't give a damn!" Say that, young man and you will be absolved.

The young man did as was directed. He slowly walked down the isle, knelt in front of the crucifix, looked around to see if his friends were watching – lots of money was at stake – and he looked up into the eyes of the Savior and began. "Lord Jesus I know everything you did on Calvary, and everything you did for the salvation of my eternal soul and frankly...frankly...frankly…have mercy on my soul." Coming face to face with Jesus just would not allow him to deny him.

The Bishop who was preaching this illustration asked the audience if they knew how he knew this story. He replied, "I was that teenager."

Jesus Christ has come from God and we will never be the same.

Second, notice how we have Jesus. We have him, according to his own words, "by water and the spirit." It is to be born anew. We don't have to fear those that Episcopalians call "Born againers…" There is nothing at all to fear. We, too, who know Jesus Christ as our Lord and Savior have been born again. [Notice in our Prayer Book, page 307 in the prayer over the baptismal waters, we read "now sanctify this water, we pray you, by the power of your Holy Spirit, that those who are here cleansed from sin and born again may continue forever in the risen life of Jesus Christ our Savior."].

How do we have Jesus? By allowing him to rebirth us. One writer (an Episcopalian) argued that the reason some of us do not want to be born again is that we don't want the responsibility of growing up again! (But that is material for future sermons).

From whence do we have Jesus? From God. How do we have Jesus? By allowing God the Spirit to birth us anew. And finally, why do we have Jesus? Jesus' own words give the hints to this. "For God sent his son into the world, not to condemn the world, but that the world through him might be saved."

God intends us to have Jesus so that the entire world will have Jesus. We are to know him and to make him known. We put on the Jesus lenses and we look at the world through him.

Margaret Hess in *The Christian Century* (May 14, 1997) writes this powerful commentary: "Think about your life, Nicodemus. What would you do differently if you had half the chance? How would you grow up differently? How would you re-edit the narrative of your life? As you enter more deeply into your puzzlement, Nicodemus, you'll find that Jesus is inviting you to be curious about your life, and to rethink your assumptions with an altered perspective. You are challenged not only to conduct an autopsy on your past, but to look to the future through the eyes of redemptive possibility. How might your life be different if you were born again? How would your life be altered if you truly believed from the beginning that God loves you with a sacrificial love? Nicodemus, patron saint of the curious, we see you in the flickering lamplight, your face an arresting admixture of confusion and interest. Jesus waits, the silence broken only by the sound of the wind banging the shutter against the side of the house. You tug at your beard and rethink your life, seeing the past and the future through the eyes of the one who loves you. You are dizzy with the possibility of it all. And so are we. Born again? The mere thought of it sweeps through us and sends us reeling. You mean to tell us that our lives might be different?"

Yes. Our lives might be different. This is the Lenten invitation.

> Christ, holding talks with Nicodemus finds
> Our knowledge shallow is and dark our minds;
> Man's everlasting welfare and true good,
> Is not by sense and reason understood.
> We blinded are, and walk as in a maze,
> Illumination is a spark of Grace.
>
> Robert Whitehall, 1677

CHAPTER 11
THE THIRD SUNDAY IN LENT

The Spanish Alliance Church, Manhattan, New York
John 4:5-42

We are given to thinking that we have more and deeper problems than civilizations and cultures of the past. We think we are unique in our circumstances and special in our needs. Along with the false notion that we are better than past peoples, we cultivate the certainty [wrongly, I might add] that our day demands new and different answers than those of the past.

We would all agree that we do not understand completely the needs of our day. Why, we can't even comprehend the ways of God at times. With all the detours God seems to lead us on: the seemingly unanswered prayers, the troublesome people he allows in our pathway, the weakness in which we must minister-God's ways are sometimes incomprehensible. The wonderful saint of Calcutta, India, Mother Theresa was once asked, "What is the first thing you will say to God when you get to heaven?" Her reply was prompt and concise: "God, you have a lot of explaining to do!"

I believe our lengthy text of the morning shows us that God doesn't necessarily have a lot of explaining to do, we have much wisdom to gain.

In this encounter between Jesus, a Jew and this Samarian woman, we are challenged with five human problems which we take for granted today as modern problems, when in reality they have existed since the Fall from Eden. Note in this text: the reality of racial division, temporal answers, hopeless circumstances, local deities, and gender inequality.

Each of these is met head on in true Gospel fashion by the author of their correction, Jesus.

First, Jesus removes racial and ethnic barriers. Jesus, a Jew, was to have nothing to do with the Samarians at all. They were the "half-breeds" of the day and he was pure Jew. This so very much echoes into the realities of our contemporary scene.

But Jesus walks decisively into the encounter and deals with the Samarian woman as an equal in need of what he has to offer. It is reciprocal as well. He needs a drink, she needs a Savior. The lessons are manifold and profound. All humanity is "shut up in sin," according to Apostle Paul, so that God might have "mercy on all." All are potential recipients of God's grace.

The human creature has three problems and these are shared by every human being. Our three problems are our past, our present, and our future. And one's race, ethnicity, nationality, or color are all irrelevant to the reality of this. Our past is a problem in that we have sinned; our present is a problem in that we do sin; and our future is a problem in that we will sin. We are all equally in need of a Savior.

And Jesus' dealing with the Samarian woman proves that there is nothing to keep us, and everything to encourage us in meeting the needs of the other by living the Christ life. It is in Christianity that we find the foundation for the race problem of the world. Jesus answers this first human dilemma.

The second human problem is our tendency to find answers in the temporal. We look at other people and hope we can model our lives after them; we look at systems and hope that the system will meet our human need; we look to the church and hope that the institution will deliver us. The Samarian woman was wanting a drink of water that would deliver her from the need to go to the well each day. And Jesus, noting her true need offered her a drink which would render the town well a mere ancillary to the life she would henceforth lead.

The great survivor of World War II, saintly Corrie ten Boom, wrote this wonderful little triplet:

"Look around and be distressed;
Look within and be depressed;
Look at Christ, and be at rest."

This Samarian woman was the workhorse of the family and evidently even of her male lover. She lived to drink (and give drink). Jesus invited her to drink in order to live. And in so doing, Jesus solves the problem of temporal answers. This life has no answers – Jesus Christ is the answer – above, beyond, beneath, alongside of all our circumstances, inviting us to drink in order to live.

The third human problem is that the human person tends first to look out for number one. This searching woman was concerned about herself and not the others in her family or village. Jesus directs her to "Go and call your husband." There is an emphasis on the evangelistic here – you don't receive solely for your own benefit, but the recipient of grace becomes the minister and evangel of grace. How much we need to hear this in individualistic, narcissistic Western culture – we who so often look inward and not outward – nationally and not globally.

The fourth problem reflected in the historic record is that humans always tend toward the localized. God is not the God of Samaria but of Jerusalem, Judea, and the uttermost parts of the earth. Worshipping in spirit and in truth makes it possible to worship anywhere for God is everywhere. Even the famed paleontologist Pierre de Chadin wrote a "Mass on the world" for those times when bread and wine were not present. Jones Very, an early American divine closed a poem with the words

The soul, forgetful of her nobler birth
Had hewn Him lofty shrines of stone and wood
And left unfinished and in ruins, still
The only temple He delights to fill.

The temple God delights to fill is the human heart – the human person. And when filled, the temple therefore is anywhere God and we are!

Finally, there is the problem of anticipation only and not fulfillment. Jesus says, "I am He!" There is always the danger of "always learning" and "never coming to a knowledge of the truth." The goal is not solely the seeking; it is, as well, the finding. Those who seek Christ, find Christ; those who are content with seeking for seeking sake, continue to seek fruitlessly. Jesus' words that He is that for which the prophets longed is a testimony of finality-culmination-sufficiency-absoluteness. And all of this is wrapped inseparably up in His person-the God-man, Jesus Christ.

May we, as we contemplate the encounter of this woman with Jesus of Nazareth, find our own problems brought into the light of the Word of God so that we, as I believe she was, will be delivered from these haunting human tendencies engendered by sin and be delivered into a viable and rewarding faith in the Lord. Amen!

CHAPTER 12
EASTER VIGIL

St. John's Episcopal Church, Kingston, New York
Romans 6:3-11; Psalm 114 & Matthew 28:1-10

One Christmas Eve, a priest mounted the pulpit, took off his alb, took out a basin, soaped his face, and proceeded to shave in the pulpit. Without a word he completed his task. When he was finished, he simply said, "You will tell your friends, 'You won't believe what our priest did on Sunday,' and when you tell them, they won't believe you. But you have seen it. Believe!"

Well, I have no intention of shaving tonight. But just as at Christmas we are confronted with the unbelievable story of virgin conception and birth, so tonight we are confronted with a physical resurrection. The Apostle Paul, in I Corinthians 15, settles quite successfully the argument, that if Christ is not raised, then we are all fools and should get back to the more mundane matters of life.

We have heard salvation history read and rehearsed for us tonight, and we celebrate how God has done it and how humanity has experienced it. Tonight we celebrate the apex of this salvation work of God on behalf of the human race.

Notice the words of the Gospel reflect for us that there is a certain continuity with all of God's dealings. It is the "Angel of the Lord" who is at the empty tomb. It was the Angel of the Lord who was providentially present at so many of the in-breakings of God onto the scene of human need.

It was important for the Jews to know that there was continuity in what God was doing. A Jew was not so much a consistent person who conformed as he was a person of continuity who cohered in his manifold beliefs. Some people think of Christians being Christians precisely because they have everything together – rather, we are Christians precisely because we have succeeded in scattering all things apart. We have continuity with God's doings even if we are inconsistent in and of ourselves.

Then in the Gospel there is the confirmation of Jesus' promise. Matthew records the Angel's words, "He is risen just as he said." The great difference between Jesus and Jeanne Dixon is that Jesus did what he said he would do. The charlatans of the world make great boasts but produce little. Nostradamus made great predictions, and they are about as precise as a shot-gun. Jesus is risen, just as he said. There is a trustworthiness to the words of Jesus Christ.

Finally, there is the creation of a new relationship. The two Marys are told to "Go and tell my brethren." Remember, we are in first century Palestine and women don't tell men anything. This is the epitome of patriarchal society. Women are owned. And we are immediately confronted with this one implication of the new creation. Jesus is not gender hierarchical. And this is a powerful argument for the inspiration of the Bible record, since Matthew, a devout Jew would not have created a story that said this! He would have been laughed out of town.

Yesterday, on Good Friday, the last of the Solemn Collects asks the Lord, "let the whole world see and know that things which were being cast down are being raised up and things which had grown old are being made new, and that things are being brought to their perfection through him through whom all things were made new…"

And so tonight we are granted this renewed continuity with the past; we are given this confirmation of the finished work of Jesus of Nazareth; and we are blessed with the creation of a new relationship. We have each other – we belong to God – and God has spoken through his inspired word. Alleluia, Christ is risen! Amen.

CHAPTER 13
THE SECOND
SUNDAY OF EASTER

St. John's Episcopal Church, Kingston, New York
Acts 2:14a, 22-23; Psalm 111; I Peter 1:3-9
John 20:19-31

The last verse of today's Gospel tells us at John's own hand, "these things are written that you may believe that Jesus is the Christ, the Son of God, and that believing, you may have life in his name." Life in his name. What is this resurrection life that we read and speak so much about in Christianity?

When I think of the life I would like to have it would include a seaside home in Jamaica, a perfect teenage physique, excellent health; an inheritance large enough that I would not have to work, a disposable income to allow me to travel and purchase all I wish, and plenty left over to share with others. Alas....

How would you fill in those spaces if you could present your wish list to God and say, "this is what my life would look like if I had my way...." It was John Wesley who once wrote to his mother saying, "I can't believe that when God created this world and put us in it that he meant for us to be permanently miserable in it."

Well, it appears that Jesus and John have other, deeper concepts in mind as we study the record of the encounters in this Gospel account. Exactly what could John have in mind when he sums up this pericope in this fashion?

First, the disciples are behind locked doors living their new life in Christ. This tells me that the Christian life is one that often counters the bureaucracy. The leaders of the Jews in cohort with the pagan Romans were still on the trail of those who followed this would-be Messiah. And it seems that this has been the case for two-thousand years. That whenever someone or a group of "someones" wants to live the Christ life, there are those who will readily attack them with all of the canon laws and constitutions and by-laws that tell them they aren't doing it right. The Christian life is always a henceforth and not a hitherto. There is a rich and rewarding sense that the resurrected life is one of countering the prevailing authorities on matters spiritual. Jesus brought nothing if it was not NEW life.

So many of the spiritual leaders of the Temple had the behavior down pat — all the time their belief was shaky at best. And so, no doubt, John had in mind that this new life in Christ, this "life in his name" was a life of counter-spirituality. [Certainly all of the parables attest to this].

Then twice in this small section Jesus appears with the words, "Peace be with you." This life possesses the procured peace. It is the peace of God that is given to the disciples, and elsewhere we are informed that this peace "passes human understanding."

Peace is never the absence of conflict-rather in the Biblical sense, peace is the knowledge of the adequacy of one's resources. And our resource is nothing less than God himself. Therefore in the midst of life as we may not wish it, there can be peace.

An old-time Anglican wrote a most wonderful hymn that places peace right where it belongs in the believer's life:

Peace, perfect peace, in this dark world of sin?
The blood of Jesus whispers peace within.

Peace perfect peace, by thronging duties pressed?
To do the will of Jesus, this is best.

Peace perfect peace with sorrows surging 'round?
On Jesus' truth nothing but calm is found.

Peace perfect peace, with loved ones far away?
In Jesus' keeping we are safe, and they.

Peace perfect peace our future all unknown?
Jesus we know, and he is on the throne!

Peace perfect peace, death shadowing us and ours?
Jesus has vanquished death and all its powers.

It is enough, earth's struggles soon shall cease,
And Jesus call us to heaven's perfect peace.

Edward Bickersteth

Believe it or not, that is not a funeral hymn but an Easter one! Peace is the assurance that our resources are adequate in God!

Finally, John seems to indicate that there is a third characteristic of this life in Jesus' name, and that is joy and gladness. The disciples were "glad when they saw the Lord." We don't often think of Jesus as gladness-inducing. We are often pushed in the direction of church being somber and serious. Rather, Jesus, the risen Jesus, in the midst of His people is a source of joy. [Now, mind you, not Western culture's shallow happiness, but true joy]. One of the most joyous persons I know is a very seriously melancholy personality. Yet even though the personality is melancholy, the spirit is joyful.

We often think of the Christian faith as a list of things we should do and a list of those we should not do. Moralism is so very much easier than the Christ life. Virtue is easier than faith; ethics easier than spirituality. Madeline L'Engle, the great writer of our generation, herself an Episcopalian in our Diocese wrote,

"Virtue is not a sign of a Christian. Joy is." Amen to that good lady.

The joy and humor of heaven has Jesus alive, and the guards at his tomb, according to the Gospel account, "fell as dead men." The joke is on death and the perpetrators of the politics of death. For the Christian who has life in the name of Jesus, there is the assurance of continued encounter with the powers of darkness; the peace of Christ which assures us that our resources are adequate; and the joy and gladness of the presence of Christ.

When we affirm "He is risen indeed, Hallelujah," we are affirming new life-for him-for us! Amen!

CHAPTER 14
THIRD SUNDAY OF EASTER

Holy Cross Episcopal Church, Kingston, New York
Acts 2:14a, 36-47; Psalm 116; I Peter 1:17-23
Luke 24:13-35

We have been through a season where we admit, contrary to reproducible evidence, that Jesus is alive. This is and has been a tenet of the Church's testimony for two-thousand years. The great poet, John Updike, whom many of us studied in high school, wrote what is called "Seven Stanzas at Easter." Two of those stanzas read

Make no mistake; if he rose at all
it was His body;
if the cell's dissolution did not reverse, the
   molecules
re-knit, the amino acids rekindle,
the Church will fall.

Let us not seek to make it less monstrous,
for our own convenience, our own sense of beauty,

> lest, awakened in one unthinkable hour, we are
> embarrassed by the miracle,
> and crushed by the remonstrance.

The entire poem is valued reading but is outside of our time constraints this morning. We are living in resurrection time. It is a qualitatively different hour for the believer in Jesus Christ. But alas, that belief is difficult at times. Times when we would want to see God at work in circumstances and situations, he seems strangely distant.

Two travelers following the crucifixion are our focus this morning. They are paradigmatic for us. They model our fears and frustrations that what ought to be possibly isn't. The philosophers tell us we are now entering the second decade of the post-modern era – where life is viewed absurdly, and chance takes precedence over design, and so many act like missing persons while all the time they are at home. Cleopas and the second person on the Emmaus road are us-wanting so much to see resurrection life and unfortunately seeing so much crucifixion. Even as we gather this morning, it has just been seven months since 9/11; there are forty-four wars beings fought around the globe, and the city of peace "Jeru-shalom" is anything but peace-filled.

In light of this, let's take a look at the record from the Gospel. First, Jesus is veiled in everyday occurrences. They are walking to Emmaus, and the last person they expect to be present is Jesus. That's us. We go about our daily duties and desires, and often miss the presence of the living Christ. When Peter speaks in today's Epistle about being "rescued from our futile ways," I wonder if this is what he is hinting at — that we be rescued from our ways being without the conscious presence of the Lord? What Jesus' presence on the road to Emmaus indicates is that everything, even an evening walk home, has purpose because He is present.

And so the mundane takes on purpose; the discouraging takes on purpose: the eating of a meal, the doing of a deed, the suffering of a loss-each has purpose precisely because the Lord is present.

As Archbishop William Temple walked through the ruins of Coventry Cathedral after the German bombing, he found, it is recorded, some piece of altarware that survived without mar. Someone in his party exclaimed, "What a coincidence." And the Archbishop keenly and wisely replied, "Coincidences are God working incognito!"

Jesus is veiled in our everyday occurrences, but present nonetheless!

Secondly, notice that Jesus is exposed in the biblical evidence. Here we have a coalescing of the Hebrew Scriptures and what would become New Testament truth. Jesus began with the prophets and expounded His own Messiahship to these two travelers.

The Scriptures become for us the sustenance we need to interpret the seemingly veiled times. Veiled in everyday occurrences, Jesus becomes more and more exposed as we encounter Him in the Scriptures. Hearing the reading of the Canon of Holy Scripture opens us up to understanding that Jesus is present even when apparently most absent.

And finally we are told that He is known to us in the breaking of the bread-not in the existence of the bread, but in its breaking. The entire passion of our Lord is reenacted in this action and we know Jesus Christ. And this is the capstone of Jesus' presence in everything. And so, to support my conclusions, I am drawn to Fr. Robert Farrar Capon a magnificent author and an Episcopal priest. Capon writes: "There can never be a completely spiritual version of the Christian religion. Not that that hasn't been attempted. There have always been itchy souls in the church who are allergic to materiality. For example, you find Christians who argue that if the deepest reality of the Eucharist is the presence of Jesus himself, then the signs of bread and wine are mere symbols that can be switched around at our pleasure. Beer and pretzels, or crackers and milk will do just that.

"Their fallacy stems from forgetting that the sacraments are precisely hats on an invisible man. To be sure, if the Word had decided to wear a beer-and-pretzel hat instead of a bread-and-wine hat, he would have been perfectly within his rights; it's his head and it's his hat. But once he has announced that the bread-and-wine hat is his choice for the late afternoon of the world, we had best keep a careful eye on *that*. It is, after all, the only one under which we *know* he has promised to make himself available.

"He's (Jesus is) available and active everywhere… you can look up the invisible man on the golf course any time you like. That's not the point. The problem on the golf course is that it's hard to be sure you've got hold of the right invisible man—or, indeed, of anything more than one of your own bright ideas. It is not a question of presence; it is a question of how to know when you've grasped it. If I'm right, for example, the Mystery that the Eucharist signifies is present throughout the creation; the Incarnate Word does not become *more present* at the Mass than he is elsewhere. What happens at the consecration is that his presence is sacramentalized for us under a device of his own choosing. We have his assurance for the device of bread and wine; the best you can say about beer and pretzels is maybe—which you could just as well say about ducks, dogs, or dandelions….

"At the Eucharist, Jesus does not show up in a room from which he was absent. The eucharistic "change," it seems to me, is neither quantitative nor even, properly, an ontological matter. It's qualitative—a clear but subtle shift in God's style that makes it possible, under the form of an occasional meal, for his creatures to effectively take the Word's constant mystery of victimization and victory into their ordinary exchanges."

I apologize for the lengthy quote but it *was* necessary. We know Jesus in the breaking of the bread. It is what makes all the rest make sense. Mountains are brought low; rough places made plain; and the crooked made straight.

Perhaps a poem would end our investigation best. Senator Jeremiah Denton of Alabama, while a prisoner of war in Viet Nam in the 1960s and 1970s, among many who sensed that God had forsaken them, wrote this poem. He thinks it was on an Easter Sunday – but since he had no watch nor calendar he could not be sure.

> The soldiers stare, then drift away
> Young John finds nothing he can say.
> The veil is rent; the deed is done;
> And Mary holds her only son.
>
> His limbs grow stiff, the night grows cold,
> But naught can loose that mother's hold.
> Her gentle, anguished eyes seem blind.
> Who knows what thoughts run through her mind?
>
> Perhaps she thinks of last week's palms,
> With cheering thousands off'ring alms,
> Or dreams of Cana on that day
> She nagged him till she got her way.

Her face shows grief but no despair,
Her head though bowed has faith to spare,
For even now she could suppose
His thorns might somehow yield a rose.

Her life with Him was full of signs
That God writes straight with crooked lines,
Dark clouds may hide the rising sun,
And all seem lost, when all be won! Amen.

CHAPTER 15
FOURTH SUNDAY OF EASTER

Holy Cross Episcopal Church, Kingston, New York
Acts 6:1-9; 7:2a, 51-60; Psalm 23; I Peter 2:19-25
John 10:1-10

Coming to the fourth Sunday of Easter, we are again encountered by a Gospel account whose entire goal is to focus our attention on Jesus Christ, the author and finisher of our faith. Christianity has many and multiple concerns, it has only one center; there are a myriad of foci of our faith, but only one central object of our faith. There are many things that Christians are encouraged to do, but only one person who has really done everything that needs to be done (for us). And so we come to the Gospel pericope which is often seen by exegetes as difficult and confusing because of the metaphor shifts. Jesus speaks here of being first, the one who enters the fold correctly; then he claims to be the shepherd who leads others in and out correctly; and then concludes with claiming to be the door of the sheepfold.

Now if we did something like this is in our high school or college writing class we would be marked incorrect for mixing our metaphors. But this is not college writing – it is the God-man Jesus Christ describing his multiple roles as fulfilling everything humanity needs.

First, Jesus enters in, when all we could do was to surreptitiously pilfer the things of God. What we could only gain through thievery, Jesus has procured for us legitimately and freely. Then when we act like sheep without a shepherd, Jesus becomes that feeding, sustaining, guiding presence which stabilizes us. And finally to assure us that there is a recognizable and repeatable method of entry, he, himself becomes the door so we will continue to recognize the way home.

J. Rufus Mosely writes of this omni-competence of Jesus this way: "The highest self-disclosure that Jesus makes of Himself is that He is Perfect Everything, giving Perfect Everything, enabling Perfect Everything, and commanding Perfect Everything.

"He is the most precious being of all because He is God, the Eternal Christ and the perfect man on the plane of our suffering and need; He is the Perfect Word made Perfect Flesh, the Perfect Ideal perfectly realized and manifested. He is the Perfect Man perfectly self-offered, resurrected, glorified, and on the throne of God and the universe. He is the perfect beginning of the new heaven and the new earth.

"He is the Perfect Body as well as the Perfect Soul. In Him the perfect spirit has attained the perfect form and concretion....He is Perfect God on the throne of man, and perfect man on the throne of God."

Here we have a sampling of an understanding that Jesus sought to convey – everything I need is summed up and made available in Jesus of Nazareth, the Christ of God. In him, teaching is summed up as truth; metaphors are given meaning; and contrarieties are coalesced.

The second teaching of this often difficult Gospel is that Jesus leads believers in and out of this pasture, through this door, that is none other than He, Himself. It is a simple truth, and often preachers have summed it up with "be like Jesus."

Now I don't know about you, but the one thing I fail at most often is being like Jesus. Jesus says give, I like to receive; he says love your enemies, I would like to annihilate them (or at least maim them badly); he says turn the other cheek, I lift the other hand; he says believe, I find solace in doubt; and on and on.

But the wonder of this passage is that it is none of the noble virtues that are applauded and encouraged. Jesus merely says, "enter...go in and out and find pasture." And what follows is life and as one translation puts it, "life superabundantly." And so I am called to live the life Jesus provides – not as he is perfect, but faithfully following him and imbibing his provision.

John David Burton, one time Poet-in-Residence at Princeton University writes this poignant poem with

which I have found great identity and I trust you will
too...

Being Like Jesus
"He was a man of sorrows and acquainted with grief."
Isaiah 53:3

The preacher says,
"Now that you are saved, go be like Jesus."
I may be lost, for I am not like Jesus.

Jesus, says the preacher, was much in prayer.
I pray now and then, but not all of the time.
The preacher says Jesus thought mostly of God.
I think of God, sometimes, but much of the time
I think of my children, and their children, of
Jean, my wife, who died, of women I have loved
and of a woman I want to marry.
I think about work and money and sex and war
and about a man I once wanted to kill.

Jesus, says the preacher, had great faith.
I have faith, but doubts, also.
I think about the world and my life in the world,
and wonder if the meaning of it all is that there is
no meaning to it all.

I had just about given up hope of "being like
Jesus," thus proving that I am saved, when I
read of my Master that He was

"a man of sorrows and acquainted with grief"
and I thought, "So am I! So am I,"
glad to be like Jesus in one way at least.

I am not the first nor only man to watch a
wife die, to see a son go mad nor to have
a grandchild suffer,
but all of these are the first time for me,
and there are times I want to say,
"It is more than I can bear,"
knowing that the unbearable must be borne.

I would like to be like Jesus in all good
things, greatness of soul, constancy in prayer,
love of foe as well as friend, full of faith
and no doubt at all, thinking mostly of God
instead of thinking of getting my car fixed.
Still, if showing that I am saved demands that
I be like Jesus, maybe it is worth it to be,
 "a man of sorrows and acquainted with grief."
Better that than not being like Jesus at all.

I don't understand everything the preacher says.

And so, men and women, Jesus has done it all, and
it is all wrapped up together. And His resurrected life
invites us to live and be like him – at whatever level
– and follow – and go in and out – and find pasture. In
a world that engenders hunger, we just might find the
food we need. Amen!

CHAPTER 16
THE FIFTH SUNDAY
OF EASTER

Holy Cross Episcopal Church, Kingston, New York
Acts 17:1-15; Psalm 66; I Peter 2:1-10 & John 14:1-14

Most everything in the canon of Holy Scripture is both intellectually challenging and personally edifying. There is the sense in which we can approach the Bible for study, and there is the very real sense in which we can and must approach it for spiritual aid and assistance.

In today's Gospel, the disciples are concerned that in the absence of Jesus there will be a cloud of unknowing – a certain lack of clarity, and certainly the absence of assurance. To counter these concerns, Jesus parallels the liturgical three things He is (in last week's Gospel) with the three most necessary elements needed by humankind.

Last week we saw Jesus as the "enterer" who got in the right way, and this is paralleled by the "way" in today's declaration-"I am the way…" Last week we saw Jesus as the door, and today this is paralleled by

"I am…the truth…." And last week we saw Jesus as the shepherd, which is today paralleled by "I am the… life."

"Without the way, there is no going…
Without the truth, there is no knowing…
Without the life, there is no growing…"

And all of these are claimed by Jesus, to be wrapped up in the "Who" that He is.

We often think of a way as a map – a planned route to be taken to get to a certain place or end. Jesus doesn't address the way in this fashion, rather he wraps it all up in Himself. He is the way-we travel in, through, by, and according to Him. We don't look for the way, we trust Him. There is not so much of discovery as there is surprise and wonder. "I am the way," says Jesus, wrapping all of our journey up in His person. And if we can't really see where we're going (and I've been there often) we look at Jesus Christ.

A little girl was making a drawing and her mother and father asked her, "what are you drawing?" She replied, "I am drawing God!" Her parents replied, "But no one knows what God looks like." To which the little one quickly replied, "They will when I am finished!"

And so when we can't see the way, we can trust the way since it is Jesus.

Then He claims, "I am the truth." Not a bunch of true statements like the fundamentalist Catholics and Protestants like to make Him. Jesus is not propositional revelation but is personal revelation. As the truth we are given the ability to know-not everything of course, but to know Him.

Following 9/11 one of the famous Country-Western singers named Alan Jackson wrote a wonderful song called "Where Were You When the World Stopped Turning?" In it he has these wonderful lines:

> "But I know Jesus and I talk to God and
> I've known since I was young;
>
> Faith, hope, and love are three things he gave us,
> And the greatest is love."

Knowing Jesus Christ as truth doesn't make us "know-it-alls," but rather we know the One who knows it all. Christian trust makes us humble not obnoxious.

Finally, Jesus claims, "I am the life…" We live, as it were, in Jesus Christ. He doesn't give us something that He Himself is not. In living the Christian life, we are living the Christ life.

When the Apostle Paul wrote, "I am crucified with Christ, nevertheless I live, yet not I, it is Christ who lives in me," he was making the profound statement that our living is the living Christ, living in us.

There are no substitutes for the way, the truth, and the life. There are not really any imitations. Substitutes and imitations work — but any substitutes or imitations of the way, the truth, and the life, leave us aimless, unknowing, and certainly anything but living "superabundantly." (see last week). No, there are many decoys, however that turn us away — things like church polity, high or low church habits, rules, laws, expectations, etc. All of these tempt us to idolatry, when Jesus seems to claim that He is enough.

The story is told of a policeman who had not gotten his quota of arrests on a given week. So late on a Saturday night he parked just around the corner from a local gin mill. No one came out. And then at last, at about 2:00AM fifteen or sixteen men came out, got into various autos and drove off. All except one man who staggered more than any other, wrestled for what seemed an eternity to try to get the key in his car door, and then once in the car proceeded to turn on and off every light several times. Finally after about twenty minutes he got the car started and wove dangerously around the parking lot before exiting into the street. Once he was in the street, the policeman was on him in a flash.

Getting the man out of the car, the policeman gave him a breathalyzer test that he passed with a 0.00. Impossible, thought the policeman as he shook the instrument and tried again. Another 0.00. Frustrated the policeman said to the fellow, "How can this be?" And the man replied, "I am the designated decoy."

Many are the designated decoys to keep us from following Jesus Christ. Give them up – take Him up, and know personally and with much anticipation for tomorrow, Jesus Christ as Lord. Amen!

CHAPTER 17
Sixth Sunday of Easter

St. John's Episcopal Church, Kingston, New York
Acts 17:22-31; Psalm 148; I Peter 3:8-18 & John 15:1-8

Just this week I was reading *The Chronicle of Higher Education*, one of those journals that goes with my job, and a retired educator wrote, "I have had the happiest unhappy life, which is better, I suppose than having an unhappy happy life." Not entirely sure what he meant, I surmise that he was saying that in the midst of much unhappiness and a less than perfect existence, he was, nonetheless, happy through it all.

Peter, in the lesson of the morning, says something about "He that would love life and see good days..." and then some admonitions follow. It would appear that Peter, the impetuous, trusting, risk-taking disciple who loved to be out in front with Jesus, continued long after Jesus' ascension to still celebrate life. It is as if Peter were setting the stage for what John Wesley would say to his mother many centuries later, "I can't believe that when God put man on this earth he meant for us to be absolutely miserable here." And Wesley's life was, on many occasions miserable.

From Wesley's diary we get these records:

Sunday AM, May 5 – Preached at St. Anne's. Was asked not to come back.

Sunday PM, May 5 – Preached at St. John's. Deacons said, "Get out and stay out!"

Sunday, AM, May 12 – Preached at St. Jude's. Can't go back there either.

Sunday, PM, May 12 – Preached at St. George's. Kicked out again.

Sunday AM, May 19 – Preached at St. Somebody Else's. Deacons called a special meeting and said I couldn't return.

Sunday PM, May 19 – Preached on street. Kicked off street.

Sunday AM, May 26 – Preached in meadow. Chased out of meadow by a bull turned loose during the service.

Sunday AM, June 2 – Preached at the edge of town. Kicked off the highway.

Sunday PM, June 2 – Afternoon, preached in a pasture. Ten thousand came to hear.

And along with all of this was a wife who would follow him around and begin riots by throwing rotten fruit at her husband. And Wesley loved life.

Jesus had placed the foundation for life firmly on a relationship with He, Himself. The Gospel record of the morning speaks of the vine/branch relationship. And contrary to popular interpretation Jesus is not giving an ultimatum here, but rather is describing the relationship believers have with him. There is not really an imperative in this lesson as much as there is an indicative.

- Jesus is the vine – believers are branches.
- Branches are integral to the vine and the vine is integral to the branches.
- Branches bear fruit.
- Branches bearing fruit prove their integrity with the vine.

The lessons are extremely simple. What Jesus is doing is telling us what disciples of Christ are like – it is natural – automatic – essential.

Later, in Galatians, Paul will describe the fruit of the Christian life with words like "love, joy, peace, gentleness, meekness, longsuffering," but Jesus is satisfied with telling us we will bear these things. The emphasis of Jesus is not on striving to produce these things, but acceptance that these will be produced in and through us.

I wonder if much Christian frustration comes, and then a lack of these fruit because we try too hard. It is a revelation through Paul that these fruit in our lives are the "fruit of the Spirit." Sometimes, I merely have to get out of the way.

Jesus is not threatening the disciples that they will be cut off if they don't produce – don't push the metaphor too far. He is saying live branches are alive. Dead ones are gone.

And so we are led to several conclusions:

Paul's words to the men of Athens, "In Him we live, and move and have our being..." The Christian life is life – not struggle; not attempt; not attainment. There is a very real sense in which Christ is now our life. Every movement, our very being is Christo-centric.

Then Peter settles that it is possible to love life. Oh, I know there are the melancholy among us – the discouraged and the depressed – I identify with you. And yet one of the most joyous men I know is a melancholy curmudgeon who was a professor of mine thirty years ago and who made the most profound impression on my life. We share temperments! But we love life. (Someone said "It beats the alternative"). But remember it is the Christ-life for the believer that we love.

Finally, Jesus' metaphor of the vine and branches is pertinent. The branch must abide in the vine. And "abide" is the key word. The difference between abiding and visiting is crucial to our understanding. When we visit, we are at the mercy of the host. We ask for what we need; we respect the home as the domain of the host. But when we abide, we do for ourselves – we keep the house, we prepare our meals, we don't ask a host to serve us. "Abide in me," Jesus says, and in saying this invites us to be at home – where faith is as natural as breath, and life is as normal as the process of inhaling and exhaling.

The lessons of this week begin to prepare us for Pentecost's celebration, and an old A. B. Simpson hymn is appropriate:

Jesus breathe thy spirit on me,
Teach me how to breathe thee in;
Help me pour into thy being
All my life of self and sin.

I am breathing out my own life
That I may be filled with Thine,
Letting go my strength and weakness
Breathing in thy life divine.

Breathing out my sinful nature,
You have borne it all for me,
Breathing in thy cleansing fulness
Finding all my life in Thee.

I am breathing every moment
Drawing all my life from thee,
Breath by breath I live upon thee
Blessed Spirit, breathe in me.

And so, as we continue to celebrate this Eastertide, we are invited by Jesus to life. To live. He is alive, and we are part of that. It is immense! Amen!

CHAPTER 18
SEVENTH SUNDAY OF EASTER

St. John's Episcopal Church, Kingston, New York
Acts 1:1-14; Psalm 68:1-20; I Peter 4:12-19
John 17:1-11

As I approached today's texts, and began to see the emphasis among them, I was tempted to wish that my interim period began next week. Sometimes, one would like to run from texts because they approach controversy.

My three sons often remind me that in thirty years, they have never heard me use "Hell" as a topic or emphasis in my sermons. I am proud of this. And this is pertinent today, because many Christians read the Holy Scriptures, and from them get caught up in warning people of Hell-rather than appealing to people with the goodness of God in Christ. [We may want to return to this on some later date!]

Hell is one of those interesting features of the Gospels. I am reminded of Gary Larsen, the great comic writer, who used to do the Far Side comics. He was most theological in many of them. And in one color,

Sunday strip, Larsen had dogs delivering mail, scooping up dog droppings, and washing fire hydrants. The only caption was "Dog Hell." That may be sufficient commentary on what Hell really is. Again, we might return to this in a later gathering.

The first confrontation in the Acts reading of the day is that Jesus expects Holy Spirit empowered people to spread the Gospel universally. It is obvious from the record that Jesus wishes all to be related to Him, and He sends the disciples with a world-wide assignment.

An interesting writing of Charles Darwin was recorded to have read, "If you ever appear to be heading for marooning on a deserted island, pray that the lesson of the missionary has arrived before you." There is something good about the message of the Gospel applied world-wide. [We won't get into the faults of the church over 2,000 years this morning – that is preachable from other texts]. The lesson of the missionary is that God loves people and Jesus redeemed the universe in a way no other deity or religion can do.

Notice the Psalm we read together a few moments ago. It supports this universal concern of God.

Peter follows along and tells us to "entrust souls to a faithful creator." When Peter says that it is difficult for the righteous to be saved, and then asks how will the impious and sinners stand? He answers himself. "By a faithful creator!" is how they will stand.

And finally in the Gospel of the day, which is the record of the Gethsemane prayer of Jesus on the night of His arrest, says that eternal life is to know God and Jesus Christ. Not a whole lot more – nothing less. This is clearly Gospel teaching.

And so, I think we must delineate several teachings from these lessons. They sum up resurrection life and prepare us for the Pentecost emphasis of next Lord's Day.

First, the provision of God is universal. The teachings of the Bible are so multiple and repeated on this that it is almost unnecessary to state it. "He is not willing that any should perish, but that all should come to repentance."

The second lesson is that universality is wrapped up in the particularity of Jesus Christ. Jesus clearly said, "No one comes to the Father but through me." It is the scandal of particularity. This has been the church's teaching for two-thousand years. And we can embrace it, when we are willing to negotiate the curves thrown to us by the first point of universality, and the following point.

And here we find that there is relatively little stated by Jesus on Heaven and Hell. [Actually, Jesus says much more about money than about Heaven and Hell combined – but more of that around October and pledge time]. There may be a plurality of religious "ends" to humanity, and the Judeo-Christian heaven may be just that, Heaven.

And this leads us to the final emphasis of the Scriptures which I would so much have wished to skip over today: Jesus says "Go into all the world and preach the Gospel," and in his John 17 prayer, he prays, "They are in the world, keep them." Christians are Christian. We will not do any favors to pluralism and multi-cultural-ism by watering down our faith, but by affirming it. I can only trust a person of another faith when I am true to my own – for to forfeit mine is to threaten yours with forfeiture.

So there. We have navigated several Scriptures. And our lesson is simple. Be a Christian believer. By God's grace we can be. Amen!

CHAPTER 19
TRINITY SUNDAY

St. John's Episcopal Church, Kingston, New York
Genesis 1:1 – 2:3; Psalm 150; II Corinthians 13:5-14
Matthew 28:16-20

Since the fourth century, the church has proclaimed her faith in the Triune God – Father, Son, Holy Spirit. Granted the church has not said she understands the doctrine, merely that she believes it.

In one of the churches I served in inner city Philadelphia, I had a man who had reworked the whole doctrine because he found it incomprehensible. He often shared his reworking with me, and I found it incomprehensible. He did nothing but confuse the matter more – not to mention he stepped outside of 2,000 years of church historic authority.

At a Roman Catholic parish in Utica, New York, a number of years ago, an elderly CCD (Sunday School) teacher had taught her eight year olds that the Trinity was the Father, Son, and Holy Spirit – in preparation for the Bishop's visitation. Rehearsing with the children, she asked one little tot, "What is the Trinity?"

And with a little lisp, he softly replied, "The Father, the Son, and the Holy Spirit." Hard of hearing, the teacher responded, "I don't understand!" To which the little tike said, "The Father, the Son and the Holy Spirit." Again the aging teacher said, "I don't understand." Frustrated the little fellow mustered all his volume and shouted, "You're not supposed to understand. It's a mystery, you know!"

Well, here we are on Trinity Sunday, the day of the Christian year when more heresy is taught than on any other day. And so I will endeavor not to add to the heresy. I want to talk about the necessity of the tri-person Godhead of Christianity and celebrate the big God we have.

In Irian Jaya, one of the large islands of Indonesia, a friend of mine served for forty years as a missionary. To translate the phrase "praise the Lord," they wrestled for several years. Finally they came to the conclusion that in the Moni language "Make God big!" was the best parallel to English "Praise the Lord." And that is exactly what the doctrine of the Trinity does – it acknowledges the immensity of God.

First century Jewish converts were caught head on with the problem of God the Father, whom they had traditionally worshipped, with the omnipresence of God the Spirit, and then with the Jesus whom they readily worshipped and to whom they cried, "My Lord and my God!" These three realities called for a statement of just who God is. God is too big for simple definition.

The creeds are therefore created in the third century (and we will read St. Athanasius's creed as our affirmation of faith following the sermon this morning).

There is a diversity demanded by personality. If God is personal as we acclaim God to be, then personality is only personality when it is manifested for other personalities to experience. Hence, before creation, God needs self with whom to communicate. It is no accident that in Genesis 1:26 the Hebrew word "Elohim" is used for God-the plural in singular-a hint at what would come in the progress of revelation.

That God is a person (having intellect, will, and emotion) demands that there be a diversity within the Godhead, and behold: Father, Son, Holy Spirit. God could hold converse within the Godhead prior to creating any intelligent beings. God is therefore self-sufficient.

Secondly, activity is demanded by eternality. God must be at work doing. And the Judeo-Christian revelation is a record of those mighty acts of God's doing. The eternal reality of God manifests in creation and continues to manifest in continued creation. Nothing can be eternal without doing something with that eternality. Action is a result of being, and God is the ultimate actor in the reality we know as the universe.

Finally, unity is demanded by plurality. The Greeks and the Romans in classical history had a pantheon of gods – these gods often were at war with one another because there was no unity in their plurality. They were not of the same substance or essence as the declaration is of the Father, Son, and Holy Spirit. And if there is no unity, there is no meaning –no ultimate purpose-no goal.

*We in the United States have on our money the phrase "E Pluribus Unim"-out of the many, one. So with the doctrine of the Trinity – out of the Three, there is one.

Humanity has postulated four essences: earth, wind, fire, and water. And from this has searched over and over for the quintessence or the fifth essence that would unify all of the others. So too, with our thoughts of God – we want in God the one who brings all into a singular meaning and purpose-the Triune God of the Universe.

Even the term "universe" tells us that out of much, there is one. (One PhD joked that he was asked during his defense of his dissertation, to "Define the universe and give two examples.") Such absurdities are funny at best.

Trinity Sunday – a celebration of God's person – God everything the human person needs, wrapped up in Father, Son, and Holy Spirit. Amen!

---

*Thoughts from this point to the end of the homily are borrowed from Dr. Ravi Zacharis.

CHAPTER 20
THE SECOND
SUNDAY AFTER
PENTECOST

St. John's Episcopal Church, Kingston, New York
Deuteronomy 11:18-21, 26-28; Psalm 31;
Romans 3:21-25a, 28; Matthew 7:21-27

Everybody likes the beginning of things and most like the ends – the arrivals. The start of a race and the finish are the high points; the first classes of high school or college and commencement day are the high points. It is the in-between times we find most trying.

These weeks in ordinary time are the weeks to help us between the high points of Christian celebration – they are weeks to help us do what needs to be done. Moses speaks to the children of Israel challenging them to lay up the words of God in their hearts and minds so as to do the work of God; Romans speaks to us of living the faith life; and the Gospel account tells us the significance of building what we build on, the rock and not on the sand. [It is interesting to note that nothing is said about the type of structure. The focus is on the foundation].

And so we are confronted with three Scriptures that challenge us with the in-between time-the time between our first steps of faith and the finality of our earthly walk. And I think that both the evangelicals with their exclusive emphasis on the "born-again" experience, and the radical sacramentalists who think if we can only get some water on this baby's head it will be saved eternally, are wrong. Both miss the reality of a life lived for Christ.

That the Christian life is a life of journey and progress cannot be overlooked. We keep at it. Louis Cassels, one time famous journalist, puts it this way: "The automatic goodness of ready made saints evidently is less precious to God than the flawed and sweaty goodness achieved by fallible men through struggling with temptations and making responsible choices in difficult situations....To regard this world as a crucible in which souls are forged makes sense, of course....We are confronted not with a riddle, but a choice."

I am intrigued with these texts that are so vague in their specifics. The outline that seems to come from them is that we are confronted by God in the crucible of life and we are thus confronted continually.

First, there is the choice between being blessed and being cursed. Blessed in being God-conscious; cursed in being conscious of everything but God. God trusts us with this choice within His grace.

Then Paul, in Romans speaks to us to be people of faith. It is interesting that we are not to be people of doctrine or people of experience or people of emotion, but people of faith. Faith believes – that is enough. Faith puts its roots into a God who became human for us. And we are given the right to believe it or not.

And finally in the Gospel Jesus says build – but build on rock. (Remember Jesus has spoken elsewhere of he, himself being the stone which the builder rejected – and Peter's words, "Thou art the Christ, the son of the living God," being the rock on which he would build his church). The type of building is unspecified. The foundation is all that is our concern. What you and I do, we do for Jesus, the Christ that is sufficient.

Henri J. M. Nouwen poignantly puts it this way: "Jesus does not respond to our worry-filled way of living by saying that we should not be so busy with worldly affairs. He does not try to pull us away from the many events, activities, and people that make up our lives…

He asks us to shift our point of gravity, to relocate the center of our attention, to change our priorities…. Jesus does not speak about a change of activities, a change of contacts, or even a change of pace. He speaks about a change of heart."

Summer brings us a new season – a season when we will celebrate a Sunday school year over; we will work an annual fair; we will honor graduates; we will plan for a rector search; and on and on. Jesus merely says, "Do it for me." And we will. Amen.

CHAPTER 21
THE THIRD SUNDAY
AFTER PENTECOST

Church of the Resurrection, Hopewell Junction,
New York
Hosea 5:15-6:6; Psalm 50; Romans 4:13-18
Matthew 9:9-13

Recently a parishioner of another parish in the Diocese cornered me and said that they liked to hear controversial sermons. I wish they were here today. We have in the texts, the controversy of God and his people being likened to a prophet and his prostitute wife, and we have the controversy, yea the scandal, of Jesus spending his time with the irreligious – the tax collectors and the sinners. Oh bless us all! And in the center of all this is Paul's scandalous declaration in Romans that there is little or no merit in keeping the law since God only deals with us by grace. If we do not grasp grace as scandalous, we do not grasp the concept of grace.

The Hosea prophecy is clearly one which tells those who will hear, that God's ultimate intent and purpose, is that guilt be removed and that forgiveness be experienced. This is uniquely Judeo-Christian. It is the scandal of God saying, even in your utter unfaithfulness, you will know my utter faithfulness and forgiveness. C. H. Dodd convincingly argues, "We believe in the forgiveness of sin, not by convincing ourselves that our sins were excusable, or remediable, or that we meant well, or that 'we won't do it again.' It is because the principle of forgiveness is built into the structure of a moral order created and determined by the character of a just and faithful God."

Then Romans reminds us that it is all by grace – we can't have it both ways – meritorious and grace both. Either God has met his own requirements in Christ Jesus or we are in dire straights. Guilt is endless if grace is absent.

And the final text is Matthew's record of Jesus and his crowd of eating and drinking buddies. The religious establishment did not approve (they never do). Jesus was saying that you can have religion without guilt, but you cannot have Jesus Christ without guilt. The sick need a physician, the sinners need his call.

I want to share two stories with you this morning which will illustrate the scandal and controversy of sin and guilt. First about a young women whose name we do not know. She committed what she felt was a terrible sin but one which society has declared legal. She was so completely overtaken with guilt that she began therapy. For months she went to a therapist who told her she had nothing to be guilty about. But she continued to be haunted by the guilt. Finally she approached a clergy-person who told her to go and buy a ticket to plush a tropical resort-travel there, spend and be spent, and after several weeks come home guilt free. You see, said the clergy-person, you are guilty of guilt and you need to free yourself from it.

Her response was "Who do you think you are-God?" You see, to endeavor to rid ourselves of guilt is to cover over that which is not an end in and of itself, but rather a means to an end.

Our second story is about a miserable, hateful, and nasty woman we will call Martha (just in case you know her real name). Martha always had a correction for her Rector and a directive for everyone else in the parish. She was the epitome of the type of person you wish would convert to the Baptists or someone else – but she never did. For almost twenty-five years, she alone, and also through her husband, ran rough shod over the entire parish-almost to its decimation. Then one day during Lent, she heard that the Sunday School was singing a song about sin and confession. She immediately secured the words and confronted the Rector about the terrible things his wife was teaching to those innocent little children. Cease and desist immediately she demanded. The kind Rector's wife ceased. There must be no consciousness of sin or confession thereof in this church – after all we're Episcopalians.

That would not be any great story if it were not for Martha's follow-up corrective to the Rector three weeks later during Easter Season when he, according to rubric, chose to omit the General Confession from the liturgy. Following the recessional she was on him in a flash. I don't appreciate your deleting the General Confession. After all it is a part of our heritage, and I expect it there next week.

Well, I won't tell you what became of Martha or the Rector, but Martha was guilty of guilt and would not acknowledge that she was guilty of sin (and so were the children in Sunday school). God has no answer for us when we are guilty of guilt. But the texts of today are powerfully reassuring when we acknowledge that we are guilty of sin. You see, Martha wanted the General Confession to show off her humility not to receive forgiveness. And there is a vast difference between the two.

If we confess for any other reason than to move on with life forgiven, we have not confessed. Notice the Hosea passage, "He has torn that he may heal; he has sticken that he might bind us up. After two days he will revive us…" The lessons are poignant and scandalous.

God says to us today, that we are sinners. Confess it, be forgiven, and get on with it. Your guilt is not my goal- your life is. Either you can settle for guilt being your landing strip where you will wallow, guilty of guilt, or you can accept guilt as your launching pad into forgiveness.

Father, forgive us our sins as we forgive those who sin against us. Amen!

CHAPTER 22
THE FOURTH
SUNDAY AFTER
PENTECOST

St. John's Episcopal Church, Kingston, New York
Exodus 19:2-8A; Psalm 100; Romans 5:6-11
Matthew 9:35-10:15

An evangelist friend of mine, a man in the know, tells the true story of the Founding Executive Director of a Christian social service agency on the West Coast. It seems the organization began well with intimate involvement by this charismatic and able leader. The organization grew to international fame, when one day a needy person came to the office of the Director.

The secretary approached the Director and said, "A person is here to speak briefly with you about a need they have." His response was, "I can't see him. Since I've gotten involved with the needs of the many, I have no time for the individual any more." The insightful secretary responded, "Sir, that is amazing, even God is not that busy!"

The entire emphasis of the Gospel account this morning is that those who should care about humanity do not, and Jesus is challenging the disciples to fill the void left by the organized and bureaucratic religion of the day. And what was true of Israel in the first century is no less true of the systemic religious establishment of the twenty-first century. All systems tend toward evil, and the very systems which are established to protect the human person become the stocks which enslave the individual.

I was in sixth grade when we heard the then President John F. Kennedy make the famous statement "Ask not what your county can do for you – ask what you can do for your country." And we all swallowed it hard. But it is diametrically opposed to the historic purpose of nations and even more to the classical biblical purpose of the church – our emphasis this morning. The organization [read "system," or "judactory," etc.] exists precisely for the good of the person and not vice versa! This is an essentially classical understanding which is sorely overlooked or rewritten as culture progresses.

Jesus is proclaiming several trans-generational realities in this encounter with the crowds. First notice the characteristics of the masses of people. They are harassed – a typical approach to people by the powers that be. The systemic tends to care for the system; the bureaucratic tends the bureaucracy. Harassment is the condition of treating people as means to an end rather than as an end in and of themselves. But remember that throughout the history of humanity, humanity continues when systems die. The enduring end is the human person. The crowds were harassed.

Then, the crowds were helpless. They were conditioned into a victim-hood which they would never consciously choose. When the system exists for itself, there is never any avenue for the individual to reach her or his inherent potential. Contemporary examples abound in certain ethnic groups of our urban centers and in certain fundamentalistic Christian circles where the dogma declares the individual as incapacitated when it comes to using intelligence to grasp truth.

Finally, these masses of people are characterized by leaderlessness. They were literally like "sheep without a shepherd." The parallels are amazing. Sheep without shepherds merely exist. They cannot find food, much less eat, and they can, in significant rain, stand looking up to the sky, and drown. There is an essential neediness to sheep – hence to the human as well in Jesus' parallel.

These are the conditions in which Jesus finds the crowds of Jews, who, indeed, had priests, scribes, Pharisees, Sadducees, and other religious persons in leadership positions. The lesson is clear – it is one thing to be in a leadership position, it is an entirely different thing to lead.

This condition then is the foundation of the harvest – it is plentiful and it is without an abundance of laborers. The harvest is the full incorporation of humanity into God and its true laborers [read "leaders"] are few.

And that is where we come in with the challenge of the texts to you and me this morning. The call to the Christian laborer (leader) is first a call to compassion. We are to do what the harassers were not able to do. We are called to see the needs of people and to become present for them. Compassion – this means to feel with (literally to have passion with as in the passion of Christ). A leader who does not feel for those she or he is leading is not a leader. You and I are called in this sense to be leading laborers in the harvest of God. You may not like it-I may not like it, but I am called with you to do it.

Then we are called to be gospellers of the Kingdom. That is we are to be living good news. It is almost as if the systemic is irrelevant and the Kingdom is everything. Gospel, which means good news, has been just the opposite for centuries in the Church, and continues to be a questionable thing today until we get caught by it.

I think with a heart of commitment and a little bit of release, you and I can be people to lead others into biblical Christian living and celebration. Amen!

CHAPTER 23
THE FIFTH SUNDAY
AFTER PENTECOST

St. John's Episcopal Church, Kingston, New York
Jeremiah 10:7-13; Psalm 69:1-18; Romans 5:15b-19
Matthew 10:16-33

I was summoned to jury duty this past week. After being called with the first group, we were asked questions by each lawyer to ascertain if we would be good jurors for this particular case. The questions went on for what appeared to be an eternity. Beginning at 10:30AM they continued until 4:00PM when eight of us were seated.

We were directed by the judge that we could have no contact with either party or their lawyers as long as the case continued. But when the case was settled mid-week, we were told we were free to speak with either or both lawyers. As I left the court room, the two lawyers seemed interested in speaking to the guy with the clergy collar on. I had no particular interest in speaking with them, but as I got closer, I could not help addressing a question to both of them. "Gentlemen," I said, "You asked each of us an inordinate amount of questions. One question you never asked was, 'What do you think of lawyers?'" And upon completing the question, I merely said, "Good day," and left.

I really wasn't being unkind, but in light of last Sunday's homily on the systemic tendency toward evil, I could not help myself. Needless to say, the systemic is diametrically opposed to Christian truth and living. This is the essence of the Gospel record of today.

Notice all the negative relationships Jesus indicates:

"sheep in the midst of wolves;" "beware of men... they will deliver you up;" "brother will deliver up brother...etc.;" "if they called the master of the house Beelzebul, how much more will they malign those of the household..." The negatives abound. The hopeful Gospel appears to be fraught with hopeless dangers.

This text is a continuation of the text of last Lord's Day, and is a gracious act on the part of Jesus to assure His disciples that the trends of the world are not congenial to the convictions of the believer in Christ. In light of the potential conflict, Jesus tells us who believe, "Be wise as serpents and guileless as doves." ["Helpless" is a poor and unfortunate translation]. The world in which we live calls for an approach characterized by wisdom – not just head-knowledge, but a wisdom which sees into and through the circumstances of life. And coupled with this is the guileless spirit which keeps itself from becoming cynical in the midst of the world's tendencies.

Jesus does three things in speaking with his disciples here: first he prepares them with gracious assurance;, then he delivers them from needless fear; and, finally, he challenges them with appropriate orientation.

That this message is a message of grace dare not be missed. Jesus is not promising some kind of a pie-in-the-sky religion which is irrelevant to the realities of life. The Christian life, the life He sets out is fraught with conflict and contrariness. Not everyone agrees with God; therefore not everyone agrees with the believer. It can be quite disconcerting, but the aspect of grace here, is that Jesus owns up to this ahead of time. Don't think of Christian living as a safe place – think of it rather as a good place, for it is where God is.

The systems of the world will not understand the values and paradoxes of true faith; family will misunderstand; some places will not welcome the believer. And since this happened to the Master, the disciple is not necessarily any better off. When our bell-ringing on Wednesday night is misunderstood, when we feed the one dying of AIDS, when we accept the outcast etc., we will be treated with disdain at times. Expect it – Jesus says.

I have had people (brothers, fathers, others) in the church leave when we accepted the unacceptable – when the outcast was brought in. Jesus predicted that we would be so treated. One brief example will serve. Upon arriving at my parish in Long Island in 1997, I needed immediately to hire an organist/choir master. I found the person I wanted, hired him, and put him to work. On the first Sunday, we were aligned for procession when one of the members of the parish who had been there the longest whispered to me, "He's black!" My response was, "I hadn't noticed," and we processed into church. Brother will deliver up brother over race, gender, ethnicity, Christian counter-culture, and on and on. Christianity can be quite disconcerting and disconnecting. Jesus prepares his disciples with gracious assurance.

Then, Jesus delivers them from needless fear. Basically the directive is to not fear the human nor the systems of humanity. They may kill the body, but the truth is only God can "kill the soul." God is owed fear; human systems are to be abided and heeded in so far as they sufficiently produce for the good of the human race. Jesus' firm command is to not fear them. And remember that he is speaking to many who will indeed lose their physical lives to the very systems to which they belong (i.e. nation and religion).

Often we move hesitatingly through the maze of threats in life, when Jesus is essentially directing that we know peace, even in the midst of peace-less-ness.

Finally, Jesus challenges his followers with an appropriate orientation. Suffering was one mark of the true church, according to Martin Luther. Jesus taught that in our fear of God, we would find an assurance and an orientation that would allow us to go on in a hostile world. One writer captures the essence of what we need to hear:

"On April 20, 1999, 17 year-old Cassie Bernall was in the school library reading her Bible at lunchtime when she first heard shots. As a boy with a gun entered the room, she reportedly knelt and prayed, angering her attacker. He approached her and asked her sarcastically if she believed in God. She paused, then said one word, "Yes." The attacker asked her, "Why?" but Cassie had no time to answer before she was shot to death in Columbine High.

"In fact, according to some counts, there have been more Christian martyrs in the twentieth century than in the previous nineteen centuries combined. Countries with the most wolf-like policies and human rights violations include China, Sudan, Saudi Arabia, Burma, North Korea, Indonesia, Vietnam, Turkmenistan, India, and Egypt. The Global Evangelism Movement estimates the number of people martyred for their faith each year at around 160,000."

In light of this, Jesus orients his disciples around his own person – he himself. Assuring them that he is a dangerous man to follow, He invites them to do so anyway. It is no secret that the Church is tolerated as long as it does things the way society feels it should.

Counter-culture Christianity is dangerous from other Christians and from the world systems. And in light of this, Jesus says that if we will acknowledge him, he will in turn acknowledge us before God.

C. S. Lewis poignantly captures this in *The Lion, The Witch, and the Wardrobe,* when he writes, "'Is—is he a man?' asked Lucy.

'Aslan a man!' said Mr. Beaver sternly. 'Certainly not. I tell you he is the King of the wood and the son of the great Emperor-Beyond-the-Sea. Don't you know who is the King of Beasts? Aslan is a lion—*the* Lion, the great Lion.' 'Ooh!" said Susan, 'I"d thought he was a man. Is he—quite safe? I shall feel rather nervous about meeting a lion.' 'That you will, dearie, and no mistake,' said Mr. Beaver, 'if there's anyone who can appear before Aslan without their knees knocking, they're either braver than most or else just silly.'

'Then he isn't safe?' said Lucy.

'Safe?' said Mr. Beaver. 'Don't you hear what Mrs. Beaver tells you? Who said anything about safe? 'Course he isn't safe. But he's good. He's the King, I tell you.'"

And that is Jesus. Safe? Heavens no! Good? Infinitely so! And this Jesus claims us as his disciples in a world where we will experience the lack of safety at the same time knowing his presence and his goodness. "Lord I want to be a Christian, inna my heart!" Amen!

CHAPTER 24
THE SEVENTH
SUNDAY AFTER
PENTECOST

St. John's Episcopal Church, Kingston, New York
Zechariah 9:9-12; Psalm 145; Romans 7:21-8:6
Matthew 11:25-30

I must applaud our excellent Deacon on her homily of Sunday last. It was a fitting capstone to the two Sundays of emphasis on systemic evil and the dangers of succumbing to the institution without always being vigilant. There is infinitely more to say about this, but to keep us from dwelling on true, but negative truths, the lectionary directs us down another path beginning today and taking us through all of July. We look at some of the parables of Jesus and each week there is a theme which supports a specific life hermeneutic – or means of interpreting the Christian's life.

Dr. Norman Vincent Peale once spoke and referred to his father who was an M.D., and a PhD. He clearly told his audience that his father was a pair-a-docs. And paradox is the hermeneutic of life we will look at over these four weeks of July. The dictionary defines paradox this way, "a statement, proposition, or situation, that seems to be absurd or contradictory, but in fact, is, or may be true."

[From the *Encarta: World English Dictionary*]

In today's Gospel, which is supported strongly by both of our other lections, there is the paradox of wisdom and understanding belonging precisely to those who lack wisdom and understanding, babes. Jesus continues with the paradoxical and tells us that the precise method of finding ease and lightening our burdens is to take his yoke upon us.

An older hymn caught this. The words were written in the nineteenth century;

> Make me a captive, Lord, and then I shall be free;
> Force me to render up the sword, and I shall
> conqueror be.
> I sink in life's alarms when by myself I stand;
> Imprison me within Thine arms and strong shall
> be my stand.

> My power is faint and low till I have learned to
> serve;
> It wants the needed fire to glow it wants the breeze
> to nerve;
> It cannot drive the world until itself be driven;
> It's flag can only be unfurled when Thou shalt breath
> from heaven.

The message is that life is completely wrapped up in the paradoxes of God: God most present when God seems most absent; believers most wise when in reality they are sometimes the least taught; the greatest leader is the servant; and on and on. The messages are innumerable and pertinent to the lives you and I live.

One philosopher, endeavoring to bring together the four essences of life: earth, wind, fire, and water, sought the quintessence, the "fifth essence," to make sense of the paradoxes these essences put forth. It was Christ, Himself, the quintessence of life. One writer said that in Christ we find the "coalescing of contrarieties." Jesus Christ – the glue of the paradox.

The Old Testament prophecy echoes the hymn quoted above and shows that the prisoner is the most hopeful while the prison guards are indeed bound. The Romans passage, at the dictation of Paul the Apostle, stresses the paradox that the mind which is most pertinent to life is NOT the one which thinks of this life (the flesh) but the one which thinks on the things of the Spirit.

Perhaps a modern hymn from the pen of Rusty Edwards (a friend who was in my cohort in our doctoral program with me) will serve to strengthen this thinking:

Before God says "Go" God says "come."
>Before the word "give" comes "receive."
Our faith is a treasure no money could buy,
>Since before the word "see" comes "believe."

Young students will rise up and teach.
>And last-in-line people will lead.
Before we can do we must know what's been done;
>By a slave who obeyed we are freed.

The Gospel is older than law.
>God gave before we were a friend.
The cross is a matter of dying to live
>Now our last breath will not be the end.

Text copyright 1997 Selah Publishing
Co.Kingston, New York 12401

And so we come to the applications of the paradoxical faith that is ours. There are several applications, and they help us interpret the Christian life we live by God's grace.

First, paradox honors the mystery. I cannot explain it all. As a matter of fact, I cannot explain most of it! Life is mysterious at best, and to define it is to diminish it. Paradox honors and celebrates the mystery – we embrace the truth that God is working His purpose out and we find it mysteriously wonderful.

The second truth is that paradox embraces both sides of the paradox, living them fully. I am a bond-slave to God and a free-man in Christ. Maybe you are suffering terrible things in life right now while at the same time there is abounding blessing through it all. Each end of the paradox must be embraced and owned if we are to know the truth of the Christian life. I call this inclusion. Some embrace their depression and their Christian joy at the same moment.

Finally, paradox in Christianity encourages me that I am not alone. "By a slave who obeyed we are freed." Jesus, the Christ of God, has been here before, is here now, and will be here tomorrow. Each and every Christian must live paradoxically and this means you and me.

In *The Pilgrim's Regress,* C. S. Lewis writes these marvelous lines of paradox;

> "Beating my wings, all ways, within your cage
> I flutter, but not out."

Embrace God's paradoxes in your life today – they are His way to make you all that He plans you to be. Amen!

CHAPTER 25
THE EIGHTH SUNDAY
AFTER PENTECOST

St. John's Episcopal Church, Kingston, New York
Isaiah 55:1-5, 10-13; Psalm 65; Romans 8:9-17
Matthew 13:1-9. 18-23

This morning, we continue with our theme of paradox in the life Christ calls humans to live. And today's Gospel seems to delineate the paradox of productivity. There is little doubt that Jesus is speaking this parable to persons who need to be receptive ground – open, willing, expectant, honest, receiving. This is Jesus' own interpretation of what he has placed in the parable. [By the way, it is the only parable that Jesus explains in the context of telling the parable]

My favorite commentator on the parables, Fr. Robert Farrar Capon calls this parable of the sower the "Watershed of all the Parables." It is only after this parable that Jesus becomes conscious in his "hidden revealing" of his Messiahship. It is intriguing. And it speaks to us.

"Well," he seems to say, "since they've pretty well misunderstood me so far, maybe I should capitalize on that. Maybe I should start thinking up examples of how profoundly the true messianic kingdom differs from their expectations. They think the kingdom will be a parochial, visible proposition – a militarily established theocratic state that will simply be handed over to them at some future date. Hm. What if I were to stand every one of those ideas on its head? What if I were to come up with some parables that said the kingdom was catholic, mysterious, already present in the midst, and aggressively demanding their response. Let me see…"

The rich insight this parable gives is that the "Word of God" that is sown is the Son of God, Jesus. The sower is God the Father and Jesus is universally sown in the world. The first paradox is that Jesus is present precisely where we could declare him absent.

First, the kingdom is whole – there is one – to use Capon's word, "catholic." Jesus sets this paradox against the "we're the only ones" mindset of his hearers. Apocryphal stories abound of how we think ourselves the only or best way to God – the elite recipients of the kingdom. I am reminded of the group that gets to heaven – gets a tour of the wonderful place and sees a high dividing wall with many voices coming from behind the wall. "Who's back there?" asks someone in the tour group. "Oh, they're the Episcopalians, they think they're the only ones here!"

The paradox of universal presence in often apparent absence is a major jolting lesson from this parable. The seed falls universally – symbolized by the four types of ground to which Jesus refers. Accepted or not, the kingdom is present.

Secondly, there is, as Capon states, the mysterious aspect of the kingdom. The kingdom is seed sown, not full-grown plants planted. There is the small, seemingly insignificant, surreptitious aspect of the little seed making the biggest difference. And though some seed is sown (intentionally, since you would only sow on good ground – anyone knows this) the seed falls, seemingly powerless on all kinds of ground. This is the power of the kingdom found in the "left-handed" power of the cross. Capon says that seeds are disproportionately small, and they disappear. So with the entire Christian enterprise. Jesus – Galilean peasant – dead and buried. World-changing. Life-changing.

The final paradox is that the sower is busy sowing. If it is God the Father sowing God the Son, then we have the paradox of God's first-rate activity in a world apparently devoid of God's presence. "The seed, and therefore the Word, is fully in action in and of itself at every step of the story." Whatever subsequently happens, it is not the fault of the seed – the seeds spring up – even those carried away by birds and scattered in another fashion.

And this last paradox of the parable is that we are not told to do anything, but to be something. We are not to become some kind of good soil (that would be a meritorious works type of salvation). Rather all we are called to do is to bear fruit. The seed is sown. We now allow it to bear its fruit in our lives. We can't force it to do what it does not have the innate power to do. And it will even do it where the "Devil" snatches it away. (We might possibly fear evil less if we realize that evil has stolen good seed and carries it around! – the implications of this are immense.).

And that ends the parable. Insignificant seed size produces largeness of kingdom; death and burial of the seed brings life and growth; eaten by birds, stolen by the Devil, kept in the rocky crags, the seed grows; apparently absent, actually present, is the kingdom. Amen!

CHAPTER 26
THE NINTH SUNDAY
AFTER PENTECOST

St. John's Episcopal Church, Kingston, New York
*Wisdom 12:13, 16-19; Psalm 86; Romans 8:18-25
Matthew 13:24-30; 36-43*

Last week's parable about seeds is often misnamed the "Parable of the Sower," when it should be called the "Parable of the Seeds."

This week's parable has often been mislabeled the "Parable of the Weeds." It is not this at all as we can see clearly from Jesus' own words, "The Kingdom of heaven may be compared to a man…" The kingdom is thus anthropomorphized into the characteristics of a human being. It is the man we must look at and from whom we must learn the paradoxes of this parable.

This Gospel text introduces us to personhood, to personality, to character. The entire emphasis is on the man who sows the seed. We miss so very much of the meaning Jesus squeezes into this little parable (or story) if we miss the integrity and purposes of the man who sows. Jesus, himself, in the interpretation tells us that the man who sows is none other than the Son of Man.

[This term is also often misunderstood as referring to the humanity of Jesus. It does not. "Son of Man" is an apocalyptic term from Daniel and Ezekiel and it is used to refer to the coming Messiah of God —a person of special relationship to God and who represents God to the human race] And so the Son of Man in the parable here is none other than the Christ of God, who is sowing seed and whose field is adulterated with tares or weeds.

Let's endeavor to take this apart and see what it tells us of the man who sows – the Kingdom man, the Son of Man.

First, the Kingdom man, the Son of Man is a sower. The work he does is seminal – full of seed – with the full intent of germination and growth. The purpose is life-giving, full of expectancy, and it looks with a positive faith to the future. A former professor of mine from college days was wont to say that every human being has the same three problems: their past, their present, and their future. And this is, of course, absolutely true. And in the parable of the morning, Jesus is assuring his hearers that there is full intent of faithfulness, integrity, and promise in what this Kingdom sower is doing.

Secondly, the Kingdom man, the Son of Man, has at least one enemy. As much as we want to include everyone in the Christocentric view of things, some demand exclusion. When Jesus interprets the weeds as the "sons of the Evil One" he is not being gender specific.

There is a very real sense of evil in the world, and it is often so very close to goodness that we mix the two. Jesus is teaching his hearers that goodness does not prevail without a battle — a battle not between persons, but a battle between good and evil. Based on his first emphasis, the triumph of righteousness, Jesus assures his hearers that until the final manifestation of victory, there is battle.

We used to sing "Onward Christian Soldiers" and "Stand Up, Stand Up for Jesus," but we've become soft. In our correct attempt to include everyone, we have often missed the fact that evil is evil and calls for discerning exclusion.

Third, the Kingdom man, the Son of Man, is temporally tolerant. This is paradoxical. When the servants want to weed out the tares, Jesus says, "Let them both grow…" The Greek word for "to let" here is *aphete* from which we also get our word for "forgiveness." As a matter of fact, the noun form always means forgiveness. Jesus is saying, "forgive them their presence until it is harvest time." This is wonderfully explanatory of the situation of our world. Good and evil grow together — often indistinguishable — often side-by-side. The end is not yet.

Finally, the Kingdom man, the Son of Man, is righteousness oriented. This is the outcome of all things. [My apologies, here, friends, as this becomes a bit academic – please try to follow and forgive me if I am too muddled in my reasoning].

The weeds will be gathered and burned. There will be weeping and gnashing of teeth. Regardless of what anyone says, Jesus is referring to the end of the age here – this IS apocalyptic.

If the burning is *purgation* then the evil ones will come out clean – THEN shall the righteous shine like the sun – those who were righteous all along, and those who were just made righteous through purgation.

If the burning is punishment, then evil ones are consumed – THEN shall the righteous shine like the sun. Either way, the focus is that the Sower's seed will shine in righteousness.

This brings up the issue of eternal punishment, which, I think C. S. Lewis deals with most successfully of all. In his book, *The Problem of Pain,* he writes, "I willingly believe that the damned are, in one sense, successful, rebels to the end; that the doors of hell are locked on the *inside.* . . .

In the long run the answer to all those who object to the doctrine of hell, is itself a question: 'What are you asking God to do?' To wipe out their past sins and, at all costs, to give them a fresh start, smoothing every difficulty and offering every miraculous help? But He has done so, on Calvary. To forgive them? They will not be forgiven. To leave them alone? Alas, I am afraid that is what He does."

And Jesus lets the seeds of the Evil One alone. I don't understand it, it is paradoxical that the God who has won the victory in Christ still lives with the presence of evil in his creation, but he does. And we are called to faithful discernment.

A final and important aspect of this and that is the weed seeds used by the Evil One, the enemy of God, is *zizania* seed – a seed that when grown looks practically like wheat. And so evil often parades as good – and we are called upon in this world, which cannot differentiate between the two, to be people who can discern the difference, and can, by God's grace, be wheat – true wheat for the harvest. Amen!

CHAPTER 27
THE TENTH SUNDAY
AFTER PENTECOST

St. John's Episcopal Church, Kingston, New York
I Kings 3:5-12; Psalm 119:121-136; Romans 8:26-34
Matthew 13:31-33; 44-49a

Today is our last day of focus on the paradoxical parables of Jesus. It seems to sum up what we began a month ago by drawing attention to things minute. Jesus speaks of a mustard seed, yeast, a hidden treasure, a pearl, and a net for fishing. The first four, at least are very small, and the fifth is small in that, though it spreads widely, there isn't much to a net.

All of the focus is on discerning the value, the true value, of that which does not measure up to the cultural valuation of secularity. We certainly live in a day and age where bigger is better. Recently I heard three men arguing over whose Harley Davidson [i.e., "Hog"] had the most power. They almost came to blows as they spoke of piston size and horsepower output. It was comical at best, and indicative of Western Society at least. In a day when a person is judged by the buttons on their suit coat sleeve, or the brand of their car, or the size and location of their house, we are confronted by Jesus with those things which truly count.

The first parable is of the mustard seed. The emphasis is that little things produce immense results. Growth is the characteristic of the kingdom of God. I think it was C. S. Lewis who said something like an egg is fine if you are looking for an egg, but if you are looking for a chicken, the egg must be left behind. Thank God we are not the Christians we were as children. Our faith, by grace, has grown and matured and continues to so do. To "grow in the grace and knowledge of the Lord Jesus Christ" is a mandate of the New Testament. Paul says in that love chapter, I Corinthians 13, that, "When I became a man, I put away childish things." Even when Jesus likens the kingdom to little children, he is telling us to have child-like faith, not childish faith. The mustard seed reinforces the small makes large growth pattern of Christian living.

Then the leaven or yeast parable speaks of influence in the interest of the minute. Yeast is one of the smallest living things. [I always liked to harass my vegetarian friends who eat breads made with yeast that they are eating little animals…They never bit on my bait, but I still think there is something to this – though the status of yeast is questionable]. Yet the Bible tells us "a little leaven (or yeast) leavens the whole lump." You can't segregate yeast. It is everywhere if it is anywhere. And so with the Kingdom of God – the influence is in places where you know it never could be. It is getting a rise out of things which otherwise would remain flat and unleavened. Yeast can physically be as undetectable as pollen and as influential as well. You know it is there even though it is essentially unseen. So is the Kingdom of God. "The world is charged with the grandeur of God," and this charging is with the yeast of the Kingdom. It is a mightily encouraging thought.

Third, there is the hidden treasure. It must be small to be so hidden. This sums up the paradoxical nature of the Kingdom. It is not manifest, it is found precisely because it was somehow hidden. It is not in the Christian right; it is not in secular politics; it is not sitting squarely in denominational judicatories; it is not even owned exclusively in churches of the world. There is a hidden-ness to the revelation of the Kingdom, and we are challenged to seek it and find it. It is no mistake that Jesus says, "Seek first the Kingdom of God and His righteousness, and all these other things will be added unto you."

The fourth parable is of the pearl — that little semi-gloss sphere which begins as an irritating bit of grit in the muscle of the oyster. The Kingdom is like that. It may best grow where irritation has done its finest work. Just yesterday I found a wonderful book titled "A Theology of Illness." It follows hard on my recent studies in the American church's general lack of a theology of suffering following 9/11. We often have no hymnody for suffering – no explanations for that which is contrary to the success orientation of secular society.

I have been amazed with my African-American students who are under 30 or 35 years of age. When I make a reference to "Negro Spirituals" from the nineteenth century, they are unaware that anything like this exists. So many are part of name-it-claim-it churches, and success-oriented pseudo-Christianity, that they miss the years of suffering that their ancestors endured for their freedom. I even had a 35 year old man in my office recently who was down-loading many of his family's problems on me. He told me, "When God gives my wife and me our million dollars, we will…" I was dumbfounded. He said this with straight face and full intent of experiencing that kind of divine provision. [And what he planned to do with that money was not necessarily a God-glorifying expenditure of it!].

The pearl says that life is hard. Belief in God is difficult. The Christian living we are called to do is contrary to the flow of the world. The pearl only comes when the grit is embraced.

Finally, the parable of the net, I believe, reinforces last week's emphasis on division based on God's enemy. It is somewhat apocalyptic. But let's not even go there today since we were there last week. Let's look at the net. There is not much to the net which catches the fish. It is merely thread that has been widely woven to keep something from passing through its gaps. There isn't much mass – as a matter of fact the best nets have very little mass. So is the Kingdom. It is a sweeping net that catches. It keeps us from going free (remember "Make me a captive Lord…). The net is a reminder that something bigger than us has us in its embrace – its catch.

These are the parables of the Kingdom. They are summed up in the Epistle reading of the day – "The Spirit helps us in our weakness…" Thank God. And to get to the understanding of that help, we turn to the Old Testament record for instruction in how to find this. God tells Solomon, "I will give you a wise and discerning mind." The Kingdom of God demands no less than discernment; for it is discernment that will sort out and understand the paradoxes of God.

Remember, "God writes straight with crooked lines, and all may seem lost, when all is won!" Amen!

CHAPTER 28
THE ELEVENTH
SUNDAY AFTER
PENTECOST

St. John's Episcopal Church, Kingston, New York
Nehemiah 9:16-20; Psalm 78:1-29; Romans 8:35-59
Matthew 14:13-21

Recently I have been teaching courses at the college in Biblical doctrines. The first in the series of courses covers the historic doctrines of God: personhood; moral and non-moral attributes – all those lovely big theological words like omniscience, omnipresence, omnipotence *ad infinitium.* The stuff heavy theology is made of is the meat of the course. But that is college.

The problem of the attributes of God comes when those of us in the church begin to act as if the attributes themselves are God, and we are the custodians of high and mighty theology. The Gospels call these kinds of people "scribes, Pharisees, and chief priests." Rather, the Gospels seem to reveal to us the character, rather than the great attributes of God.

Our texts of today are texts which tell us something wonderful about the God of the Jews and the God of the Christians. These texts also tell us about ourselves

– that we might be considered the unfaithful at times, "stiff-necked and sometimes disobedient." Many years ago in one of my former parishes, I was speaking on the sin nature – that it is not optional, but standard equipment. Immediately following the service a young father came to me to assure me I was wrong and that his son was not a sinner, but rather was perfect, and though he might sin in the future, it was not an inevitability. I, having three children already knew him to be dead wrong, but we did not argue. Several years later after a Christmas away at Grandma and Grandpa's, this father came to me saying, "Oh, Pastor, you were so right. We didn't teach Kyle to be so bad. With all his cousins around for Christmas, his only word as he grabbed everyone else's toys was "Mine!" We didn't teach him to be selfish – it must be built in!" And, of course, it is – standard equipment.

But it is not our human sinfulness that is the essence of the texts today, and it is not the attributes of God that are on theological display. Rather we are shown the character of God; we are given glimpses of the glory of the God we are privileged to serve.

In our Old Testament lesson, we are told that God is a God who is "ready to forgive, gracious, and merciful, slow to anger, and abounding in steadfast love." And this God did not abandon those who abandoned Him! There is no "kicker" here – like those famous "churchy" sayings like "God loves you, if you love Him." Or there are those statements like "God will never forsake you, if you remain faithful." (And there is much more to say on this "kicker" theme in a few weeks – stay tuned!) Of course this text is recorded for us so that we will NOT act as Israel acted. But the essential truth of the text is a revelation of who God is, not what we must do to earn His being who he is. Of course in light of this type of God, whose character is gracious, our response must be gratitude. It will define us!

Paul, in the Romans passage, tells us that the love of God (in Christ) cannot be severed. Not "anything…in all creation" can separate us from the love of God. Now the church has not always been faithful to this truth. We like to hold threats over the heads of the members. "If you don't…God will not be pleased." [I am convinced that Jesus Christ of Nazareth pleased God eternally for all of us. Ours is not to earn his pleasure, but to enjoy the pleasure Jesus purchased for us]. Nothing can separate us from the love of God in Christ. The character of God is not called into question – His love is steadfast!

Then Jesus reveals the character of God in Matthew. Remember, Jesus said, "Those who have seen me have seen the Father." And here is Jesus, not like his disciples, selfish and wishing people to go away, but rather quite committed to having compassion and to healing them. Compassion – to come up alongside of others to go through a passion (such as Jesus' last week) with them. It is to be with people. And Jesus healed them. Then He fed them. The character of God is one of provision and compassion. Nothing earned – everything given.

We can have the big theological concepts (which are often irrelevant to our most basic needs and experience) or we can have the God of Scripture whose character is immensely and perfectly summed up in love – not that quaint and cute "God loves you and so do I" kind of bumper sticker religion, but rather a love that assures me that God is ultimately *for me* and not *against me*.

Many years ago, I was approached by a sixth grade student from St. Peter's School as I walked down Wall Street. Allow a poem I wrote to tell the story:

Predestined Interruption

Tousled hair and anxious voice
(Inquisitive, in fact)
A little tot stopped me cold -
A stranger:
And holding up his recording box
Inquired: "Would you help me mister?"

It appears an assignment has
Been dealt by a wise insightful mentor
Where little ones would
Inquire of strangers, "Is there

174

a God? And what or who is He?"
I was asked.
Without a hesitating thought I
Answered "Yes, I'll answer," then
Mustered ministerial voice and said
"Yes, there is a God, and I believe!"
Then tried to fine-tune my chosen speech.
I let him know I knew and God did too!

Oh, what a futile task – I guess I
Quoted some memorized cerebral statement;
Orthodox, of course, evangelical, no doubt –
To him, however, it was more than he
Could stand and so he said, "Thanks, mister,"
And moved along with hurried pace to another.

What I had said was so far above him, I
Had to laugh. He didn't. It was heavy stuff!
And after he walked away I thought, it
Was above me too! What kind of flop would
Drop such tonnage on a one so innocent and search-
    ing?
A cleric would, and did – yes, I did!

And so I mused, alone, in clouds of unknowing,
Of God, and what or who He is;
Light, yet often shrouded in the dark;
Judgment, yet always love-love incarnate;
Knowing all, yet not all revealing;
Predictable and always surprising.

My mind began to whirl in the wondrous
Paradoxes of my Maker-God, incorporated
He and She and They and It and all that I can't
Fathom – More than myriads of lifetimes and
Genius minds could once or ever fathom.
I worked – I thought – I pondered heard – God.

Then on and on the mind engaged to
Understand God's peace, God's rage –
Commanding right, inviting all who will,
Rich in poverty, order in chaos, joy
In solemnity, redeeming life through death.
Thank God for that boy – thanks, boy, for my
  God!

CHAPTER 29
THE THIRTEENTH SUNDAY AFTER PENTECOST

St. John's Episcopal Church, Kingston, New York
Isaiah 56:1-7;Psalm 67; Romans 11:13-15, 29-32
Matthew 15:21-28

Many have misunderstood this Gospel account and thought that it was Jesus putting women and non-Hebrews down. It is no such thing. Rather, it is a celebration of a woman's faith, and a stating of a fact that Jesus will universalize what had previously been parochial and private to the Hebrew people. All of the Old Testament prophecies of God pouring out His Spirit on "all flesh" is beginning to take place as Jesus walks the dusty roads of first century Palestine.

The facts are fascinating. This woman is a Canaanite. [Remember, these were the people Joshua was to have driven from the land when Israel captured the land many centuries before]. Jesus is again impeccably insightful as he allows a non-Jew to practice the faith which was to be exemplary to the Hebrew people. He has used a Samaritan woman, a stealthy Pharisee in the night, ignorant fishermen, despised tax collectors, and on and on. Now we have a Canaanite woman. She has two significant strikes against her.

A certain sect of Jewish men would pray every morning, "Thank God I am not a dog, a Gentile, or a woman." He would repeat the prayer at night. And here is a Gentile woman who likens herself to a dog to get what she wanted from this Messiah figure.

Both the Canannite woman and Jesus understood the covenant and its restrictions. The Covenant, though given to and through the Hebrew nation, was circumscribed by faith. Jesus looked for faith; the Canaanite woman exemplified it. Understanding the program of God is half the insight. Once we see God's purpose, we can meet God's requirement. This woman is a saintly example of humility – Jesus doesn't call her a dog, she uses the metaphor and gets what she longs for.

Secondly, this woman knew the loop holes. Faith grasps that which is seemingly nothing and finds immense substance. "Faith is the substance of things hoped for" according to the writer of The Book of Hebrews. Crumbs are sufficient – even abundant when they are from the table of the Lord. Need grasps for supply.

Third, Jesus allows this woman to universalize a previously national provision. The Book of Romans is all about this opening of the covenant to the non-Hebrew people of the world. Jesus is here allowing this Canaanite woman to give a foretaste of that which is now for everyone. There is the significant disregard for protocol, nationality, ethnicity, religious background, gender. Her request is for mercy, help, and crumbs. These are about the only things any of us need. God's mercy, God's help, and crumbs from his table.

Finally, this woman becomes a model. Great faith is manifested – intense desire met. No doubt the disciples who would have sent her away are again amazed at Jesus' so easy acceptance of all people. An acknowledgment of Jesus as Lord prioritizes oh so many areas of life. The model life is intent not outcome, faith not certainly, action not conclusion. The daughter's healing here is not the focus of the record. We are pleased with the result. Jesus is pleased with the method. In an "ends" oriented culture and society, it is good for us to sit back and see that God makes ends out of means all the time [and the implications in our sick consumeristic greedy capitalism can learn much from one who is satisfied by and exemplified by her acceptance of crumbs].

But there I go into that systemic theme again; it just seems to keep popping up.

Alas, what a woman! What a faith! What a Lord! The implications of Lordship are vast. This lesson helps us scratch the surface. Amen.

CHAPTER 30
THE FOURTEENTH SUNDAY AFTER PENTECOST

St. John's Episcopal Church, Kingston, New York
Jeremiah 15:15-21; Psalm 26; Romans 12:1-8
Matthew 16:21-27

If a human being's three greatest problems are the past, the present, and the future, the person who gives us those three great problems might be called "me, myself, and I." Back at the beginning of the twentieth century, the great writer G. K. Chesterton was reading through a London newspaper where the question was being asked of the reading public, "What's wrong with the world?" Readers were to submit their conclusions.

Chesterton, in his curmudgeon-like ways wrote to the editor of the paper: "Dear Sir: What's wrong with the world? I am. Yours truly, G. K. Chesterton." And many of us who have wrestled with ourselves would be happy to add an "Amen!" to his conclusions – merely changing his name to ours.

In the Epistle for today, Paul seems to conclude that to deal with the self we present it to God. "Present your bodies a living sacrifice…" Some insightful soul has concluded that "the only problem with a living sacrifice is that it keeps crawling off the altar…" Alas, many of us have been on and off many times in our lives. But Paul's conclusion is right. There is a commitment issue at stake in Paul's teaching and in Christ's invitation. Notice Jesus' words, "If anyone would come after me, let him deny himself, and take us his cross, and follow me." It is the first step that fowls us up so often because we have not learned to deal with the self in a sufficient manner.

Jesus tells us that in the faith into which he has come to invite everyone, there is a perspective to deny, a burden to shoulder, and a person to follow. Let's see if we can cut this up into manageable pieces.

First, there is the perspective to deny. Jesus was not telling his disciples to forget about themselves, but to come to the realization that their individual person was not the end all of human existence. The universe does not exist for any one person – no matter how much to the contrary we may argue. And the two ways we naturally try to deal with self is forgetfulness (which leads to pent-up frustration) and indulgence (which leads to self-defeat). Jesus employs the term denial-to keep one's self from being in the way. We don't work at forgetting, we don't play at indulging, we deny.

This may take the many forms: holding the tongue; keeping a contrary opinion to one's self, putting off a personal priority for the pure refreshment of seeing someone else benefit. It may even mean making myself uncomfortable for the sake of another human being.

T. B. Matson was a professor of ethics at Yale for many years. He tied this denial matter into Christian maturity. He wrote, "The more mature a Christian is, the more willing that Christian is to give up his freedoms for the benefit of others." Parents do it to raise children all the time. There was even a time when people going into business would do it to see the business thrive [no one told the Enron executives, however].

Mine may not be the only conviction, opinion, or position. I need to deny the self to realize the self according to Jesus, and I need not appear perfect all the time. Max Lucado (a writer a number of you are enjoying) writes, "God would prefer we have an occasional limp than a perpetual strut..." There is a perspective to deny, for God may call me to do something I dislike. If so, St. John Vianney counsels, "When we do something we dislike, let us say to God: 'My God, I offer this in honor of the moment when you died for me.'"

Second, Jesus directs that there is a burden to shoulder. "Take up your cross." Elsewhere Jesus tells the disciples to take up HIS cross, and I think there is a parallel or an equal to the two. A cross is a cross. Jesus is saying, carry the burden of being a Christian. Think of everything Christian-ly. Make the effort to apply the Christ perspective to everything in life. God is a different problem than no god at all. We have someone to whom we must answer. Be a Christian – love God, serve others, be yourself in Christ.

A. W. Tozer, the famous Chicago preacher around the time of World War II wrote about the verse, "I am crucified with Christ…" He said there are certain characteristics of a crucified person: they are only looking in one direction; they have no further plans of their own; and they have made up their minds they are not going back. Jesus says "take up the cross."

Finally, Jesus tells the disciples there is a person to follow. There is not in his call a set of rules, no canon law, no creed to adopt, no policy to manage or follow, no denomination to which one must pledge loyalty, no board one must please – nothing… "Follow me." The easiest thing is to follow the Lord Jesus Christ. The most difficult thing is to follow the Lord Jesus Christ. We like everyone to do it our way, and they want us to do it their way.

I love to watch the faces of Pentecostal students when I enter class the first day (this Tuesday) with a clergy collar on. Many of them are petrified. Unless you are Pentecostal you are not Christian. We sometimes feel the same way about the splinter Episcopalian groups, or the Baptists, or, well, you get the idea. Jesus makes very few moral or doctrinal claims on the lives of the would-be disciples. He makes a major invitation that they leave what they are doing and follow _Him_.

A woman by the name of Monica Furlong writes this prayer. I know nothing of her, but I know it sums up the denial of perspective, the shouldering of a burden, and the following of a person we have been discussing:

"God of the city, God of the tenement and the houses of the rich, God of the subway and the night club, God of the cathedral and the streets, God of the sober and the drunk, the junkie and the stripper, the gambler and the good family man; dear God help us to see the world and its children through your eyes and to love accordingly." Amen.

CHAPTER 31
THE SIXTEENTH
SUNDAY AFTER
PENTECOST

St. John's Episcopal Church, Kingston, New York

Ezekiel 33:1-11; Psalm 119:33-40; Romans 12:9-21
Matthew 18:15-20

There would be a plethora of answers if we asked the general question, "What are the marks of the church?" The answers would be many and varied. There have been two-thousand years of practice in finding the marks of the community of God, and many are good and insightful and true. Many are parochial, pedantic, and provincial – worthless to the Kingdom of God and meaningless to the world in which we are called to live and minister.

The Gospel record of the day is a verbatim of Jesus' direction to his followers as to what constitutes community experiences. He predicates everything on a fundamental understanding that everything will not be perfect. Human beings are seldom universally compatible and Jesus takes this seriously into account. (I love to talk to young couples when they are planning to get married and to hear them, with stars in their eyes, try to convince me that they are totally compatible and that they never disagree on anything. I remind them, that if they agree on _everything,_ one of them is unnecessary)!

But, back to Jesus. Taking into account that even believers remain sinners (at once saint and sinner), Jesus outlines a community series of exercises which help community to exist, even if they can't guarantee success all the time.

First, the community exists with a manifestation of tough love. Some things need to be addressed, handled, confessed, forgiven, before the community and its individual constituents can go on. Believer against believer, is a contradiction in terms. Withholding forgiveness, withholding confession (apology) is inconsistent with the Christian faith. Jesus takes for granted that there will be disputes, and he concisely gives directions for the manifestation, within the community, of tough love. The church is a place not only of privilege, but of immense responsibility. I cannot afford the luxury of not being in good faith communion with you!

Jesus follows this up with an expectation that the church execute cooperative justice. It takes the church to uphold the justice issues between persons. Before one Christian can have ten houses, each worth millions, there are many Christians who are owed their first home. Christian organizations which continue to fill hefty upper level administrative positions, all the while keeping lower paid persons unfairly compensated or terminated, cease to be Christian, and demand ecclesial justice be done. Justice is not something the church is fond of, but justice is justice precisely because it is a part of the tough love demanded by the Scriptures.

Two businessmen in one parish had decided, based on the writings of Paul, that their differences should not be settled before unbelieving magistrates of the state. They asked the elders of their parish to mediate their business differences, promising that they would strictly abide by what the elders decided. Days of testimony were followed by days of prayer and deliberation by the elders. When the decision was handed down, each party trashed what the elders had decided and moved ahead with their animosities. It was a poor, poor testimony to church and world.

Jesus then challenges the believing community with the practice of ecclesial discipline. Binding on earth and loosing on earth will cause things to be bound in heaven or loosed in heaven. The church is called to make decisions, state findings, hold fast to convictions. Universal, Biblical laws bind always – human ones are applied as wisely appropriate – and sometimes these can and must be loosed. Other times, binding decisions must remain binding. It is discipline not dictatorship that Jesus enjoins here.

Finally, the community of believers must welcome divine presence. Where two or three are gathered in Jesus' name, there he is. We dare not forget that there is the presence of Jesus when in his name we make community. Several years ago when I made my Cursillo, (and I will not comment positively or negatively on that), there was the image of Jesus being present every time we gathered for a community meal by leaving a vacant chair. It was a reminder of his presence.

The lives we live, the way we treat each other, the decisions we make are in his presence. And that is an awesome truth. It should impact our ways.

I am reminded of two illustrations that will give breeze to these difficult inhalations. First, there is a negative example where these things were not followed. A person in another Diocese went through the process for ordination to the priesthood. The psychologist (who made lots of money on the Diocese for giving honest evaluations) clearly decided that this person was unfit for the ordained ministry. The Commission on Ministry unanimously forwarded a decision to the Bishop that this person was not only unfit, but would be a negative influence for the church. Ignoring all of this, the Bishop ordained this person. Disaster followed, and as a result of this person's ineptness, one man died a violent death because he was ignored in a moment of need. When confronted, the clergy-person ripped off their collar and threw it on the floor saying,

"I don't want anything to do with this lousy vocation anyway!" All of this occurred within four months of the person's ordination.

Today that person is a Canon to the Ordinary in one of the Dioceses of our Church – not our Diocese! The Church was not heeded and hell resulted and continues to offend the church.

The second illustration is more encouraging and less involved. A young, unwed mother took classes at our college last Fall. Come Spring, she had so many demands with family and work and school, she dropped out, failing. Just weeks ago she wrote a letter appealing to the Academic Affairs Committee that we allow her to return because, since June, things have turned around in her life. The Committee deliberated long and hard, and after reading her letter, prayed, and decided to counsel her to wait until January and allow her life to settle just a little bit more. I conveyed this to her several days ago, and I received an email on Friday, thanking the Committee for its insightful forethought on her behalf, and that she would take this as direction from God that she wait one more semester and work on her life and situation.

I ask you, which of these is a model of the church manifesting what Christ calls the church to model? Which one listens so as to manifest tough love, execute cooperative justice, practice ecclesial discipline, and welcome the divine presence? The answer is obvious.

Our call is ominous – let's cooperatively answer it! Amen!

CHAPTER 32
THE SEVENTEENTH SUNDAY AFTER PENTECOST

St. John's Episcopal Church, Kingston, New York
Ecclesiasticus 27:30-28:7; Psalm 103;
Romans 14:1-12; Matthew 18:21-35

A few weeks ago Betty Jean Stinner called to tell me she had been asked to be the president of the Regional E. C. W. I encouraged her to take the job, be creative, and do new things and work "outside the box," so to speak. In return she called to tell me she had been elected and that on October 21 I was to be the first speaker at the regional meeting. Her word to me was, "Keep them laughing." Thank you, Betty Jean! I have chosen my topic and I am going to speak on the subject *The Humor of Jesus and the Relative Unimportance of Most Things.* The relative unimportance of most things...something most of us in America know little about. We like to make everything of utmost importance – everything in America is an "issue."

Today's texts deal with the various levels of the importance of things. I like to call it the difference between opinion and conviction. Whereas we human beings hold many kinds of opinions, convictions, on the other hand, hold us. I can no more change a conviction than I can change who I am – I am held by my convictions. But my opinions can and often do change. Verse 10 of our Psalm today assures us that "He has not dealt with us according to our sins…" and this makes an immense difference in what we have to, or, don't have to do! If God deals with me according to my sins, I have meritorious actions I must complete – I must earn something – I must be a law-keeper. If I am not dealt with according to my sins, I am free to be a "be-er" and not a producer. [Of course there are behavioral requirements for the believer, but they are not meritorious, they are manifestations of what is real inside of us – and that is much fodder for other sermons]. Today, we are called on to understand the relative unimportance of so very much.

The prophetic word in Ecclesiasticus calls on God to "overlook ignorance…" Praise God. This gives hope to many! With American law, ignorance of the law is not bliss; whereas. with God, ignorance of the ways of God is a given. God expects it

The Epistle reading from Paul's letter to the Romans reminds us that there are varieties of what we honor – some honor one day – some another. "Let everyone be convinced in their own mind," says Paul. Paul, under divine inspiration allows choice in non-essential matters.

I am reminded of St. Augustine's powerful triplet:

"In essentials: unity;
In non-essentials: diversity;
In all things: charity!"

Can it be more simple than this? Even the ignorant can understand the allowances of ignorance and difference and the call to be loving of one another.

And then we are confronted with the Gospel message which makes its mark on our convictions. There are some things that are inviolable. I cannot, not, forgive. I have no choice in the matter. This is a matter of conviction – opinion has no place.

And so, I delineate three levels of conviction. Scripture really leaves the matter of opinion to-well-opinion! Convictions – those verities which hold us rather than us holding them fall into three stages.

First, there are those universal Christian convictions based on the clear statements of Scripture which are really without question. We have the verities of the commandments, the beatitudes, and the clear propositional statements like this morning's Gospel. You can't really argue with Jesus here! These are universal convictions and they are found everywhere the Church is found. If they are not found, there is a distinct chance the church is not present there. That is about what Jesus is so firm at the end of this periscope-God doesn't take lightly those who claim to belong to him not acting like him!

Then there are conditional convictions-those of a particular body of believers who have formed their corporate identity in Christ. That is why Episcopalians don't worship and minister in the same way Baptists do-and this is completely acceptable. For in the conditions of our Church, certain convictions apply when they do not apply elsewhere. We are who we are by corporate conviction, and this calls for embracing other believers who are different from us.

And finally, as Paul says in Romans, there are such things as personal convictions. These are always based on one's own strengths and weaknesses and often address personal moral or behavioral issues. Some have convictions on what day of the week to worship, what holidays to honor, what beverages do drink, what foods to eat, what entertainment to participate in. These are formed when one considers their own lust factors, and then understands the things they can and cannot do. To this level, Paul says, "Let everyone be convinced in their own mind."

These issues are large issues and I am not so naïve to think that they can be settled in a Sunday morning sermon– but I trust they are thought issues, and that I have added a bit to the matrix in which universal, conditional, and personal convictions are formed.

May God grant us the discernment to sort out the relatively unimportant issues of life from those that are critical and matters of life and death. Amen!

CHAPTER 33
THE NINETEENTH SUNDAY AFTER PENTECOST

St. John's Episcopal Church, Kingston, New York
Ezekiel 18:1-4,25-32; Psalm 25:1-14; Philippians 2:1-13
Matthew 21:28-32

Today's lessons are best illustrated with a story. I will call our key player, Don, to protect the innocent. Don was my best friend. I buried Don in June of 1997. He was the finest Christian man I have ever, to date, met. At his funeral of 500 people, I was invited by his Rector to preach the homily – probably the hardest work I have ever done. Don was seventy-seven years old. During the service, four young men in their early twenties came into the church dressed in construction work clothes. When asked after the service what their relationship to Don was, they responded, "We work out in the gym every morning from five to six o'clock, and we met Don there. He was the kindest, most gentle, real man we have ever met. We couldn't let him go without saying good bye."

But Don's story does not begin with his sudden heart attack and unexpected death in 1997. No, he had been a trained opera singer who sang with the Metropolitan Opera, and made his debut at Royal Albert Hall in London. He was an exquisite vocal performer. Alongside all of this talent, he took a degree in anthropology and a graduate degree in divinity, and was an ordained minister. (Upon retirement, he joined me in a move into the Episcopal Church, for which I am ever grateful).

Don spent his entire ministry as an assistant pastor to four very famous men in four very famous and large churches – first in Chicago, then in Ocean City, New Jersey, then in Manhattan, and finally in another large northeastern city. His faithful service as the "second man" was unparalleled in Protestant church history in America. Everyone sang his praises. He was the model, the paradigm of what a loyal assistant should be. (I was privileged to use him as my mentor when I became the associate rector of historic Grace Church in Utica, New York in 1991). Everything came crashing down, when, in his last assignment, in one of the nation's most prestigious churches, Don went to the doctor. He had been faithful in this parish for almost eight years, when the doctor, a member of the board of the church, asked Don, "Don, are you gay?" Don hesitated a moment, and replied, "I have wrestled with this all my life-all the while remaining single and celibate." Don thought that was the end of the matter. He left the doctor's office to return to the church office. When he arrived, he was locked out, and told by the parish secretary: "You have been fired. Your office will be cleaned out and delivered to your home next week."

It seems that the doctor had called the senior pastor, told of the discussion in the privacy of the office, and the senior pastor took unilateral action. Don was devastated.

Where, though, does this story enter into pertinence with the lections of the day? In three ways.

Don *never* was anything but completely humble and Christian in his attitudes and subsequent actions. Dozens of friends told him to sue the church, the senior pastor, and to sue the doctor and have his license taken away – all of which Don could have won, hands down. But none of that occurred.

Rather, Don manifested what our lections challenge believers to manifest.

Ezekiel records God's invitation to "turn and live." The emphasis is on living, not revenging, not harboring hatred, but getting on with life. Don did this spectacularly. Whereas there might have been defeat, vengefulness, or other negative emotions, Don lived. He traveled, performed, and ministered with immense success in churches. (At his funeral, it is estimated that persons from 300 different churches and six countries attended to make up the crowd of 500 present). Don was living godliness.

Then in Paul's Philippian passage, we are confronted with the *kenosis*, or the emptying – the humbling of
God the Son to become human. The lesson is humility.
Only we can humble ourselves; others may attempt to
humiliate us, but if we will be humble, we cannot be
humiliated. Don proved to be the most humble of men
– gracious, kind, patient, and humble. Don was living
Christ-like.

Finally, the Gospel confirms to us that actions
speak louder than intent. And Don was a man of action. I like to look at the pious-ass attitudes of a doctor and a minister – who, obviously not wrestling with
the issue of sexual identity, think they will get into the
Kingdom before Don who did wrestle with the gender
identity issue. Well, men, you are dead wrong. Don is
light years ahead of you because his intent was to do
the will of God-to believe-not to exclude and remove.
Don lived with intent.

In the Gospel, Jesus asks, "Which of the two did
the will of the Father?" The one who acted as the Father requested. Position, priority, prestige, all fall into
insignificance. The one who ___did the will of the father___ is
the one Jesus lauds.

Men and women, today we are absorbed on many
fronts with many demands of loyalty and performance.
I challenge us to be people who do the will of the father
– to be Don to our generation – to "work out our own
salvation with fear and trembling," not because we can

do it on our own, but, as Paul says, "it is God who is at work in you, both to will and to work for his good pleasure." God was pleased with Don's doing – may He be pleased with ours. Amen!

CHAPTER 34
FOUNDERS' DAY CHAPEL

Pardington Hall, Nyack College, Nyack, New York
Matthew 18:1-6

"Unless you are converted and become like children you shall not enter the kingdom of heaven..."
—Matthew 18:3 NASB

Just before God reveals to the disciples the messiahship of Jesus, Jesus puts the disciples in the place whereby they must recognize their need for conversion and child-like-ness. It is incredible that it is in this context that Jesus makes this invitation. [It is interesting, as well, that it is child-like, Peter, to whom and through whom the revelation is given!!] Paul, in I Corinthians 13, tells his readers to not be childish, and then lauds the eternal value of child-like traits of faith, hope, and love.

Coupled with the text of the day, is my assignment to make this a "Founder's Day" homily or sermon. I want to focus on several of our founders.

A. W. Tozer speaks of A. B. Simpson, and his subsequent movements of the C&MA, as "The man grown large." Simpson, in all his fullness is what Nyack is; this has historical precedence:

- To understand Judaism we must study the patriarchs;
- To know Christianity you cannot do so without Jesus Christ;
- To know the spread of Christianity into the Gentile world, you must begin with the Apostle Paul;
- To know Nyack College, we must begin with the man, A. B. Simpson.

But our focus on Simpson, and two of his colleagues, will be through the lens of child-likeness.

I wish us to look at Albert Benjamin Simpson, Dr. Kenneth MacKenzie, and Dr. Henry W. Wilson-Simpson the Presbyterian, and MacKenzie and Wilson, each Episcipalians.

It is imperative that we see them as real human beings. We must demythologize their history so that we see them for who they were. No pedestal will do; they must come down to earth. And we will find that indeed, they were human, had feet of clay, they were sinners saved by grace, and they carried the anointing of God upon them.

First look at Albert Simpson with me, and we find his Christ-like, child-like trait of FAITH. "It will work out…" was the focus of his trust. And in that child-likeness, he began a movement that continues now many years later.

While traveling through Europe he writes, "I am not going to the Irish Assembly…I am tired of Assemblies and want rest…" (Soon after writing this, he writes that he took the day at Wimbelton and had just returned.) Simpson would address his wife as "Maggie" in letters and sign off as "Bertie," Bertie, the founder of our college!! While doing ministry in England he writes home, "I have already visited the exhibition, the zoological gardens, and the Royal Academy. I think of going to the British Museum and Crystal Palace tomorrow…" (And we won't even mention what he says about trying European foods and fine European wines).

Once, while writing home, his faith shows through in his paragraph, "Remember me lovingly to dear Bertie and Mellville and give them a great big hug for their papa. I can't trust myself to speak much about them or I would get very sad, but I pray God to watch over you and them as a husband and father ever present, and in due time to permit us all the great joy of meeting in an unbroken circle in our happy home once more…"

His was a faith that was child-like. Criticized later by colleagues and family, he simply believed God to do what God has said he would do. This is childlike faith.

Then there is The Rev'd Kenneth MacKenzie, a man who had great physical weakness and disability at times in his life, shows us the child-like trait of hope. Dr. George Pardington, after whom this building is named, wrote, "never vigorous physically, his preservation and health are truly remarkable..." When pushed to make a statement as to how he could, with hope, handle the circumstances of life, he would quote Dr. Simpson's hymn:

> There's a little secret, worth its weight in gold;
> Easy to remember, easy to be told:
> Changing into blessing every cause we meet,
> Turning Hell to Heaven – This is all – keep sweet!

> Make us kind and gentle, harmless as the dove,
> Giving good for evil, meeting hate with love;
> What though trials press us, what though tempests
>   beat?
> Naught can move or harm us, if we just keep
>   sweet.

A child-like hope carried MacKenzie through physical stress and deficiency and brought him well into mid-century of the 19th century – able to see great growth in the C& MA and Nyack College.

Finally, a favorite of mine, a founder of the Christian & Missionary Alliance and Nyack College, Dr. Henry W. Wilson. Wilson was nothing, if he was not child-like in his love. Simpson himself, said of Henry Wilson that he was "radiantly cheerful and joyous." He possessed a personal gift of wit and humor that enlivened his public address and made him a genial and charming companion.

Hear what Dr. Pardington says of Wilson: "It is in connection with his work for the children that Dr. Wilson will live longest in memory and affection. Shall we call him the apostle to children? Surely we may, for he was their sympathizer and interpreter, their friend and lover. Not only the children of the Gospel Tabernacle and the entire Alliance, but the children of the whole world were on his heart. Five thousand children at home he enlisted in the support of 5,000 children in other lands, he himself assuming responsibility for 1,000. Every week for years he edited a Children's Page in the Alliance Weekly, under the initials, B.B. B., signifying "Big Baby Brother."

He was often called "The Sunny Man." (Not a name often thought of in relation to clergy as a whole!) What a man of the child-like trait of love.

When Karl Barth was touring the U.S. some years ago, in an academic setting he was asked the question, "Dr. Barth, with all your study of the Bible, what is the greatest truth you have ever learned?" Without hesitancy, Barth declared, "Jesus loves me, this I know, for the Bible tells me so."

Again, I turn to A. W. Tozer who warned us: "There are areas in our lives where in our effort to be right we may go wrong, so wrong as to lead to spiritual deformity. To be specific, let me name a few: 1]When in our determination to be bold we become brazen; 2] when in our desire to be frank we become rude; 3] when in our effort to be watchful we become suspicious; 4] when we seek to be serious we become somber; and 5]when we mean to be conscientious and become over-scrupulous."

We must take care, lest in our sophistication we lose our purpose; lest in our worldly acceptance and approvals we surrender our mission; and in our adulthood we do not lose our ability to wonder. Great vigil must be kept to insure that we are not ministering out of a false abundance and not out of a mutual dependency. Is it not amazing that Jesus chooses a child as the metaphor for the kingdom inheritor? We have the examples in Simpson, MacKenzie, and Wilson. They belong to us, let us follow them as they followed Christ. They teach us that "A man in Christ," to use Pauline terminology, is childlike!

In a history book on Nyack and the C & M A, one author refers to Dr. Gregory Mantle taking a group of people through St. Paul's Cathedral in London. Someone asked where the memorial to Christopher Wren was. Dr. Mantle responded "Look around-all of this is his monument." Men and women, look around, and when you see child-like faith, and hope and love among us, then you see the monument our founders would wish. Amen

CHAPTER 35
THE TWENTY-FIRST SUNDAY AFTER PENTECOST

St. John's Episcopal Church, Kingston, New York
Isaiah 25:1-9; Psalm 23; Philippians 4:4-13
Matthew 22:14

If God's posture toward humanity is one of grace, you would expect that now and then, his written revelation, the canon of Holy Scripture, would have something encouraging to say to the recipients. And it does! All of today's texts are wonderfully positive texts – confirming the gracious posture of God on behalf of the human race.

I call them the "In Before Out" scriptures. Oh, yes, there is the respectfulness of God which allows a person to say "No," to God and go on their own. The Biblical God is a not a God of force or undo coercion. The person who wants to be put out is obliged, just as those who wish inclusion are graciously welcomed.

Note the Old Testament emphasis on the wonderful things God has done – the strong, the poor, the needy, are all met with the provisions of God. There is something in this God's provision for all. It culminates with the reminder that this God, on His mount, will make a feast for all peoples – a feast of universal invitation! A glorious chorus will be sung of this universal provision by all who gather on that day.

Then what can we say about our wonderful morning Psalm – Psalm 23? It is that universal Psalm that invites all to know the shepherding of the chief Shepherd. Even when we walk through the valley of the shadow of death, God is there.

And the old curmudgeon, Apostle Paul, in the epistle of the morning celebrates the goodness of God that leads to rejoicing. Paul concludes with the insightful comment, "I have learned the secret..." And that secret is that whatever the circumstance, God is there to meet us in it.

These wonderful, universal truths are predicated on and find their foundation in the teaching of the Gospel record this morning. It is a classic parable of the "In before out" hermeneutic or principle of Bible interpretation.

The lessons are simple: rich man holds wedding banquet for child. All guests are invited, all provisions are made. And as would be the case in first century Palestine, wedding garments would be made available to you as you came through the gate or door of the house. You didn't travel in celebration clothes. When the initial guests (the bureaucratic leaders of the Jews) are invited and find excuse to be absent, the host invites everyone (even the Gentiles) to come to the banquet. (The essential purpose of this parable is to judge the religious leaders of Jesus' day. He was constantly putting it to the system-but that is another sermon for another time.)

All those subsequently invited come to the party, enter and are clothed-they are in, before they are out. One guest refuses to be clothed (clothed in righteousness, we might interpret) and is put out. There is only one result of refusing the host's offer, and that is the consequence of refusing the host's offer. Grace is still grace – it is merely refused. God only excludes those who exclude themselves. This is a clear and essential teaching of the Scriptures which show us the God of integrity who honors the choices of those He has created.

There is an old Gospel hymn called "My Hope is Built on Nothing Less." Two of the stanzas go like this:

My hope is built on nothing less,
Than Jesus' blood and righteousness,
I dare not trust the sweetest frame,
But wholly lean on Jesus' name.

When He shall come, with trumpet sound,
Oh, may I then, in Him be found.
Dressed in His righteousness alone,
Faultless to stand before the throne.

The lessons are so simple to be almost obvious. It is all of grace, and we are called to gratitude. We put on the robes of righteousness. We take off the old robes; we put on the new; and we celebrate our being "included" the invitation of God.

Multiple other parables suggest the same truths and support this claim, but, they too, are for another day. May God make us thankful that He is gracious, and may we say with the prophet, "You are God, we will exalt you for you have done wonderful things!" Amen!

CHAPTER 36
THE FEAST OF
ST. LUKE
THE EVANGELIST

(TRANSFERRED TO SUNDAY,
OCTOBER 20, 2002)

St. John's Episcopal Church, Kingston, New York
Ecclesiasticus 38:1-4. 6-10, 12-14; Psalm 147;
II Timothy 4:5-13; Luke 4:14-21

Once in a while when we come to portions of the Holy Scriptures, they open themselves easily for our study and outline. Today's Gospel breaks into our series from Matthew, so that we might celebrate the feast of St. Luke which we transfer from October 18. The Gospel of the morning is Luke's record of Jesus' initial teaching in the synagogue in his hometown of Nazareth. Jesus reads from the Isaiah scroll and says that his presence in the synagogue that day, reading that prophecy, fulfills the prophecy. This is an amazing thing. We, with sly sophistication, stop the reading where we do so that we can miss the reaction: those of the leaders of the synagogue rise up to cast Jesus over a cliff and kill him. But this isn't nice, so we pass it by.

217

Nonetheless, it is historic, and there is a reason for it. Whenever there is a fulfillment of prophecy, those expecting it the most accept the fulfillment the least. There is more comfort and safety in the expectation than in the fulfillment; for when the fulfillment comes, we are implicated and expectations then are put on us. This is almost universally true in the Bible. People, including us, like our safety boxes, and we don't want anyone, much less God, mucking that up!

So just what is fulfilled and how is it fulfilled that day 2,000 years ago in Nazareth? First and foremost, the fulfillment is in the person of Jesus. Just as Jesus doesn't answer when Pilate asks, "What is truth," so Jesus doesn't have to do anything but be as the fulfillment of this prophecy. Pilate should have asked, "Who is truth?" but the wrong question solicited only the answer of presence.

Here we see Jesus take a portion of Isaiah that says the Spirit of the Lord, on the right person, will manifest the Messianic fulfillment of accomplishing five things. They are:

- To preach good news to the poor;
- To proclaim release to captives;
- To proclaim recovery of sight to the blind;
- To set at liberty the oppressed;
- To proclaim the acceptable year of the Lord.

These are Messianic expectations of Israel, and they are then and there fulfilled in Jesus. By reading this, Jesus solidifies his audience. Anyone who is not poor, captive, blind, or oppressed is outside the purview of his purpose. And certainly the systemic leaders were anything but poor, captive, blind, or oppressed. What Jesus is saying is that the only requirement to enter his kingdom is that you acknowledge you don't meet the requirements. The work of Jesus is not a restroom for saints but a hospital for sinners.

Let's dissect these five commissions of the Lord Jesus and see what they hold for us in the whole Lukan emphasis of the day:

First, the work of Jesus to preach good news to the poor is an affirmation that those who are overlooked by the secular and religious societies of which they are members are indeed recipients of good news (gospel). We are not pounced upon with ethical or sacrificial requirements. The good news is that the requirements have been met. A contemporary gospel song goes something like this:

> Oh be ye glad, be ye glad,
> Every debt that you ever had;
> Has been paid up in full
> By the blood of the Lamb,
> By ye glad, be ye glad, be ye glad!

And the only requirement is that we number ourselves among the poor. (Remember, in the sermon on the mount, Jesus emphasizes that "Blessed are the poor in spirit for they shall see God!).

Second is the teaching that there is release for the captives. The state of one, slave or free, has little, ultimately, to do with their real state. I think of Good Friday, that the freest person alive was Jesus, and the second most free person was the repentant thief. The more I ponder the slavery movement in England and America in the 18th and 19th Centuries, the more convinced I am, that as horrible as the whole sad history is, the freest people were, indeed, the slaves, for they were the most like the Messiah. Paul said that he had found contentment – and whatever state in which he found himself had no bearing on this.

Third, there is the Messianic recovery of sight to the blind. What Jesus is saying, is that everything is not as it appears. The media moguls do not necessarily represent truth. Facts can mislead and truth go undiscovered. The human being is created to see through our eye with our conscience, and Jesus effectively takes away the blindness of conscience. William Blake put it this way:

Life's dim windows of the soul,
Distort the world from pole to pole,
And force us to believe a lie,
When we see with, not through, the eye.

The sight Jesus gives has little or nothing to do with physical eyes, and everything to do with spiritual insight, discernment, and integrity.

Fourth, there is the liberty to the oppressed. No one is more free than when her spirit is free. And Israel should have known this. Some of the greatest saints and victors for the Hebrew faith found their victory, their liberty in the midst of oppression: Esther, Daniel, and the three Hebrew Children. Ezekiel cannot be excluded. Jesus is the perfect example. Liberty, also, has nothing to do with the issue of captivity. Israel is never more at liberty than when she believes and acts successfully on that belief.

Finally, there is the acceptable year of the Lord. What Jesus is saying is that there is no longer a wait for good news, release, sight, or liberty. They are present realities. "Behold now is the time of salvation – this is the day that the Lord has made…" There is the present reality, in Christ, of all these provisions of his Messiahship. These are the reasons for Calvary. If true strength is not in powerlessness (as in the cross) then true strength is in the size of our weapons, or in our positions of power over one another. Paul tells Timothy to "endure suffering…fulfill your ministry."

What has all of this to do with Dr. Luke? Precisely this, that Luke as a Gentile convert, finds in Christ all that the human really needs: good news, release, insight and vision – liberty. The condition of the body is ancillary to the condition of the soul. And Dr. Luke celebrates this. Alas, there is the provision in the atonement for the healing of the body, and in the resurrection we will all get a new one (thank God). But the deep, life changing truths necessary to meet this afternoon, are found in the life changing provisions of Jesus – recorded for us by Dr. Luke. Amen!

CHAPTER 37

JESUS CHRIST AND THE RELATIVE UNIMPORTANCE OF MOST THINGS

Regional E.C.W. Meeting – St. Andrews, New Paltz, NY
John 21:20-22

This little talk is not so much a sermon – it is really not a sermon at all – it is a fun talk to a group of dedicated women in the Episcopal Church in Ulster, Orange, and Dutchess Counties in New York State. It is included in this anthology by request.

What is that to you (Peter), you follow me." It is so easy to get caught up in concerns over all kinds of things and sorts of people in life. Today, I would like to speak to this and challenge you ladies to be women of single-mindedness in a world of fragmentation.

First, however, I must establish my right to be here. I am here by invitation of your new President, Betty Jean Skinner – and when she invited me, I was told, "Keep 'em laughing!" (She's heard enough of my sermons to know that I like a good story!) And there is a warrant for humor, both in Scripture, I believe, and certainly in the church. A favorite author of mine, G. K. Chesterton, writes that Jesus hid something when he walked this earth; and Chesterton surmised that Jesus hid his mirth.

And I found this wonderful little book by the author of *O Ye Jigs and Juleps,* and it is called *Credos and Quips: The Jigs and Juleps Girl Has Grown Up.* It records some of the mirthful things the church has done in its history. And I am particularly taken by what this author, a woman, recalls of the old English Book of Common Prayer.

What's a woman to do? She is to be!

There is the example of Mary: Mother of Jesus – "The Jewish Mother…" This Mary is found to be faithful and fruitful in the life entrusted her by God. She is completely at ease with herself, whether we read her spiritual compilation in The Magnificat, or if we see her in her "nagging" way at Cana of Galilee. There is a reality to this woman that no other can match. She is most like Jesus in a "coalescing of contrarieties.

Mary Magdelene – The strong, some-think, reformed prostitute (though the evidence is questionable). There is no doubt she is sensual, creative, and possibly a little bit cunning. And these are not all bad. The resurgence of interest in her history is evidence that men and women want to reconnect to the physicality of their spiritual walk. Mary Magdelene will not allow Gnosticism to creep in, no matter what the contemporary theologians try to invent!

Finally, there is Mary, sister of Martha & Lazarus – Friend of Jesus. She is the practical one. She is contemplative – "Behold he stinketh!" she says of her brother, now some days dead and buried. And she proves to us the reality that stinky stuff comes before the resurrection.

And if a woman is to be, what exactly is a woman's place? Could it be that a Biblical focus on women is enticingly parallel to a Biblical focus on men? Just what is a woman's place? Compared to being (a gift of God) there is necessarily a relative unimportance of most things. Period. Hear John David Burton.

A Woman's Place

On a jet plane from Seattle to Chicago,
a voice on the intercom informs us,
"This is your First Officer, Nancy Martin."
She must know how to drive the airplane.
We get from Seattle to Chicago in one piece.

At the hospital in Chicago, the doctor comes
to tell my son, his wife, and me what is going
to happen. The doctor says,
"I am Dr. Susan Luck. I will be taking care of
Matthew today, doing the right lobectomy on his
liver, to see if we can take the tumor. I will

be back when we are done and tell you more."
Six hours later, Dr. Susan Luck, Pediatric
Surgeon, comes to tell my son, his wife, and me
about Matthew's blood, and she says:
"We took all the tumor we could find. Now we
will see about radiation and chemotherapy."
Then she goes with us to watch as they wheel
Matthew, nine months old, small and still and
white, down the hallway to Recovery.
I call my other children to say it looks O.K.
for Matthew. My lawyer/daughter, defending the
U.S. in a multimillion dollar suit, says it
sounds as good as it can sound, and my doctor in
Seattle says that Susan Luck is the best for
taking care of Matthew.

I go home to Presbytery in Seattle where they
are debating what to do about a Pastor and a
Session refusing to ordain women as Deacons,
Elders, Clergy.
The anguish of my life boils up to anger and I
offer to make a motion to depose the Pastor,
dissolve the Session and have Presbytery take
the Church, thus throw out each weakling male
on his chauvinist ass. Cooler heads than mine
prevail. In more polite arrangement the Pastor,
Session and part of the Church are allowed to
depart in peace.

A woman's place? When life hangs in the balance,
a woman's place is wherever she is needed.
A woman's place, it seems to me,
is any place a woman wants to be.

CHAPTER 38
THE TWENTY-THIRD SUNDAY AFTER PENTECOST

St. John's Episcopal Church, Kingston, New York
Exodus 22:21-27; Psalm 1; I Thessalonians 2:1-8
Matthew 22:34-46

A person's motives equate with their intent, obviously. The lawyer in today's Gospel record is ignorantly unaware of this. What you are is fundamentally more important than what you do in God's eyes – this has been true throughout all of Hebrew history, and yet this lawyer of the Pharisees misses it altogether. Jesus masterfully steps way back into the book of Deuteronomy in the Hebrew Scriptures and gives this lawyer exactly what he should have known:

- There is no such things as multiplicity of laws – law is necessarily singular (after Jesus' owning of this greatest commandment, all else is commentary);
- There is no keeping of law seriatim – all law exists "as simultaneous responsibilities rather than sequential priorities (precisely because we would hierarchicalize them according to the ones we're best at keeping);

- Love is pre-eminent in the universe – "Love is God's essence, power is his attribute; therefore his love is greater than his power." [Richard Garnett]

The commandments as *laws* have always intrigued people. As commentary on love they are generally ignored or explained away. Note our Psalm of the morning:

"Blessed are they who have not walked in the counsel of the wicked, nor lingered in the way of sinners, nor sat in the seats of the scornful! Their delight is in the law (singular) of the Lord…" This is powerfully noteworthy. The Psalmist is synthesizing, coalescing laws into law-the law of the Lord to love God and love others as self. This is the epitome of commandment studies.

The story is told of a professional man who quite arrogantly announced to Mark Twain, "Before I die, I want to make a pilgrimage to the Holy Land. I will climb Mount Sinai and read out loud the ten commandments." Twain, not known for holding back criticism when it was due, keenly observed, "I have a better idea. You could stay at home in Boston and keep them!"

The lessons Jesus brings to these religious professionals are strikingly simple. Love God. How? Why? Simply because the presence of Jesus in our midst proves that God works on the principle of love. Elsewhere the Scriptures tell us that "God first loved us…"

The second lesson is that we are to be taken out of ourselves into love of God and others. Essentially the self-centered person has no center and therefore is entirely unbalanced. Everything must revolve around me to the self-centered (and I am not saying selfi<u>sh</u> – many self-centered people are anything but selfish – doing good to others so that they themselves will look good)!

I do not know where I found this poem many, many years ago, but it sums up contemporary society's insistence on self-centeredness:

I went to my psychiatrist
    To be psychoanalyzed,
To find out why I killed the cat
    And blackened my wife's eyes.

He put me on a downy couch
    To see what he could find,
And this is what he dredged up
    From my subconscious mind.

When I was one, my mommy hid
    My dolly in a trunk,
And so it follows naturally,
    That I am always drunk.

When I was two, I saw my father
    Kiss the maid one day,
And that is why I suffer now
    From kleptomania.

When I was three, I suffered from
    Ambivalence toward my brothers
And so it follows naturally,
    I poisoned all my lovers.

I'm so glad that I have learned,
    The lessons it has taught,
That everything I do that's wrong,
    Is someone else's fault.

Now I wouldn't take all this too far, other than to say, self-centeredness is diametrically opposed to the great commandment.

Finally, we have no choice; as God's people we must love God. There is absolutely no other relationship a human being can have with God. Either there is love or there is lack of relationship. St. Augustine wrote that "God is the only goal worthy of the human's efforts." And the love that God calls for in Jesus' commandment here is a special term – a special type of love. "The Greeks had a word for it: 'Eros' (physical love) is all take; 'Phileo' (friendship) is give and take; 'Agapao' (Godly love) is all give." [G. B. Caird] It is from the root "agapao" that Jesus draws his commandment. Love gives.

Will D. Campbell in *Soul Among Lions* records the following encounter. It speaks of Miss Velma's truth about love. It is powerful.

"Thirty-two years ago the home of a black family in Hattiesburg was doused with gasoline and set afire. The father, Mr. Vernon Dahmer, stood firing his shotgun through the front door so the family could escape out a back window. Today the children remember being huddled with their father in a nearby barn, his lungs seared from the intense heat, skin peeling from his body like willow bark. He soon died in the arms of his wife.

"Recently the Imperial Wizard of the White Knights of the Klu Klux Klan was tried. The prosecution left little question of guilt. But during the trial, as I visited both the accused and the Dahmer family, something troubled me. The rationale for another trial, after three hung juries, was that thirty years ago, was that Mississippi was a police state and getting a conviction was impossible But a police state has higher ups directing it, not everyday Klansmen. So when will the governors, the rulers be tried?

'How do you feel?' a journalist asked as the convicted Klansman was led away?

'I feel deep compassion for him,' I answered.

'Why?' he added.

'Because he's a prisoner of the state,' I explained.

"Jesus said nothing about ideology or gravity of offense. We are to be with the prisoners because they are prisoners — be they governors, Klansmen, or innocent victims. The notion began with a sweet child in a manger. It was sealed with a swarthy, sweaty, bloody convict hanging on a cross.

"Miss Velma Westbury used to say, 'If you just love the folks what's easy to love, that really ain't no love at all.' She said 'If you love one, you have to love 'em all.' ...Of course, some people said Miss Velma was crazy."

CHAPTER 39

THE TWENTY-SIXTH SUNDAY AFTER PENTECOST

St. John's Episcopal Church, Kingston, New York
Zephaniah 1:7,12-18; Psalm 90; I Thessalonians 5:1-10
Matthew 25:14-15, 19-29

Beginning last week, we wind down the Christian year as we prepare for Christ the King celebrations next Lord's Day, and then four Sundays of emphasis on the first and second Advents (or comings) of Jesus our Lord. In preparation for the second coming, or the return of Jesus to this earth as he promised at his Ascension, Deacon Sue focused our attention on readiness last Sunday – in what, I believe, was an outstanding homily (as they always are, Sue). Readiness involves activity, and staying with the stuff of life and ministry until we see Jesus in person – either through our death or through his return.

Today, the emphasis is on finishing. It is all right to not be an over achiever, as long as we are a finisher. Jesus' harsh words in the Gospel are only to the person who did nothing at all to be a finisher. He hid that which was placed in his care.

Too often, the focus on the return of Christ is on our being super saints. Men and women, as I said on All Saints' Day, we are believers by virtue of our being made Saints by God, not by being good. God knows, the list of Saints would be lots shorter if Saints were saintly! Saints are average – not a one of them normal (someone recently said "Normal is the setting on a dryer!). Let's then, in light of this, see what these texts say to us:

First, the Zephaniah passage tells us that "The day of the Lord is at hand." This is nothing new. It always is! There is an immanence about the great Day of the Lord. And until that day comes, we are reminded that "This is the day the Lord has made, let us rejoice and be glad in it!" Someone once asked John Wesley what he would do if he knew early one morning that Jesus was going to return later that evening. His response was, "I would do exactly as I had planned to do all along – nothing different." The fact that the Day of the Lord (an eschatological – end of time term and concept) is at hand, merely calls us to a confident affirmation. Things will not always be as they are, and there will be a time, as the song says, when "all wrongs will be made right." In that confidence, we go on. As horrid as circumstances may sometimes appear, the Christian has a confident affirmation that all is not as it appears.

LaVonne and I ride the Amtrak train with an anchor from CNN news TV. This person indicated that she fully expects that we are on the verge of World War Three. Those prospects are frightening at best. What is the believer to do? Go on – the Day of the Lord is at hand.

Secondly, the letter of Paul to the Thessalonian believers tells them, in essence, they have no need to know the times or the seasons. There is a certain allowed agnosticism as to the details of the end.

Now, not everyone likes this. The "Left Behind" series of books and movies that are sweeping the nation don't like agnosticism as to the specifics of the second advent of Jesus.

I am sure most of you were not aware in 1988, that every minister in the U.S.A. and Canada received a free book called "Eighty-eight Reasons Why Jesus Will Return in 1988." And when he didn't, the author rewrote his book after a recalculation and wrote and freely distributed to every clergyman again "Eighty-nine Reasons Why Jesus Will Return in 1989." He didn't again, and the fellow crawled silently away.

Another person publicly announced in the mid-1990s that this second advent will occur. It was a specific day announcement as well. And, well, we all know what didn't happen. The fellow is still preaching on the radio and still has his sadly misled followers. (It is a good thing we are not living in Biblical days, or these false prophets would be stoned, and we would be put out of their misery). What about all of this? Simply that Jesus, himself, does not have the specifics of the future return, by his own words, and Paul assured us that neither do we.

Finally, the Gospel record brings to us a practical application. Do something with what God has given you. Do it – either with lots of results, or little results; that is not the issue, and do it faithfully until the Master returns. Just because one servant didn't make as much as another is not the issue. Each receives their "well done." It is the finishing with something that is the issue. Well, really, it is the finishing itself that is the issue. [As a matter of fact, last week's Gospel that Deacon Sue so aptly applied is an excellent example of this]. All of the virgins fell asleep. And it was not really the oil that was the issue either. Rather, half of the sleepy virgins left for new oil and weren't there when the Bridegroom arrived. They were not there at the goal or the end, the purpose. They are judged not for lack of oil, but for lack of presence. That Gospel is a lively commentary on the theme of today.

Be God's person when Jesus returns; and don't involve yourself with the ancillary arguments and guess work.

A personal illustration, if you will. I think it the perfect example of what God expects of us when God plans the return of Jesus.

In 1974, I was finishing my baccalaureate degree in Bible and Christian education, with an emphasis also in music. I had enrolled in a choral-conducting course with Dr. David Sheng, who had his Doctor of Musical Arts from the University of Shanghai, China. He was a very short little man in stature, but a man wise in music and with a great heart. He was not great with the English language, however. Three of us enrolled in the class, and by mid-semester, the other two had dropped out. I was the only person in the class, so got personal attention for seven weeks.

The day came for the final examination, and Dr. Sheng handed me a piece of music I had never seen. He said, "Mr. Mackey, Sir, you have five minutes to learn the piece. I will then return, sit at the piano, and you will conduct me. I will follow you, so you will know if it is right or wrong." He left, I studied, he returned.

When he sat at the studio piano, all I could see were his dark Chinese eyes peering at me over the top of the piano. He said, "Ready?" I replied that I was, and with correct positioning, I began. Honestly, I think I did a commendable job. We finished the piece (by the way, I had never seen or heard it before and today could not begin to tell you what it was). Dr. Sheng stood, came around the side of the piano, took my right hand and said, "Ah, Mr. Mackey, Sir, I must give you 'A,' you only one who finish course!"

I got an "A" for finishing the course. He never commented on my conducting! And today, that is just like the Lord-less interested in our performance than in our successful completion of the course of life. Men and women, let us allow the Lord to deliver us from the need to achieve (he already did that for us) and focus on finishing the course. Amen!

CHAPTER 40
THANKSGIVING EVE

St. John's Episcopal Church, Kingston, New York

I t's easy to miss the purpose of the holiday we plan to celebrate tomorrow, particularly since the focus is now on "turkey day," and the T. V. ads yesterday (Tuesday) began advertising the post-Thanksgiving sales at major department stores. Everyone lives through tomorrow's overeating so they can watch football (not bad in and of itself) and then shop until they drop on Friday (maybe bad in and of itself).

The history of our celebration is common knowledge, though I think the native American Indians get left out of much of the ceremony we remember and celebrate. But that is for the historians with convictions to address and challenge us.

Biblically, for believers, thanks holds a central part. We have the historical model of Israel; the incarnate presence of the Christ; and the mandate for the church.

These all lead us to be people who are people of thanksgiving.

First, we have the historical model of the nation of Israel. Each time there is a major victory, Israel gathers for a celebration of the faithfulness of God. There is no mere human sufficiency in the individual Hebrew or in the nation as a whole. The radical monotheism of the Jewish nation, coupled with the radical humanism of the Jewish mind, marry in the response to and responsibility before Jehovah God. They model this quite vividly in the Hebrew Scriptures.

There is a pattern, a paradigm for believers of 2002 to follow – we need not wonder what to do in thanksgiving; we have before us the model to follow. God's people gather for the giving of thanks – for the verbalizing of and actions of gratitude. Those to whom much is given, give much. Our response to God is a noteworthy way of thanking the God who sustains us.

Then we have the incarnate presence of Christ as a challenge to our thanks. Jesus Christ of Nazareth is a man who continually lives a life of gratitude. His gratitude comes through his giving of himself and not in his receiving unto himself. This is a key to understanding thanks. *Charis,* the Greek word from which we get "charismatic" and "Eucharist," "mean beauty, the 'grace' of the human form, favor, gratification, homage, gratitude, gracefulness – all things which delight." It is a big word, for gratitude (or thanksgiving) is all inclusive. The life of Jesus, the incarnate Son of God is all inclusive. He lived thankfully! This is the one who says, "Follow me." What we do tonight and tomorrow must be our pattern each day of the year.

Finally, thanks is the mandate for the church. Apostle Paul, in I Thessalonians 5:18 clearly directs, "Give thanks in all things, for this is God's will for you in Christ Jesus." (And I have not taken this out of its context. This verse is the context for all that Paul is teaching in this particular chapter). Simply give thanks with a grateful heart, Paul admonishes.

Paul Tillich, in *The Eternal Now,* captures the transformative power of thanks when he writes, "The abundance of a grateful heart gives honor to God even when it does not turn to Him in words. An unbeliever who is filled with thanks for his very being has ceased to be an unbeliever!"

St. Ambrose boldly stated, "No duty is more urgent than that of returning thanks!" And our thanks is to be directed to God – above and beyond all thanks we would make to others. As Christina Rossetti confides, "Were there no God, we would be in this glorious world with grateful hearts, and no one to thank!" And so, thanks be to God for God and for all the good things from heaven's hand! Amen.

CHAPTER 41
THE FIRST SUNDAY
OF ADVENT

St. John's Episcopal Church, Kingston, New York
Isaiah 64:1-9a; Psalm 80; I Corinthians 1:1-9
Mark 13:24-37

Have you ever felt like Isaiah the Prophet? First, you understand that God has called you to do something. You try to argue your way out of it, but God prevails. Then as you are about doing what you know needs be done, God doesn't seem to pitch in and help you do it? God doesn't seem to have the same agenda, the same schedule, and his *modus operandi* is so very, well, different! Isaiah's complaint in this morning's prophetic word is the complaint we all make when God doesn't or won't do it our way. Sometimes I am reminded of the child who awakes on Christmas morning at 5:00AM and has to wait to open gifts until parents arise at 8:00AM or so! It just isn't right – why can't they do something sooner? Advent is like that – an incessant longing – a repetitive itch calling for scratching! Why, God? Why not now?

Paul, in I Corinthians seems to tell us that we are in a waiting mode for two reasons. First, we wait so that we are spiritually complete, "not lacking in any spiritual gift." There is a certain awareness on the Apostle's part that there is an ultimate plan or purpose, and until we have met that level of spiritual giftedness we will not see the end. And then secondly, we wait the "revealing of our Lord Jesus Christ who will sustain us to the end." There is something in all of this of endurance, perseverance, longsuffering, expectation. The end (as in purpose or goal) is found in waiting for the end (in time).

And unfortunately, most advent thinking only looks at the end as a time termination. There is an end before the end that is often missed. That there will be an end is a critical and crucial part of Christian affirmation. We affirm it in the creed, "He will come again to judge the living and the dead;" we pray it at the memorial acclamation, "Christ has died, Christ is risen, Christ will come again;" and we pray it in the Lord's prayer, "Thy kingdom come." There is no denying that the church, for 2,000 years has affirmed the second advent (or coming) of Jesus the Christ to earth. And that is important. But it is not the focus of the Scriptures – what we accomplish until then is the focus. What are we to do in light of this truth? Are we to naval-gaze? Set times? Watch for signs? Proselytize? Are we to go off to a high mountain, sell all we have and live as a cult?

What are we to do in light of the imminent return of Jesus to this earth?

It is important to note that the answer is simple, yet profound. And the Gospel record of this morning gives us insights into the believer's posture in all of this. And this posture is paradoxical. It is a posture of both activity and inactivity, of doing and of being. Precisely being on watch is doing the work of waiting. I think Jesus' words give us the outline, the hooks on which we can hang our advent thoughts.

First, "take heed." That is, listen to the whole of the advent emphasis. Note that it is doing the work while waiting for the return of the Master. It is indeed doing the work of the ministry – seeing Christ in others and ministering to them. Last's week's Gospel is keen on this – as much as we do to the least, we will do to Christ – and to leave the needy in their need is to miss the Christ in every person. (There is nothing, by the way, in last week's Gospel of justification be faith. There is the need for Christian works as an accompaniment. Just thought I would throw that in to knock us off our Protestant leanings!).

Take heed means to do what we are told to do, whether it be to work, to watch, to wait. One writer puts it this way, "Watch and wait; imagine and dream. The signs of the season are all around, pointing us to the beginning of our end. God with us!"

I remember an adolescent, juvenile interpretation of the imminent return of Jesus, when college boys who were planning on getting married were convinced that Jesus would return to earth sometime between the "I do," of the marriage ceremony and the consummation of the marriage that night. They were sure Jesus would ruin their first sexual time as husband and wife. Some thought, why bother, Jesus will mess it all up in the second advent. But the "take heed," tells us to go on anyway. And most of us did! Take heed.

Then Jesus says "watch." This is a simple directive for the believer to know that the promise is to be fulfilled. Watch for it in the midst of doing our daily work as believers. It means living in belief, hope, desire. It means wanting God to come again and make things right. It is not a retreat into false piety and an ignorant "hope-so-ism." There is nothing of retreat here and certainly no room for the Pollyanna-ish notion that I'm right and you just wait to see how God deals with you! Many of you remember wading through the play, "Waiting for Godot," in high school – the play that was just the opposite of the watching Jesus is speaking of. The Godot play is "existing without faith, without hope, and without life, really, (it is) graceless and empty. This is the distressing opposite of Advent's attentiveness and aliveness that we are invited to experience in the coming weeks." (from *Advent, Christmas, and Epiphany,* by Megan McKenna).

Finally, Jesus gives the indication that we should wait. Really wait. We should invest our expectations that peace will come; earth's wrongs will be righted and all good that has been unrewarded will be fully rewarded. And though there is certainly the "do something" nature to the second advent, there is the wait as well. The turn of the phrase also works, "Don't just do something! Stand there!"

Henri Nouwen captures this in his work *Watch for the Light.* "Waiting is not a very popular attitude. Waiting is not something people think about with great sympathy. In fact, most people consider waiting a waste of time. …For many people, waiting is an awful desert between where they are and where they want to go. And people do not like such a place. They want to get out of it by doing something."

But alas, waiting is part of the advent call. And so, the Master has gone away and left us in charge. That is somewhat scary! (I'm reminded of the first time LaVonne and I left all three boys home alone – but we won't go there). But this is true – we are left in charge and told to work, and watch, and wait. The implications are manifold; the rewards indescribable. Amen!

CHAPTER 42
THE FOURTH
SUNDAY OF ADVENT

St. John's Episcopal Church, Kingston, New York
II Samuel 7:4, 8-16; Psalm 132; Romans 16:25-27
Luke 1:26-38

To live above with saints we love, oh say, that will be glory. But to live below, with saints we know, well, that's another story!" Samuel, in our Old Testament lesson today makes repeated reference to the *people of God*, that somehow the individual, be it David the King or others, exists in the midst of the called community. Paul's great benediction from the epistle to the Romans is wrapped up in the plural "you," with the hopes and anticipation that the Christian message will include "all nations." There is something radically communal about the faith delivered to us through the Messiah Jesus.

There is nothing in this Christian faith of a mere "I'm in, you're not" kind of faith. Christianity did not parallel the modern world very well; and thus becomes so apropos to the postmodern world you and I are entering.

Will you allow me a brief history lesson? Up to the mid seventeen hundreds, the world existed in the mystery of pre-modernity. These were the days before scientism and industrialism. The mystery of religion was embraced and reason was not the end all of everything considered. Then with the Enlightenment, the revolutions of the eighteenth century, the industrial revolution, the rise of scientific method, rational humanism, the world moved into the modern era. This was a time of decline for true faith - much of Christianity became deism (God is watching us from a distance) and individual faith took precedence over corporate faith. The church of the Reformation became a place for individuals to find God, but not necessarily to find each other. Thomas Oden of Drew University calls this modernist mentality "inordinate hedonic self-assertiveness."

Then something radical happened. The individualism of the modern era began to be shaken by the beatniks of the 1950s, the hippies of the 1960s, and the free love movement of the 1970s. The 1980s produced a Ronald Regan who, despite whether you like his politics or not, in orchestration with Pope John Paul II, brought down the Berlin Wall and ushered in the postmodern mind when persons again started to think that modernity was not all it was cracked up to be. [By the way, George W. Bush is a thorough-going modernist who has not moved in his thinking into post-modernity].

People are not sure progress is inevitable; that science has the answer for everything; that all things are explainable by sensory facts. Mystery is again entering into humanity's thinking, and consideration is being given that I might just need you and you might just need me to live in this world which often is unfriendly to us.

The incarnation of Jesus Christ of Nazareth anticipates these kinds of needs. Authenticity within the community is what Advent anticipates. Jesus comes as the hub of a wheel whose spokes, when they get closer to him, necessarily get closer to each other. There is something centripetal to Jesus of Nazareth - something that pulls us together.

When Mary is told she will give birth, the entire encounter is shrouded in others - Mary, baby, Joseph, Elizabeth, Zechariah, John the Baptist, and on and on. This is not an isolated individualistic occurrence. It is something earth-shakingly radical. God with _us_ (notice the plural).

There is a plethora of teachings in the Gospel record of what Jesus requires. He seldom requires some grand and glorious doctrinal statement. But he often and repeatedly requires that relationships with others be mended before one intends to follow God.

We have the Pharisee and the poor sinner in the temple praying. Jesus has little time for the Pharisee who dismisses the penitent without seeing himself like him.

We have Jesus saying that if we have something against another, we dare not go to the altar unless we leave our gift at the altar and then go, reconcile, and then return to the altar.

There is the teaching that two must agree together to walk together.

There is the parable of the Prodigal Son (and the real prodigal is the older brother who stays home and does everything right except welcoming his brother upon his return - and this cancels out all his doing of good!).

There is the story of the rich man and Lazarus where the rich man is sent away from God after death, not because of lack of faith, but because of lack of love.

And we could extend this list almost endlessly with the same exact teaching. Jesus is "God with *us!*" The "us" is the important place where God dwells - not in my modernistic selfish, my-way only kind of faith. The Protestant Reformation made that kind of faith central - my relationship with Jesus....Postmodern catholic (not Roman Catholic) faith will see each of us as precious to God and special to us.

If indeed I cannot graciously and self-sacrificially give myself up (my opinions, my preferences, etc.) for your sake, then I have missed the model of Mary in the gospel record, and the description of her response to

God is wasted on me. Notice what Luke records Mary saying, "Behold I am your servant Lord, let it be to me according to your Word." If you and I are indeed the servants of God, our vocabulary will change, our methodology will change, and I guarantee our productions will change.

Now let's make one disclaimer here. This is no Polly-annish be nice to everyone truth. There is nothing of saccharin sweet non-offensive Christianity here. But there is common Christian decency and Godly love. No, I don't like everyone - I don't even like all the Christians I know; there are people at work I wish were not there - but this does not grant me the permission to treat them dismissively. I have no Christian choice but to receive them into the company of the redeemed.

This is something you and I promised, yea, vowed to God we would do! Notice page 308 of your Book of Common Prayer, "We receive you into the household of God." I may not like you, I may not want to spend overt amounts of time with you, I may not even think you are the kind of Christian I would want you to be. But "I receive you," and before God, "I am your servant." "Lord, be it unto me, according to your word."

May our lives following the first appearing of Jesus be lived as He plans, in the expectation that he will soon return and find us being Christian to one another. Amen!

CHAPTER 43
THE EVE OF THE HOLY NATIVITY

St. John's Episcopal Church, Kingston, New York
Isaiah 9:2-4,6-7; Psalm 96; Titus 2:11-14
Luke 2:1-14 (15-20)

We're in church tonight, so we really ought to be honest. As much as most of us like giving things at Christmas, watching faces as happiness spills upon them as packages are opened, we also, down way deep inside, like to receive things as well. I like getting.

Each day at work when the daily mail is delivered, there is usually a package or two brought to my desk by my secretary. They usually contain books, and I like getting books! But, frankly, I like getting, period. Now be honest - you do too!

Tonight's Scripture from Isaiah tells us that "unto us a child is born, unto us a Son is given." Paul tells Titus that the "grace of God has appeared bringing salvation to all people..." And in the Gospel we are reminded that born to us today is a "Savior, who is Christ the Lord." These are gifts to us - things we receive - things we take and make our own. It is a receiving in the fullest sense of the word.

As I contemplated these Scriptures, I began to outline what we get when we really "get" Christmas - when we get past the wrapping paper, the needle-dropping tree, the ornaments broken by our various pets, our ham or turkey dinners which give us post-lunch slump (a full stomach and a light head). When all this is past, have we really received; have we really gotten Christmas? When we do, there are numerous startling gifts that become ours.

First, in the Christmas event, we receive a Savior. This tells us, first of all, we must need one. We are not merely dirty people who need to be cleaned up; we are not weak people who need to be made strong; we are not poor people who need to be made rich; we are not bad people who need to be made good. We are lost people who need to be saved. And the gift is salvation. The bad news of our lostness is met with superior news of a Savior. In the Christmas event, I am given the gift of lostness that I might know the gift of being found - salvation is to be found. T. S. Eliot reminds us that this is like coming home and finding it again for the first time. Salvation as a gift is something that puts us at home, really at home.

A second gift we receive in this entire Christmas event is a God who invades every part of our lives. God doesn't merely visit in Jesus, God comes to dwell among us. Emmanuel is "God with us," we can't get away from God. The Incarnation celebrated tonight is "God in the flesh," or "God in the meat" (from "carne" meaning flesh or meat). As much as I would like a spiritualized Jesus, I get one who cries in the night, wets and messes his swaddling clothes, and has to grow up, go through puberty, withstand temptation, and bleed and suffocate to death on a cross on the public garbage heap of Jerusalem. And Isaiah tells us that this one is called "Wonderful counselor, Mighty God, everlasting father, prince of peace."

As the wonderful counselor, I encounter one who knows more than I do and from whom I may receive counsel and direction. He puts me directionally in my place.

As the Mighty God, I am encountering one who is transcendent as well as imminent - one whose big picture can be set over my small time-encapsulated life and give it meaning.

As the everlasting father, I receive one who receives me back and makes me suffer the pains of being forgiven, freely, when I would like to meritoriously work my way back to God! The prodigal's father simply took him back; and that is grievous to those of us who want credit for coming back.

And in Jesus, as the Prince of Peace, I am given a God in Jesus who calls me to an existence which I cannot produce myself, peace. I am given the knowledge of the adequacy of my resources and that God is a God of peace, whose sword only confirms the human sword and is never wielded at its own motivation. Peace - a concept, particularly for us after 9/11/01, we would most like to jettison.

I am given other gifts according to Apostle Paul. I am given the gift of renouncing "irreligion." God delivers me from being a pompous ass - and invites me to bask in the greater passions of a life of belief and not to be mired in the worldly passion of unbelief.

I am given Mother Mary who declares herself the "servant of the Lord;" I am given frustrated, yet patient Joseph who stays with his engaged wife and step-child to raise him to the glory of God; I am given smelly shepherds, noisy angels, and foreign Magi or kings who don't even speak good English. In the Christmas event I am given the gift of discomfort in who I am naturally in the invitation to become who I can become supernaturally. I am doomed to hear prophecy and know that it was fulfilled; I am challenged to look at myself and realize how far I have to go; I am indicted as one who must see these things that have come to pass and then return to a mundane life, praising God for all I have seen and heard.

In Christmas, I now know and am known by a God in Christ Jesus who makes me run counter to the values of the world; who makes me embrace the poor and the needy who call for ministry; to wrestle with

Scriptures I don't always understand; to live in a community of faith which often argues over the most petty things imaginable.

Christmas implicates me in what God is doing; it baptizes me in mystery, forcing me to submit my rational explanations; it thrusts me into witness, making me live a life of integrity; it indicts me as a person, made in the image of God and now redeemed by God's grace.

And my response is, "I can't handle all of this!!" And Isaiah, who would have agreed with all I have shared tonight, anticipates my frustration and assures me, "The zeal of the Lord of hosts will perform this!"

Christmas gifts from God deliver me from the painful and haunting incessant need to do and frees me, by grace, to be just another one of God's redeemed.

Unpack these subtly haunting yet awesome gifts, and find the Christian life the most disturbing, adventurous, mysterious, and yet fulfilling life on planet earth. "Unto us is born this day, in the City of David a Savior who is Christ the Lord..." "You shall call his name Jesus."

"Come on, Jesus, let's wrestle and have some fun." Amen!

CHAPTER 44
THE FIRST SUNDAY AFTER CHRISTMAS

Isaiah 61:10-62:3; Psalm 147; Galatians 3:23- 4:7
John 1:1-18

The world thinks Christmas is over. The church says we are only fives days into the twelve day celebration which ends next Sunday with our celebration of Epiphany. Whereas Epiphany is God coming clean with who the Divine really is, Christmas is the hint that the Divine is not what we normally think a God should be.

The gods of the Greeks, the Romans, and even to some degree the Hebrews, were gods who were somehow known by their otherness, their distance (or transcendence), the revelation of their likes and dislikes, and the dark shrouds that covered their abodes. The gods let you see certain attributes, and even Moses in the cleft of the rock only gets to see the "hinder parts of God" (God's *glutious maximus* in other words).

Then along comes this infant named Jesus, claimed by heavenly host and spiritually insightful humans alike as the God-man; God incarnate, God now in the very flesh the Hebrew Scriptures indicate God created many millennia ago. Now we find a God with urges and needs and all that a human nature possesses. He hungers, thirsts, needs rest, relieves himself, is tempted, gets frustrated, is often angered, and on and on. This is no self-respecting god of the past; this is a new vision of God. And later we would be told that, "Whoever sees me has seen the Father!" Can you even imagine!

And now, here is John reflecting on this incarnate God, Jesus. And in what is known as "The Prologue to the Gospel of John," we have the text read for us this morning. And there are at least four captivating new realities with which we are confronted.

First, "the word (reason, rationale, philosophy) became flesh..." This is scandalous at best. Spirituality is now wrapped up in materiality, never again to be separated. Suddenly the human frame becomes something that is inherently spiritually important. This body that we drug out of bed this morning to worship in this place is of inestimable value. My five senses, though limited, are not perverse. My needs for rest, food, drink, relationship, thought, emotion, etc., are not illicit realities, but part of the wonderful *imprimatur* that God places on the human body in the incarnate act of Bethlehem. The controversial Episcopal priest and writer, Matthew Fox insightfully writes, "Flesh itself dispenses grace and healing, liberation and forgiveness. Spirit is at home in flesh and loves to dwell therein." (And I heartily recommend his new book *Sins of the Spirit; Blessings of the Flesh*).

John continues with the fact that this word not only becomes flesh, but "dwells among us." This is not the divine visiting his creation, but coming to dwell in it. We have presence rather than absence. We have a God who can be implicated in a discussion (prayer); who can be seen in paradoxical ways; who can be, and often is, as present in seeming absence as in conspicuous presence. God, in Jesus dwells among us. That means to make one's home here. Jesus is God at home in the world. It's a dangerous place, but not such a bad place after all. And we may abhor its climates, its politics, its proclivities and the like, but there is a certain reality that God is at home here.

This certainly runs counter to what 2,000 years of Christianity have taught, but those who have taught the opposite of this have missed the revelation in John chapter one. God is here. There is no need to invite the Presence; we merely move within the Presence who lives among us. (Alright, for those who want to be theological purists, when Jesus is resurrected and ascended, He is technically no longer here, but tells us that He will send "another" Comforter (of the same substance/essence - *homoousias* - in the Greek) to take His place. Holy Spirit is God still dwelling in creation.

And so we have this wonderful affirmation of flesh and this reality of divine presence.

Further, John tells us that "we beheld his glory." Now the gods of the ancients allowed humanity to see their happiness and their anger. You were either blessed or judged and cursed. There was nothing of sublimity, awesomeness, delight, or glory. Now in Jesus we have the invitation to bask in the absolute wonder of God. To the beatnik generations, God may be seen as neat, keen, groovy; and a little later on in contemporary history we might even stand back and say, "awesome, man!":

And then John tells us that "In Him was light." This is not an ethereal "enlightenment," but rather some horse sense - a common sense, that if there is a god, this is how he would do it just to throw everybody off. "Oh, I see..." is the reaction to revelation not self-congratulatory insight. Light was the first element seen in the creation process in Genesis, and is foundational to and precedes all the other creation. Light may be the essence of all matter as well, we are told by modern physics.

And here we are at Christmas, celebrating a birth that brings us these things. And maybe this is what makes Christmas so fleshly, so present, so glorious, so filled with light.

A reportedly true story puts Christmas into its flesh and blood context:

Soon after the completion of the Verazzano Narrows Bridge over New York Harbor, a pastor was decorating his church on Christmas Eve afternoon for the midnight service. He looked up and noticed that a major roof leak had made a terrible stain behind the alter and drew attention away from everything else. Frustrated, he went for a walk, and during his walk he passed a pawn shop, where, in the window was this lovely hand-embroidered brocade tablecloth. It looked like the right size to cover the stain, so he entered the shop, negotiated the price and left with the lovely table cloth.

Proud of his purchase, he immediately went to the church to hang it. It did the trick - looking wonderfully liturgical and new for the Christmas Eve celebration. Just then, he turned and noticed an older lady sitting in the front pew praying. When he approached, she said to him, "Father, were did you ever get such a lovely piece of hand embroidered fabric?" He told her the story. She replied, "May I approach it?" "Why certainly," said the priest. As she did, he noticed that she lifted the corner and looked intently on what she saw there. "What is it?" he asked. "These are my initials, I embroidered this tablecloth many years ago in Germany before the War."

Absolutely taken aback, the priest offered to take the cloth down and give it to her. She assured him that using it in the Lord's service was far superior to any-thing she could use it for, and so it was left.

The priest asked her where she lived and she re-plied, "Across the bridge in Staten Island, I only do housekeeping here in Brooklyn." He offered to drive her home and she accepted.

The service that night was glorious. Wonderful attendance, great singing, a moving homily-all was blessed. As the priest and the altar guild were clean-ing up following the service, the priest noticed an older gentleman sitting in the front pew. When the priest approached, the old man commented on the loveliness of the hanging behind the altar. "My wife embroidered a table cloth much like that back in Germany many, many years ago. But we were separated during the War and I have not seen her in many years. Is there any chance that there are three initials in the lower cor-ner?"

The priest, completely undone by this story assured the man that the initials were there; and sure enough, when they approached the tapestry there were the ini-tials he predicted. The priest compelled the old gent to take a ride with him across the bridge to Staten Island. It was now one o'clock in the morning, but the man, having no family and nothing to do went gladly along for the company.

When they arrived at the home where hours ago the priest had dropped off the housekeeper, they approached the door, where-well, you can guess the rest of the story- husband and wife separated by war and many years were re-united as an indescribable Christmas present.

Here is God in the coincidences living among people who have deep and longing needs. Here is a God who allows us to see glory in table clothes. Here is a God who invites us to say, "Oh, I see...that is how God works!" May it always be! Merry Christmas! Amen!

CHAPTER 45
THE FIRST SUNDAY AFTER THE EPIPHANY

St. John's Episcopal Church, Kingston, New York
Isaiah 42:1-9; Psalm 89:1-29; Acts 10:34-38
Mark 1:7-11

How often, when raising children, when we want them to really hear what we are saying, we say, "Look at me!" The story is told of a leading world theologian of the last century, who was questioned by a student during a lecture. When the professor began to answer, the student began an intense conversation with a fellow student next to him. Frustrated, the professor said, "Sir, look at me!" The student continued his rude conversation and the professor again demanded, "Look at me!" When the student refused to look at the professor, the professor ceased his attempt at an answer and continued his lecture.

It is hard to know what one is talking about if we do not look at them. And this is exactly what Epiphany is - this is the time, Jesus, in so many words says, "Look at me!" As we survey the Christian year, we see that Advent and Lent are the seasons when we look at ourselves; Pentecost is the season when we look at what needs to be done; and Christmas, Epiphany, and Easter are the seasons when we look at Jesus.

This true story is recounted in the Preface to a book called *Dimensions of the Faith*. An international conference of students and faculties of Protestant theology was held in which Karl Barth, the Swiss theologian was present. The account goes like this: "At the very first session of the conference, Dr. Barth filled every expectation of controversy. The first paper, presented by a theologian from the University of Geneva, dealt with the concept of religious experience and it employed the language of psychology as well as of Christian theology. Before the speaker was well under way, however, Dr. Barth suddenly arose in the audience, interrupted the speaker, and addressed the chairman. 'I shall not wait any longer. I want to ask the speaker a question now,' he said, thereby of course throwing the meeting into an uproar of consent and dissent. The chairman replied that it is customary for questions to be withheld until a paper is finished, but that he would leave the decision to the speaker. With questionable judgment the theologian reading the paper agreed to accept the question immediately. Barth thereupon made a frontal attack. 'Is the speaker reading to us a paper on Christian theology or on the psychology of religious experience? If the paper is on the psychology of religion, why should we here listen to it? This is a conference of Christian theologians; only the Word of God, not talk about psychology and religious experience, is appropriate here.' Immediately the assembly plunged into heated argument, a debate on the place or lack of place, of secular science and even of apologetics in a Christian discourse. The heat of the controversy pervaded the remaining sessions of the conference."

As a Biblical person, Barth wanted a Biblical focus. Too often we talk about the application of the story of Jesus and not enough about Jesus, himself. Episcopalians, particularly, like to speak highly of "Christ," or "the Christ," but are uncomfortable with Jesus. And yet, we are confronted with the Jesus person, an historical figure who tells those who follow him around the dusty roads of Palestine, "Those who have seen me have seen the Father." There is that something about Jesus that demands to be seen.

And on this first Sunday after the Epiphany, I think we might hear Jesus saying to us, "Look at me!" Certainly I am more and more convinced that this is what people are expecting of the Church. If they want psychology, there are therapists; if they want Islam there is the Mosque; if they want Torah, there is the Synagogue; if they want entertainment, there is the theater. But if people apply themselves to the Church in our day and age, I believe they are demanding that we give what we believe and affirm those things that make us different. And that is Jesus.

These weeks of Epiphany we will spend delineating some of the simple things the Gospels tell us about Jesus, and this morning there are several.

First, we must acknowledge that Jesus said of John the Baptist that no greater man has been born by woman. There was an elevated reality to the man John as Jesus' forerunner. Based on this, when John says what he does in today's Gospel record, it is of all the more import.

The first thing we learn of Jesus is from John's mouth, and that is that Jesus is greater than the greatest man ever born. There is a priority to Jesus. He is, after his resurrection, known as "the first born among many brothers and sisters." There is a pre-eminence that is manifested even in the relative obscurity of his Galilee ministry. John acknowledges that Jesus is "mightier" than he himself is, and that he, John is "unworthy" to untie Jesus' sandal.

The attention of those who follow Jesus is on Jesus. The great survivor of World War II German prison camps, Corrie ten Boom reminds us:

"Look around and be distressed;
Look within and be depressed;
Look at Jesus, be at rest."

Something there is, that unquantifiable something, in this one to be baptized by John that would later lead

John to say, "He must increase and I must decrease." This is that which we learn of Jesus today. We serve a mighty one.

We are then told that Jesus is baptized not only by water, but by Holy Spirit, and affirmed in a voice from God. God is pleased with this Jesus of Nazareth. This is purposeful. There is design here.

This is why Epiphany follows upon Christmas. It is not all made up! As a matter of fact, one insightful philosopher in examining all this historic give-and-take said, "It takes a Christ, to invent a Christ!" In other words, it is too far out to imagine it all.

Dr. John David Burton, one time Poet-in-Residence at Princeton University, writes *God + Mary = Jesus; A Christmas Poem.* He begins with the quote from Galatians 4:4, "God sent his son, born of a woman."

> God, we have found You out, learned You could
> not do on Your Own what You wanted done above
> all else, to let Yourself be seen in a Form so
> fair that human eyes would look again, again, and
> yet again, to let Your Voice be heard in a voice
> so clear that —above the sounds of hate – human
> ears would listen, listen for the love.

> All of this You wanted, and You could not do it
> on Your Own, unable – earthworm-like – to
> reproduce Yourself with Yourself alone. Even You,
> the Lord of Life, cannot do it on Your Own.

For You to be made Flesh, a peasant girl is
needed, a girl quite like all the women ever
born to bear daughters and sons, to nurse them in
the night, watch them grow, then let them go to
a world which often slays the children.

You, O Lord, cannot come among us except as
    You
are birthed as we are birthed, "of a woman made."
You, Who rounded the earth in the hollow of Your
    Hand,
could not come to earth except as You were willing
to round the belly, swell the womb of a peasant
    girl.

All year long the preacher's word tells of God,
high and holy and lifted up, apart from us.
The Christmas word is "God Plus Mary Equals
    Jesus."

This is the Epiphany word as well. Jesus has come
among us. We have a Savior who "takes away the sin of
the world," and we have an impeccable example who
says, "follow me." The new year is upon us and we have
loads of work to do. Lead on Jesus. Amen!

CHAPTER 46
THE SECOND SUNDAY AFTER THE EPIPHANY

I Samuel 3:1-20; Psalm 63:1-8; I Corinthians 6:11-20; John 1:43-51

Today is one of the few days in our three year Lectionary cycle that we read from the Gospel of John. It is the more theological of the four Gospels, and reveals Jesus through his teaching more than through his action. Today's Gospel tells us something of Jesus; it is again an Epiphany or a revelatory Scripture.

Epiphany is that season, not when the light bulb goes on because we have thought-up something ourselves, but the lightening bolt shatters the darkness and allows us to see with supernatural light what we cannot see by human reason alone.

God uses the ordinary to reveal the extraordinary. God uses the normal to accomplish the miraculous.

The, no doubt, apocryphal story is told of a fellow who is going through a flood and has climbed as high as possible to the pinnacle of the roof of his house. He prays to God to miraculously deliver him when a row boat comes by and the chap in the boat says, "Climb aboard!" "No, God will take care of me," is the reply. Just then a helicopter comes overhead and drops a line. The stranded man waves him off with a, "God will take care of me." Then a fellow on a raft floats by inviting the stranded man to join him and float to safety and again the word is, "No thanks - God will deliver me."

After the fellow has drowned and gone to judgment, he asks God why he didn't answer his prayers. God, amazed, says to the fellow, "I sent a rowboat, a helicopter, and a raft and you rejected them all, so I let you drown."

If the ordinary doesn't teach us, we are uneducable. There is little for us to learn. And here we are confronted with the Gospel.

First, Jesus allows the disciples to reveal that Jesus Himself is, indeed, the fulfillment of Jewish prophecy. He is the one Moses and the Prophets foresaw. He is in the direct line of God's salvation history and all we have to do is see him and follow him. God, in doing something new in Jesus, is doing the same thing God has always been doing and that is calling people to follow.

For thousands of years, the Hebrews first, and the church subsequently have made theistic belief difficult when Jesus makes it simple. It is not easy, it is simple. The incarnation is God's coming among us to say, "follow me."

She was sixteen and he eighteen when they met and married. Within five years there were four children and life overtook the young couple. He worked two jobs to support the family and she took care of the house, her husband and the four little ones. One day as she was doing the dinner dishes, she took off her apron, dried her hands and walked out the door.

No one could find the young wife and mother, and for months the devastated husband looked in vain. Each week she would call and ask about the children and he would plead with her to come home. We love you - we really love you and want you home - and she would hang up before the call could be traced. After many months of weekly calls, the husband hired a private investigator to find his wife. He found her in a run down hotel in down town Des Moines, Iowa. The husband left the children in the care of his parents and drove across the country to the hotel. He parked the car, walked in, found her room number, and slowly climbed the stairs. He didn't know what he would say, but he knocked on the door anyway. She opened the door and he said, "Honey, we love you, come home with me." She melted in his arms and he walked her to the car and they went home. As they drove he said, "Why would you return with me now and not with all those months of pleading?" Her reply is classic. "Before today it was all words, and then you came."

Epiphany is that season that follows hard on Christmas, when that which had been all words was now come. "In the beginning was the Word and the Word was with God and the Word was God,...and the Word became flesh and dwelt among us." Before, this was all words; now Jesus came.

Then Jesus assures us that something good <u>can</u> come out of Nazareth. Nathanael asks the question and finds his answer in Jesus. And each of us asks if anything good can come out of____and we fill in the blank with places, and situations, and circumstances where we are sure nothing good at all abides. And then Jesus proves us wrong by answering our negative question with Himself.

And finally, Jesus allows Nathanael to call him the "Son of God," and the "King of Israel." And though Jesus asks him about the logic with which he reasons this, Jesus never squelches the declaration. We have in front of us the very Son of God and the King of Israel and this person is the revelation of God to us.

Many throughout history have made statements such as the one Ghandi made, "I would be a Christian, but for Christians." And the problem is that we look at Christians and we are disappointed. It is Jesus, the Christ who does not disappoint and to whom we must look. It is the lesson of Epiphany. It is the revelation we are confronted with during this season.

Benjamin Disraeli said, "Who can deny that Jesus of Nazareth, the incarnate Son of the most high God, is the eternal glory of the Jewish race?"

Fedor Dostoyevski writes, "I believe there is no one lovelier, deeper, more sympathetic, and more perfect than Jesus. I say to myself that not only is there no one else like him, but there could never be anyone like him."

This is the revealed Jesus. This is our Lord. Amen!

CHAPTER 47
THE FEAST OF THE PRESENTATION

St. John's Episcopal Church, Kingston, New York
Nyack College-New York City, Chapel Service
February 4, 2003
Malachi 3:1-4; Psalm 84; Hebrews 2:14-18
Luke 2:22-40

We are in the midst of Epiphany when we are confronted with the Feast of the Presentation. This is not often on a Sunday, so we are enabled with a special privilege today. The Presentation is always celebrated on February 2, and it is the remembrance that Jesus was taken to the temple in obedience to the laws of Moses and there this infant encounters Simeon and Anna. The record tells us much of Jesus, and the lessons with which we must wrestle are not easy.

Christianity is nothing if it is not an invitation to change. Conversion means to change. There is an essential and incontrovertible reality to the change which Jesus Christ causes in the human heart and life. And here we have hints of that change

The two who are present in the temple, Simeon and Anna are the instruments of revelation - instruments used by God to bring new, challenging, and life-changing elements into our lives.

That Simeon knew that he would not die until he had "seen the Lord's Christ (or Messiah)" is of particular note. We are told, in essence, that this faithful Jew knew this Child was the promised one. But his Messiahship would turn the common concept of the Messiah on its head. Listen to the predictions:

First, this Christ or Messiah would be a light - light is more than law - for the religious always want rules and this new Messiah would, in the fulfilling of Moses' law, institute the revelation of light. Now we can see this means there is insight, understanding, and a rationale of redemption rather than a rationale of sin and ignorance. It is utterly different than anything hitherto expected.

Then this light would not be for any one group but would be available to and applicable to the Gentiles (a generic word for all non-Hebrews). What scandal - a Messiah, a Jew, with pertinence for everyone? How absurd! How real, however and how true. There is no truth unless it be universal truth; if it is not true for everyone it cannot be true for anyone. Regardless of what our Postmodern society may say, I cannot make up truth as I go along, because at some point I will have an unsolvable confrontation with someone else doing the same thing.

Certainly the religious would keep all the truth for themselves, but Simeon reveals a new and wider and broader way.

A true story is told from the 1960s. Bill was a college student, probably one of the "Jesus Freaks". He is described as having "wild hair, torn jeans, shoeless feet, and tie-dyed T-shirt, all of which testified how recent was his conversion to Christianity." Listen to how Leonard Sweet of Drew Theological Seminary in New Jersey relates the story:

"His appearance, though, belies his unusual intelligence, and on a particular Sunday soon after his conversion, Bill attended a local congregation for fellowship and nurture beyond his college Bible study. Across the street from the campus sat the college church, filled weekly with well-dressed and conservative members.... Picture the scene as Bill enters. He has no shoes. He is clad in his jeans, T-shirt, and sports that wild hair. Their service has already started, so Bill ambles down the aisle looking for a seat. The pews are full, so he keeps walking. By now, people are a bit uncomfortable, but no one says anything. Bill continues down the aisle, looking for a seat, but finds only perplexed gazes. When he realizes there are no seats, he simple squats down on the floor. At the college fellowship, this is perfectly acceptable, but no one has ever done it at this church.

"The people grow nervous and the tension thickens. Then a deacon rises from his seat and slowly makes his way toward Bill. This particular deacon is in his eighties, has silver-grey hair, wears a three-piece suit, accented by a pocket watch. Known as a godly man, elegant, dignified, and courtly, his gait is aided by a finely crafted cane. As the deacon walks toward Bill, many are thinking, *You can't blame him for what he is going to do. How can a man of his age and background understand some college kid?*

"It takes a long time for the deacon to reach Bill. Silence reigns; one can almost hear the tapping of the deacon's cane. All eyes focus upon him and the people are thinking, *The minister can't even preach the sermon until the deacon does what he has to do.*

"Suddenly the elderly man drops his cane to the floor. With great difficulty he lowers himself and sits next to Bill. When the pastor has regained his voice he says, 'What I'm about to preach, you may never remember. What you have just seen, you will never forget.'" The Messiah that Simeon holds in his arms is for Bill as well as the old time deacon.

This Messiah is the glory of the people Israel. One of the hardest things today for Israel to understand is that Christians are fellow believers with Jews. The Apostle Paul tells Christians that we are grafted into the tree that was Israel, and that ours is not to convert Israel but to make them jealous of what we have. Instead, we have turned the Jews off to Christ by obnoxious evangelism.

Finally, Simeon tells Mary that this one is appointed for the rise and fall of many. There is a particular danger in following Jesus. He upsets the comfortable apple carts of societal mores. No one could have ever convinced me that I would become anti-death penalty and pacifist. But Jesus confronts us and changes us. I am about to write to our President and ask him, as one Christian to another, that, before he tries to kill Iranians and Hussein himself, that he invite him to lunch - break bread together, and then see if he can still go to war. Remember, later Jesus would say if we have anything against another, leave your gift at the altar and go and try to make it right first. President Bush, break bread with Saddam Hussein!

Then there is little old Anna. She sees Jesus with Mary and Joseph; she gives thanks and recognizes the Savior. We do a lot of things in our Christian churches, but probably the most lacking is a consistency of gratitude and a recognition of salvation - simple things often sacrificed on the altar of the difficult and expedient.

The Feast of the Presentation reminds us that this incarnate God, Jesus, the Christ, was truly human as well as truly divine, and that to circumvent this is to circumvent our own salvation. C. FitzSimmons Allison, a retired Bishop of our Church, has written a compelling book, calling us to take Jesus as the Church has taken Jesus for 2,000 years - to reject the deconstructed Jesus of so much modernity, and to regain the mystery of the Biblical Jesus whom we cannot always explain. That is the foundation of discipleship. His book is entitled *The Cruelty of Heresy.* Heresy keeps us from the Jesus presented to God in the temple; keeps us from God among us; and man in the presence of God. This screaming baby boy is none other than God the Son. I didn't write this stuff - no one could. Believe it to your benefit! That's God's intent! Amen!

CHAPTER 48
THE FIFTH SUNDAY AFTER THE EPIPHANY

St. John's Episcopal Church, Kingston, New York
II Kings 4:8-37; Psalm 142; I Corinthians 9:16-23
Mark 1:29-39

To focus on the healing aspect of today's Gospel is to unfortunately miss the true lesson that is part of the movement of Jesus in his ministry. Remember that Jesus is ministering during the time called "Second Temple Judaism," named for the temple built years before by Ezra and Nehemiah after Solomon's temple had been destroyed by the Babylonians. This is a puny and second-rate temple, as well compared to what Solomon in all his glory had done; but it was, nonetheless, the temple of God.

However, the temple had been taken over by bureaucrats: scribes, Pharisees, Sadducees, and priests. Each of these groups, though good in their intent, had to some degree become exclusivistic and separatistic. They had inflated their understanding of themselves and grown to appear threatening, at best, to the average Jew on the street. They were the aristocracy of the religious Judaism of the day. Not bad people, in some ways too good for others; and, therefore, irrelevant to most others.

The temple system had grown to exclude the poor who could not purchase perfect animals for sacrifice; the lame, since it was argued that if only pure animals were acceptable, then only whole humans were acceptable; and the blind were discouraged from approaching the temple as well. Women, particularly, who had long standing diseases where blood might be involved were ceremoniously dismissed from temple involvement, even in the court of the women or Gentiles. And all of this says nothing of what the poor demonized of the day might face. There simply was no place for them in what had become a religious system - a system of the well, the whole, the spiritual, the "righteous." And Jesus makes a startling statement when he claims that these are the very people who do not need him; rather the sick, the unrighteous, the partial, the unspiritual - these are those, the lost - whom Jesus comes to seek and to save.

Jesus, therefore is, in the line of his cousin John, a counter-temple movement. He is not anti-temple, but rather, counter-temple. He is the option for the masses, the choice of the disenfranchised. He is the Messiah for those who know they need one. And this is precisely why Jesus makes every effort to go and meet with those who could not in other ways go to the Temple of Mount Moriah.

Jesus doesn't just walk around Palestine looking for opportunities to do flagrant miracles for miracles' sake; rather, his are visible statements that those who are rejected by mankind are those who are accepted by God. Whereas the wood and stone temple excludes, the flesh and blood temple includes. That is why the message Jesus speaks is called "Good News!" It is not that Jesus is healing; not that Jesus is being compassionate; it is that Jesus is being, well, God!

Note first that Jesus removed the healing sacrament from the temple or synagogue to the home of Peter where Peter's mother-in-law is sick. Whereas no respectable temple priest or leader would enter a house with a sick bed, Jesus boldly enters with fixation of intent. He touches her and raises her up (another no-no!). And then he is served by her, which no self-respecting Jew would allow since she is unclean for a time; she needs to be purified.

In all of this, Jesus universalizes what had hitherto been localized. Now a person goes to Jesus of Nazareth, the Messiah of God, rather than to the temple. He is, for all intents and purposes, a counter-temple. Everything you would expect to find in the temple, you now find in Jesus, only it is made available wherever there is need.

So Jesus universalizes what was localized; he includes those who were excluded; he relates to those who were disenfranchised; and we see that he de-nationalized what had hitherto been for the Jew only. He invites his disciples to go with him to other towns and, in doing so, to go through Galilee where he would encounter many persons of every possible nationality.

And so, the lessons from this Epiphany revelation are simple. Bureaucracy tends to bureaucratize; systems selectively segregate; temples tend toward totalitarianism. Jesus smashes these tendencies. He de-localizes the deity; he makes ministry personal and not career-driven; and he universalizes the provision - "to the Jew first, and also to the Greek."

The lessons for the church in the twenty-first century are manifold. God works where God works; human need is an opportunity for ministry; the message is not the possession of any one group. There are times, many of them, unfortunately when the denominational has become detestable. There are times when we would rather support others in ministry than do ministry ourselves. And there are times we think God only does God stuff in "the church." All of these are abominable, and the lessons of the day call us to follow Jesus. Paul says it this way, "I became all things to all persons, in order to win some." This is the goal. We do not exist for our own luxury coach-ride to heaven, but to be disciples of the one who would not let the system keep him down. Amen!

CHAPTER 49
THE SIXTH SUNDAY AFTER THE EPIPHANY

St. John's Episcopal Church, Kingston, New York
II Kings 5:1-15; Psalm 42; I Corinthians 9:24-27
Mark 1:40-45

We must be reminded during Epiphany that God is telling us something, revealing as it were, something new and unique. And so too, this morning. Leprosy was the most dreaded disease in biblical times. It separated the leper from the community; there was absolutely no contact. It became, through many centuries, a symbol for sin, and is often interpreted in the metaphorical sense.

But today, let's look at Naaman from the II Kings story. There are some striking things about him. Naaman is a person who is relatively important in Syria, yet there is this stigma of leprosy. There is no getting around it. Let us see what the story reveals to us.

First, the two people who influence him the most are slaves; the Israelite slave girl who first directs him to the prophet, and then the male slave who challenges him to do something simple since he is sure he would have done something difficult. It is precisely those who are equally insignificant to society who are most significant to the situation. The implications are enormous! The persons involved in the purposed ends may often not be those we think are most influential. In God's economy there are no little people, no little places. A slave girl or a servant man may be the instrumental person used to thrust us in the right direction. [This is precisely true of the Palestinian peasant named "Jesus of Nazareth," is it not?].

Second, to get to the desired end Naaman needed to transcend national boundaries. There was and is no localized truth. One must, as a 20th century prophet once said, "be like the bee who takes his "nectar from many flowers." We have been unwilling in our Biblical beliefs to learn anything from other faiths and religions, often to our detriment. [See the book *What Christians Can Learn from Other Religions.*] Naaman needed to transverse the border and go to a Prophet of Israel to find his deliverance. It was external to himself and wrapped up in identity with (a washing such as in baptism) and an obedience to the God of Abraham, Isaac, and Jacob. It was in a very real sense a conversion. Notice what he says when it is all said and done, "I know that there is no God in all the earth but in Israel." God is not known in Word only, but in experience of healing, cleansing, and deliverance.

Traveling through India a number of years ago, we went to the Ganges River to see the bodies being burned early in the morning and the ashes being spread on the sacred river. As we walked through the town, we found a Hindu holy man washing a life-size cement elephant. This elephant was his god. It was painted bright orange, and he was washing off the food and flowers of the offerings of the previous day. As I watched this man, I sensed the difference, the remarkable difference, between Hinduism and Christianity. In Hinduism, you wash your God; in Christianity your God washes you. The stains of sin and guilt are gone as we step over the boundaries, the borders and dare to take the provisions of God.

One of the chief frustrations of teaching in a Christian environment is the repeated encounters with those who will not know the delight of forgiveness and the removal of guilt. There is something in both Catholic and Protestant Christianity that likes to stay within the borders of guilt and fear and disdains the thought of forgiveness, acceptance, and the lightness that comes with them. Naaman crossed that border and found all of these.

Finally, there is not only the sense that God uses the least likely persons, in least desired places, God also uses least desirous methodologies. The ways of God are queer at best. One spiritual hymn-writer put it this way:

God moves in a mysterious way
His wonders to perform,
He plants his footsteps on the sea
And rides upon the storm.

I wouldn't make it quite so poetic, nor would Naaman. Sometimes God's ways are downright indescribably strange. The Scriptures are full of the paradoxical movements of God in the lives of people that would have rather done it all another way.

God's instructions are often vague;
God's directions are often reversed;
God's values are inverted;
God's purposes are masked;
God's methodologies are questionable;
God's friends are disreputable;
Yet God's ends are desirable.

There is no challenging this truth as we encounter the stories of Scripture. Naaman is the Hebrew Bible's predecessor of the Gospel account of the healing of the leper. Society leaves lepers alone, God uses them in his plan. And in the Gospel the leper and Jesus trade places - the leper is alone and Jesus is public at the beginning of the story; after his healing the leper goes public, and according to Mark, "Jesus could no longer enter a town..." Isn't that always like the incarnate God? Tak-

ing our place? Another one of those inexplicable methodologies.

Sometimes it is good not to know where God is
going or how God will get us there. It might just call
for faith. Amen!

CHAPTER 50
ASH WEDNESDAY

St. John's Episcopal Church, Kingston, New York
Psalm 51; Joel 2:1-2;12-17; Psalm 103
II Corinthians 5:20b-6:10; Matthew 6:1-6,16-21

Often overlooked in the Ash Wednesday liturgy is the context and teaching of the Psalm we are about to read after the homily. This is Psalm 51, and there is a specific context in which this Psalm is written. King David, the greatest of Israel's monarch's has sinned and when confronted by Nathan the Prophet, David repents and then composes this Psalm which we use as our poetic lament for our sinning as well. It is not meant to be deep and heavy theology; it is a poetic rendering of the act of sin and the delight of forgiveness.

II Samuel 11 and 12 record the following: "*And David took Bathsheba, the wife of Uriah the Hittite, and she conceived and David wrote a letter saying, 'Set Uriah in the hottest battle, that he may die.' The thing that David had done displeased the Lord and the Lord sent Nathan the Prophet to David and Nathan said to David, 'Why have you despised the commandment of the Lord to do evil in His sight? You have killed Uriah the Hittite and have taken his wife to be your wife.' And David said to Nathan, 'I have sinned against the Lord.' And Nathan said to David, 'Thou shalt die...'"*

Of course David repents, receives forgiveness, but suffers consequences as well. Part of his own penitence is to compose what have become for us Psalm 51.

I am often criticized by people who tell me that I take sin too lightly. My response is the same as the great Reformer, Martin Luther who aptly said, "Sin boldly and much more boldly repent." This is a one line commentary on David's life and action - and I am afraid a good commentary on ours as well. Sin should only be taken as seriously as to bring us to repentance and forgiveness; if we carry it with guilt, we have missed what Lent says to us.

John David Burton, onetime Poet-in-Residence at Princeton University, wrote an account of the encounter between David and Nathan. Remember, David has just had his greatest General killed and he could do the same to Nathan the Prophet. But maybe, just maybe, the encounter went like this:

Nate, you s.o.b., I might have known that you
would find me out, but I want you to know – my
prophet friend – that this was not just one
more time my head was turned by a pretty face
and a shapely ass.
This, my prophet friend, was the real thing.

"Yes, I know, Bathsheba was Uriah's wife.
That, by God, is the worst part of it all.
My trusted Hittite chief would not touch his
wife even though I called him from the front.
He said his men could not get home to lay
their women and he would not sleep with his,
thus no way to have the child seem his and
not my own.

"Well, the deed is done, and I have shamed
my throne and now I am found out by you of
breaking those two laws which Moses commanded
to be kept by kings and slaves alike:
'Thou shalt not kill or commit adultery.'
How many times I read them out for all the
clans to hear the king affirm what God said
midst the smoke on Sinai so long ago!
"All right, all right, what say you I am now
to do to make the best of the sorry mess?
jumping off the palace will not help. There is
no one with strength to take my place.
I must gut it through, bite the bullet of my
shame, repent before the people, pick the
pieces up and see what I can do to make amends.

"And Nathan, by the way, I know you had to
call me to account. You would not be my
prophet nor my friend were you not to care
enough to lay it on the line. I am grateful
that you care enough to risk what we two have.

There was no other way, there may be no way
now but if there by a way to make it right and
remain king I will find that way only
if you care enough to tell me when I miss the
mark.

"Come on, Nate, my boy! There
is just time for a drink or two
before we tell it true to God and all the people."

CHAPTER 51
FIRST SUNDAY IN LENT

St. John's Episcopal Church, Kingston, New York
Genesis 9:8-17; Psalm 25; I Peter 3:18-22
Mark 1:9-13

Today is the first Sunday "in" Lent. We have Sundays "of" Easter; "of" Pentecost; "of" Advent and "of" Epiphany; but Lent has not Sundays, because in the midst of penitence and sorrow, a Sunday is *always* an Easter celebration. There is resurrection even in the midst of Lent, and so today is that first Sunday surrounded by the Lenten starkness.

And the starkness is enforced by the emphasis on baptism, Jesus' own baptism. Baptism, literally the Greek word meaning to "dip so as to dye" is a change agent in the life of the person who submits to baptism. Jesus' own baptism was one of the steps in his re-interpretation of religious symbols that were precious to the Jews of his day, but which had become stagnant and systematized almost to the point of having no meaning.

Just this week our new Archbishop of Canterbury published his newest book, *Lost Icons,* dealing with the lost symbols of Western culture and calling for their rediscovery. This is exactly what Jesus was doing in the first century.

Jesus calls for the re-discovery of and redefinition of three symbols of the faith: Torah, Temple, Sabbath. The systemic religious leaders of the day had turned the Torah into intricate legalistic laws, ignoring the fact that it was the story of God's search for humanity. The same bureaucratic leaders of the religious movement of Jesus' day had taken the Temple to heights never ordained, excluding from it the weak, the impaired, etc., and making access to God limited only to those who could come into the temple; thus significantly excluding those they wished to exclude (i.e. Gentiles, women, and other imperfect ones). And finally, Jesus sees the religious system of the day making Sabbath-keeping a measurement of all law-keeping, which placed the human being as an agent of law rather than the law as a servant of the human creature. When Jesus says, "Don't you know that the Sabbath was made for mankind and not mankind for the Sabbath," he was in essence saying that the law was made to fit who we are and not vice versa. It is a stark reversal of the commonly held views. (No wonder they seek to silence him - he brings it on himself!).

And so, to sum up:

Torah to Jesus is more than law; it is story;
Temple is more than exclusivity; it is acceptance;
Sabbath is more than law; it is rest.

And this is precisely where Jesus' baptism by John comes in. Up until John the Baptizer, all ceremonial washings took place just outside the temple in specially prepared pools for such ritual. You would wash so as to be clean to go into God's presence. It was a stepping into the presence of God as clean as you could be.

The message of John and therefore of Jesus is that God accepts you, unclean, and then the washing and cleansing is done to you. You do not baptize (or wash or dip) yourself - God does it to you. So here is John, dressed funny and no doubt smelling funnier, baptizing all sorts of people, ceremoniously washing them as a proof of their acceptance to God. No longer is approach to God localized, it is rather universalized to wherever one can receive baptism.

This is picked up in the Book of Acts when a eunuch from Ethiopia is led to conversion by Apostle Philip, and the eunuch asked, "What hinders me from being baptized?" And Philip takes him, then and there, into the water and performs the ritualistic washing on him.

This happened to me a decade ago on the mountains of the Mohonk Preserve in New Paltz. A woman found out that I was a priest and she told me that since she had come to believe in Jesus Christ she had not had the opportunity to be baptized and would I do it. I said of course, and we went into the Coxingkill Creek and she was baptized.

There is nowhere where God is not - is the message of John and Jesus.

But there is another, more dangerous lesson to the baptism of Jesus; and, that is, loyalty is no longer to a temple system gone dry but rather to the God to whom the temple was meant to point. God had voiced displeasure over all sorts of ritual when hearts are far from God. Obedience, it was clearly said, was better than sacrifice. And now John and Jesus take this to heart and many religious leaders are threatened.

The lessons are abundantly clear - follow the Lord your God. Your loyalties and commitments are higher and deeper and richer than loyalties to the systems of religion popular in our day. And though we love the Church, it is not our ultimate loyalty. It is frail and it has often failed and is shot through and through with weakness and the systemic; but we serve a Master, who is bigger than the Church and who is the builder of the Church, and who will make the Church in due time what the Church will ultimately be.

So let our criticisms be tempered with patience as our loyalties are proclaimed. "The Church's one foundation is Jesus Christ her Lord," is not merely a nice hymn-lyric. It is the grounding truth of what we do.

N. T. Wright, Canon of Westminster Abbey in London, expounds the redefinition of symbols by Jesus in a wonderful video series called *Jesus: The New Way.* And Jesus doesn't dismiss the old ways, he merely shows up their shortcomings in the invitation to do it a new way.

May we, today, as we begin this Lenten journey together, commit to Jesus Christ of Nazareth, knowing that all other loyalties and commitments are secondary at best. Amen!

CHAPTER 52
THE FOURTH SUNDAY IN LENT

St. John's Episcopal Church, Kingston, New York
II Chronicles 36:14-23; Psalm 122; Ephesians 2:4-10
John 6:14-25

L ent is not the time one particularly thinks of the concept of peace. Rather we are stirred up by priest and appointed readings to be less than peaceful. Somehow Lent is the time of the Church year to give us the bad news first so that the good news of Easter can follow.

But, as you can see, today is "Rose Sunday." Sometimes this is known as "Refreshment Sunday," and a flower or two are allowed on the altar to remind us that we are halfway to our goal. Our texts of the day also say something to us of peace. The Psalm tells us to pray for the peace of Jerusalem, and our texts encourage us to be people of interpersonal peace and support.

So it seems that peace is one of the many themes of Lent. [Particularly poignant is this today as we are in the midst of war.]

Peace is the enabling, given by the grace of God, that we know the adequacy of our resources. In praying for the "peace of Jerusalem" we are praying for God's *shalom*. It is infinitely more than the absence of conflict; it is for the immense well-being of the City of God.

The cross stands as the final battlefield of the God of the Ages and the forces of evil. The "seed of woman" has bruised the head of the serpent and he is mortally wounded. The throne of eternal kingdom is occupied by the Victor, Jesus Christ.

It is in light of this that we approach Lent. It is in light of this that we accept forgiveness as we acknowledge our sin. It is in light of this that we find that forgiveness is sweet and makes us spiritually, in the healthiest sense of the word, "carefree." In "casting all our cares" on God, we become delivered people – people who know the lightness of being that comes from being redeemed.

An often ignored hymn in the 1982 Hymnal is appropriate to remember here, for truth is best communicated, at times, through poetry. Singing it sometimes comes across as frivolous, so let's look at its poetry together:

> Now quit your care and anxious fear and worry;
> For schemes are vain and fretting brings no gain.
> Lent calls to prayer, to trust and dedication;
> God brings new beauty nigh;

Reply, reply, reply with love to love most high.
Reply, reply, reply with love to love most high.

To bow the head in sackcloth and in ashes,
Or rend the soul, such grief is not Lent's goal;
But to be led to where God's glory flashes,
His beauty to come near.
Make clear, make clear, make clear where truth and
    light appear.
Make clear, make clear, make clear where truth and
    light appear.

For is not this the fast that I have chosen?
(The Prophet spoke) to shatter every yoke,
Of wickedness the grievous bands to loosen
Oppression put to flight,
To fight, to fight, to fight till every wrong's made
    right,
To fight, to fight, to fight till every wrong's made
    right.

For righteousness and peace will show their faces
To those who feed the hungry in their need,
And wrongs redress, who build the old waste
    places,
And in the darkness shine.
Divine, divine, divine it is when all combine,
Divine, divine, divine it is when all combine.

Then shall your light, break forth as doth the
    morning;
Your health shall spring, the friends you make will
    bring
God's glory bright, your way through life
    adorning;
And love shall be the prize.
Arise, arise, arise and make a paradise.
Arise, arise, arise and make a paradise.
Percy Dearmer (1867-1936)

This is the central feature of our Lenten fast and
practice. The doomsday mentality of the guilt-rid-
den is left behind (no pun intended) and the forgiven
find's his burden lighted. So today, half-way through
our practice of Lenten discipline, we are graciously reminded that Lent ends with resurrection. Jesus lives,
and so shall I. Amen!

CHAPTER 53
THE FIFTH SUNDAY OF EASTER

St. Gregory's, Woodstock, New York
Acts 8:26-40; Psalm 66:1-11; I John 3:14-24
John 14:15-21

The record in the book of Acts is of witness; this is supported by the other texts of the morning. Witness - an oft-times scary word and concept because it congers up all kinds of fanatical people who go out "witnessing for Jesus!" But we will try to get a Biblical perspective on this reality this morning.

First, allow me to give credit, where credit is due. I am reminded of the preacher who made the victory sign [V] at the start of his sermon and then again when he finished. Someone asked during coffee hour why he had done this, and he said, this was not the victory sign - these were quotation marks! The credit I must give is to an old-time professor at Dallas Seminary whose outline this is. The "meat" is of my own gathering, but I must say the outline is not original.

So, back to our theme: witness. Just this week I heard of a man who told a horror story of his youth, when he was forced to ride in the car with his witnessing grandmother. Before they would leave home, they would wrap us "Gospel bombs" which were tracts rolled together with heavy rubber bands. They would then drive to schools and stores where there were crowds of people and they would throw these from the car. He admits now, as an adult, that he would throw them and hide so no one could see him. He was embarrassed by this ritual. But this was grandmother's way of being a witness.

And years ago there was a movie about the "Gospel Blimp" where a group of over-zealous Christians rented a dirigible, and scattered Gospel tracts across a neighborhood. This, again, friends, is poor witness.

So let us see a scenario from the Word of God. Philip, the Apostle encounters a eunuch from Ethiopia who is, no doubt, in Jerusalem for his master to worship at Temple there. He is reading from the Isaiah scroll when Philip arrives. By looking at the record we can see the tools of witness and what they provide.

First, to be a witness, you need *a generous amount of glue.* The Holy Spirit leads Philip to "go and join yourself to that chariot." Witness consists of joining ourselves with those who are asking, seeking, knocking. We are called to be committed to those who are in a search. The task may take lots of time and command immense amounts of effort, and sometimes we may see no results of our efforts and yet the witness "joins" the one in the chariot. Witness is a life-long commitment to "practice what we preach." It is a giving of oneself to the integrity of being what we claim, and that in the presence of others. We stick to our witness.

Second, Philip shows that in being a witness you need *a keen sense of wielding the inquisitive knife.* "Do you understand what you are reading?" asked Philip. This is where we often fail. Christians are best known, unfortunately, for telling people things about their faith rather than waiting to ask or be asked the right questions. By asking the eunuch a question such as this, Philip essentially answers the question of whether or not this person wants to talk about his faith or not. If he does, you proceed, if not, you move on or wait until ready.

Third, Philip needs *a bucket with a long rope.* Philip, begins where the Eunuch is - in Isaiah - and preaches to him, Jesus. The bucket needed a long rope to reach into the past and make the past wrap itself up in the revelation of God in Christ. It is not our agenda we thrust on someone; it is their need we are called on to meet in our Christian witness. Do not miss this fact. Philip begins where the Eunuch is; we must also.

Fourth, to be a witness, Philip needed to possess *a ready willingness to get messy.* The Eunuch wanted baptism now; Philip needed to oblige. Often when we join ourselves to seekers after truth, we will get messy in the process. Interpersonal relationships are often messy, and much more so when you throw the faith and belief issue into the mix. Even when things turn out right, as with the Eunuch, still there is the messiness of baptism. Here, in Baptism, one's ultimate commitment is declared. Faith in Christ now is in ascendency.

Finally, in being a witness, Philip finds he needs *a suitcase packed and ready to travel.* When the work was done with this Ethiopian man, Philip is snatched away and placed somewhere else where a work for God must be done. You and I may not physically be moved, but God will place us in situations that call for us to be witnesses. We are to be ready to testify to what we know.

And so, being a witness is not so much in what we do, but rather in what is done with and to and through us. As Easter people, we cannot help but being witnesses. The question ends up - what kind of a witness do I bear?

Cardinal Emmanuel Celestin Suhard [1874-1949] writes this:

> "To be a witness
> does not consist in
> engaging in propaganda
> nor even in stirring
> people up...
> but in being
> a living mystery.
> It means to live
> in such as way...

that one's life
would not make sense
if God did not exist."

You and I are God's witnesses. Gather your gear
and let's be what we are called to be. Amen!

CHAPTER 54
THE SIXTH SUNDAY OF EASTER

St. Gregory's Church, Woodstock, New York
Acts 11:19-30; Psalm 33; I John 4:7-21
John 15:9-17

To live above with saints we love,
Oh, say, that will be glory.
But to live below, with saints we know,
Well, that's another story.

The story is told of a new rector on her first Sunday at her new parish. She mounted the pulpit steps at homily time and said, "Love one another." She dismounted and continued the service with the creed. The next Sunday this was repeated, "Love one another." After about six weeks, the Wardens approached the new rector to ask when she would move on and elaborate in her sermons. Her reply was, "When you all learn this first lesson, we can go on to lesson two."

It has become so very trite to say that the Gospel is about loving one another. Liberal Christianity in the twentieth century degenerated into this being the only message, and soon it became innocuous and mediocre. But there is no getting away from the fact that the Scriptures deal concretely with our loving of one another. As a matter of fact, the Scriptures clearly delineate that it is the love that Christians have for one another that is the testimony that we belong to the Christ. "By this shall all know you are my disciples when you love one another."

So, my friends, there must be something to this matter of love. And I am sure it is more than bumper sticker theology!

There are three matters of love that surface in the texts of this Easter season lection. First, there is no disputing that love is a command of the God we serve. This is not optional, peripheral, nor is it open to discussion. So far is the love theme taken by Christ, that we are commanded to even love our enemies. [Now can we talk? I have other emotions for my enemies, be assured. And I could list the very people I cannot love.] And in telling us to love even our enemies, as well as our brothers and sisters, Christ clearly implies that the power and ability to do this comes from our intimate relationship with Holy Spirit.

The command transcends place and locale and is implicit in the very work the church does. We exist to be an incarnate love organism. Living to love. So we have to rationally, even when we cannot emotionally, agree that we are commanded to love.

The second major implication of this love is that it is indicative of the church. An unloving church gives away its antichrist allegiance. The love commanded by Christ is indicative, descriptive of the company called believers in Jesus Christ. This cannot be side-stepped with excuse - "But you just don't understand the situation..." or with hierarchy of blame, "Well, he (or she) started this..." There is absolutely no place for the self-justification we all seek when we would rather not do the loving thing.

The first thing outsiders should say about the church gathered is, "Behold how they love one another." It is really cutting to realize the infinitesimal matters that we allow to separate us in light of all of life and eternity. I have seen churches split and large numbers of people make an exodus over types of music, color of choir robes, length of sermons, and colors of the ladies' room. And I am sure with a bit of research I could list dozens more insane reasons to not love another sister or brother in Christ.

Scripture has none of this, and even the pious, often self-righteous Apostle Paul, after breaking fellowship with Barnabas, must take him back at some point; and he does. Because love is indicative of the body of Christ.

Finally, the love spoken of in all three of our readings today is productive, active, and involved love. We cannot love without doing. The integrity, we manifest in being who we are in Christ, must be engaged to show that what we are sets the stage for what we do.*

And so we are brought back to the love issue. Jesus elsewhere tells that if we come to the altar to sacrifice, and have something against a brother or sister, we are to leave the sacrifice and go and make things right. It is as if our relationship with God is strained when our relationship with God's people is strained. I'm not sure I like it this way, but it appears Scripturally and existentially to be the case.

We can call many witnesses to support our case. The great George MacDonald wrote, "The love of our neighbor is the only door out of the dungeon of self." And C. S. Lewis assures us that, "Next to the Blessed Sacrament itself, your neighbor is the holiest object presented to your senses. If he is a Christian neighbor he is holy in almost the same way for in him Christ, the glorified, Glory Himself, is truly hidden."

And we could go on and on. But I think I will side this morning with that new rector who repeated often, "Love one another." Amen.

---

*[Elsewhere in this series is the account of my needing to ask my eldest son's forgiveness before I could take the Lord's Supper. It is a humbling thing for an adult to ask forgiveness of a teen.] I used this illustration again here in the sermon.

CHAPTER 55
THE FOURTH SUNDAY AFTER PENTECOST

St. Gregory's Church, Woodstock, New York
Ezekiel 2:1-7; Psalm 123; II Corinthians 12:2-10
Mark 6:1-6

We have entered what the Church has called "Ordinary Time." As if anything in life can be ordinary. I read once that the American Psychological Association gathered for their annual convention and their theme was "Normalcy." Normalcy is no more normal than ordinary is ordinary. Neither of these things are ultimately definable.

But alas, we are in "Ordinary Time." The Church envisions this time to be a teaching-learning time for daily living. There are no major events in the life of Christ to celebrate, and we are called to discipleship.

The texts appointed for today remind us that we are living in a post-crucifixion/post-resurrection time and that things did not stop with Palm Sunday. Often the battle-hungry among us like the victorious nature of the Palm Sunday ritual, but would stop there and not enter into a post-crucifixion ordinary time. William Stringfellow aptly puts it this way:

"The substance of consternation is the desire for the Gospel to end in the political triumph of Palm Sunday. If the work of Christ would only end in THAT way, Christians would be spared the betrayal of Judas, the apathy and cowardice of the other disciples, the mystery of the Last Supper, and Gethsemane's sweat and agony. They would also avoid the accusations of the authorities and the ridicule of the crowd; the Cross and the descent into Hell; the embarrassment for man in God's power in the resurrection and the awful gift of Pentecost."

But the Gospel does not end there. We are dragged through the week we call Passion week; and just when we are delighting in the freedom of the resurrection, we are again brought to the recklessness of Pentecost when the Spirit blows where it will. I am again out of personal control. So "Ordinary Time" is reckless, risky, and challenging at the least, and we must put our roots down here until the end of November.

Today's lections tell us what is given to the believer in God. There is an essential givenness to the Christian life. And in the call of Ezekial we see that the believing life is defined by being distinguished-distinguished not in the sense of being elite, but in the sense of being conspicuous. Even those who don't like prophets (or don't believe in them) have to somehow acknowledge when one has been in their presence. They will "know that there has been a prophet among them."

There is a distinguishing mark among believers that something is lacking in every ideology, every theology, every finality. That sort of God revealed in Jesus tells us that everything else is relative, everything is fleeting. The good is not the best, and the better is not our lot. There is a longing in the mind and soul of the believer that in and of itself is the mark of belief. It is even true that to ask certain questions is to note that one is a believer, for unbelievers will not ask.

And so we are people who are given the gift of being distinguished. And that is why, when we act like unbelievers, others think us hypocritical.

Then in the New Testament lesson we are given grace. Grace is the ability to grasp truth and to make it applicable in our lives. Do we really get this? We think of grace as being God's niceness, when in reality is it God's standard of integrity held out in front of us with the enduement to meet the standard. Grace gives us Pentecostal power in Ordinary Time. Grace is the enablement of believing and doing. It, too, is a distinguishing mark of believing.

Finally, in the Gospel there is the mark of frustration. That all is not well seems incongruous with the finished work of Jesus Christ. Believers have more trouble with the continuing reality of evil and disbelief than with almost anything else. Jesus, the Son of God is left without power due to the unbelief in Nazareth. Why must God put so much on our part in this whole thing? Protestants like the salvation by grace alone, but the Gospels seem to indicate that there is an element of our belief if we would see the work of Christ completed.

A distinguishing mark of belief is belief. There is no argument to justify it. We cannot use the old arguments of logic to bring the mind to what the heart should be leading - there is nothing to do but to come. Come and believe. Often we will have to believe without evidence; act without reward; pray without answers; decide without guidance; and live without instructions. It is called the graced life - a life of enabled integrity that distinguishes those who believe from those who do not.

Unfortunately it is not in law keeping or in keeping the Canons of some denomination, it is belief enabled by grace that will bring us through Ordinary Time. Amen!

CHAPTER 56
THE FIFTH SUNDAY AFTER PENTECOST

St. Gregory's Church, Woodstock., New York
Amos 7:7-15; Psalm 85; Ephesians 1:1-14
Mark 6:7-13

Many things, well, most things in life happen in Ordinary Time. The good, the bad, and the ugly are all part of Ordinary Time. And you and I are here in Ordinary Time. We have lived this past week in this time period - and much came our way - some of it requested, much of it preferred, much of it not preferred.

Jokingly I share with my friends, that when I cannot sleep at night, it is because God needs a rest and God puts me in charge for an eight hour period. I was so very angry about this one night this week, that I answered everyone's prayers with exactly what they wanted! And people were not happy with me!

Amos, the prophet of this morning's Hebrew Scripture lesson gets exactly what he does not want. He has no aspirations to be a prophet. He is a simple, wealthy herd owner from another country - called to cross the border and to speak God's words. "I think I'd rather not!" is the response of any sane person to such a call. But God is persistent, and to the believer, often gets the Divine will done! It can be exasperating at best! Amos, history informs us, obeys and is rewarded with blessing, with peace, with Shalom. People hear the message of God. That is all. There is no need for there to be success when God wills blessing.

Then Jesus in our Gospel record sends the disciples out two-by-two [an important matter in ministry by the way], and guarantees that there will be both success and failure. And it is the creative use of failure which makes the Christian enterprise of the first century so successful. In the midst of rejection and hatred and false accusation and imprisonment and death, the Christian blessing to the world is indescribably enlarged. Some places receive, some reject, and the ministry of the faithful was to minister. The blessing of God was on the intent and action, not on the result.

Now this is hard for us to hear in a utilitarian society where everything is bottom line results. I have a close friend who told me that several weeks ago he had won $14,000 at Atlantic City in one slot machine. Yesterday he told me that his total winnings over the years has been about $24,000. Someone else in the conversation asked, "What did that $24,000 cost you?..." There was no answer. But the bottom line was sought.

And here is where the central lesson of these texts in Ordinary Time take their cue - believers are blessed people, according to Apostle Paul - "Blessed be God who has blessed us with every spiritual blessing." The word is employed three times in one phrase. And we, utilitarian as we are, seek the bottom line. What does blessing do for or what does blessing give us? Most times, nothing at all.

In the 1980s a famous TV preacher's wife sang a song that went like this, "I'm blessed, I'm blessed, I'm blessed, I am blessed, I have comfort clothing and warmth I am blessed...." It continues *ad infinitum [or ad nausium].* The point of the song missed the point of blessing altogether. If we read the Scriptures rightly we will find that to be blessed is to be made God-conscious. [And you will hear this from me again, one or twice during my tenure here!] Blessing has nothing to do with outcome and all to do with relationship.

Weymouth, one of the great New Testament exegetes of the early 20th Century, wrote: "Blessedness is of course infinitely higher and better than mere happiness. People who are blessed may outwardly be much to be pitied, but from the higher and truer standpoint they are to be admired, envied, congratulated, and imitated."

The Confederate Soldier's Prayer or the poem, "The Ways of the Lord," goes like this:

I asked God for strength that I might achieve;
I was made weak that I might learn humbly to obey;

I asked for help that I might do greater things:
I was given infirmity that I might do better things.
I asked for riches that I might be happy;
I was given poverty that I might be wise.
I asked for all things that I might enjoy life;
I was given life that I might enjoy all things.
I got nothing that I asked for
But everything I had hoped for.
Despite myself my prayers were answered,
I am of all men most richly blessed.

This is the blessed life. We, in the Catholic tradition, have been led to believe that beatification comes after death; Scripture leads us to believe that it is the way of life here and now in Ordinary Time.

Prophets who would rather be shepherds are blessed in being prophets; disciples who would like to do things individualistically are blessed as they go forth two-by-two. [The lessons here against indivisualistic Congregationalism are manifold.] And believers are not to-be-blessed; rather, Paul assures us that we are blessed.

David Spangler, in his wonderful book titled *Blessing*, writes, "A blessing is a relationship in which at some level of awareness we celebrate and experience the sacred within us, between us, and around us in the world. It's that experience that underlies our sense of enchantment, unobstructedness, and connection.... Real blessings in everyday life are more like peasants than nobles; they move and mingle within the commonality of our daily experiences, sometimes going unnoticed or unrecognized for what they are....The ultimate objective is for blessings to be normal and commonplace." [Might I add, *Ordinary Time!*].

And so, my friends, we come to the realities of life - reality in which we live - it is there that the blessings flow and, therefore, I pray that you be blessed. Amen!

CHAPTER 57
THE SIXTH SUNDAY AFTER PENTECOST

St. Gregory's Church, Woodstock, New York
Isaiah 57:14b-21; Psalm 22:22-30; Ephesians 2:11-22
Mark 6:30-44

Here we are, again in Ordinary Time. I know, I really know, that such a designation sounds boring, especially to those of us in Western culture where everything must be extraordinary. Living in a society that values the biggest, the best, the superior, the abundant, the most expensive, we are relegated to oddity if we endeavor to turn against that system. Modernity taught us that if one was good, two was better, and many was best. That popular philosophy turned America into a nation of consumers and the Western mind-set into an uncontrollable materialist mode.

Much of post 1989 thinking is changing. Postmodernity, as it is being called, is secularly challenging a re-valuation of the material only mentality. Roots and heritage and genealogical investigation are seeing renewed interest and commitment. Indeed, the twenty-first century is quite different than the post-World War II era into which I was born, and many of us lived.

The texts appointed for this morning are texts which call a people of God back from wandering mentally and spiritually, they emphasize the truths that transcend time restraints; they challenge us to the self-evaluation that is realistic and not inflated; and they clearly report that the work that is valuable, and that remains and lasts, is a work that is done in community as over and against individualistic endeavors.

There is so much here that is calling the believer to go back, exactly what postmodernity is doing in secularity: pre-date the rationalistic, materialistic, individualistic ways of modernity, return to that spirituality which calls for mystery instead of explanation. As one critic said of the modern theologians when they tried to explain the real presence of Christ in the Eucharist, "It was a mystery and we defined it!" And from this came: many answers, little meaning; much theology, shallow spirituality; much organization little inspiration. And so today's readings are indeed contemporarily relevant to you and to me.

First, there is an overarching theme of *remembering*. Isaiah is intent on calling the people of God to a remembering of the goodness of God and the corresponding evilness of wickedness.

Just recently a leading professor of history, renowned for her relativistic interpretations, was asked if Hitler and his movement should not be considered evil. Her answer was, "That is a very difficult question to answer." Men and women, I propose, that if we cannot remember the goodness of God and the wickedness of evil, we are of all persons most to be pitied. My good friend from New Delhi, India, uses the story of being marooned on an uncharted island. He says it makes a vast difference as to whether the natives of the island serve you a meal or serve you as the meal.

And so, the good prophet, Isaiah, calls us to be people who remember.

Then Apostle Paul takes us through a deeper step as remembrance is broadened into reflection. The facts of the remembrance are interpreted into an existential meaningfulness. This is what God means in my life; this is where I was; this is where I am now; and there is a fearful and wonderful anticipation of where I may be tomorrow.

Believing reflection takes the facts of life and makes them facts of eternal life. Reflection places me within a scheme, a purpose, a meaningful movement of human history. God is, as a old saint insightfully wrote, working out the purpose of God. The nineteenth century noted atheist, John Ruskin speaks rightly when he said, "Not only is there but one way of doing things rightly, but there is only one way of seeing them, and that is, seeing the whole of them." Reflection is seeing the whole picture; God included.

And notice at the end of Paul's pericope from the Ephesian epistle, he is adamant that we are built together, joined together, and grow together. So that when we read the reporting of the disciples to Jesus in Mark chapter six, they are reporting what happened as they went out two-by-two. There is no "fly-by-the-seat of your pants" individualistic my way here.

The Gospel account brings us full circle from remembrance to reflection to regrouping. Everything with which we are gifted by Holy Spirit is for the body, not for us alone. When believers regroup they are in a posture to receive; hence corporate worship. The feeding of the thousands has been ridiculously interpreted while all the while missing the meaning of the narrative, and that is the provision of God for the people of God. Jesus is the focus of the text, and His followers and disciples are together. For God's people to be out of fellowship is a contradiction of terms. When I remember, reflect, and regroup, I have no choice but to include you, and vice versa.

The Ordinary Times of the Christian are times to remember, to reflect, and to regroup. There is a world needing our wholistic message. By grace we will meet its call. Amen!

CHAPTER 58
THE SEVENTH SUNDAY AFTER PENTECOST

St. Gregory's Church, Woodstock, New York
II Kings 2:1-15; Psalm 114; Ephesians 4:1-7, 11-16
Mark 6:45-52

It is noteworthy to recognize what makes human beings tick. In the Hebrew Scripture lesson today, we find that which makes Elisha tick is staying with Elijah - tradition. Tradition is the living faith of the dead while traditionalism is the dead faith of the living. Elisha had it right. He didn't want only what Elijah had, he wanted a double share of the same Spirit. So a living tradition made Elisha tick. What made Paul, the Apostle, tick was legalistic measurement. Paul wanted measure, stature, growth - all those good things which Christians seldom attain individually and have never really attained corporately as the Church.

Then we come to the blessed Gospel record of the day. The disciples show that it is fear that made them tick; a recurring theme in the Gospel accounts. Fear, fear, fear, fear, fear - that which has been the foundation of so much of Calvinistic and Roman Christianity for centuries. It has a noble foundation in a wrong mind set and emotion - that of the Apostles. It was when Jesus (who they thought was a ghost) appeared that they got afraid. Isn't that so very church-like!?

Finally, in all these texts, there is Jesus. And what makes him tick is his implicit trust. He trusts those who just experienced the miracle of the loaves and fishes to return to daily life; trusts the disciples to cross the Sea of Galilee with relative safety; trusts the disciples to receive him when he comes to join them; and trusts them to trust him when he calms the sea. His trust in others is often thwarted.

What we bring from these realities is a list of challenges, challenges that we understand the ways of God. If Jesus shows us anything in the Gospel records it is that God does not act as we anticipate; as the old hymn-writer put it, "God moves in a mysterious way all wonders to perform."

Note the progression in the Gospel account.

First, miracles precede the mundane and do not emanate from it. After the miracles, it is back to basic living. It is ordinary time most of the time. Michael D. O'Brien, a new author to me, writes this:

"There is a missing component in all human beings. The rural masses seeking the metropolis; the urban young fleeing to the woods. Women pretending to be men; men becoming more like women; everyone aping divinity in his desperate attempt to escape creature-hood. Western youths seeking the Orient; Orientals seeking capitalism? Monks abandoning their monasteries; married men pining for solitude. Liberals seeking to demythologize the Scriptures in an attempt to flee the exigencies of biblical faith; fundamentalists seeking to fill the empty void in their religion by a return to the Old Testament, fleeing the tasks of the baptized intellect. Was the promise always to be found *elsewhere*, always just beyond the next horizon? Why this persistent need for signs, wonders, new pillars of fire, arks of the covenant, tablets of stone—anything other than the demands of raw, laborious, darkest faith?"

The faith expected by Jesus is a faith that is - it is not marvelously overcoming, it just is the gift of faith given us by God - the same faith that has been given to God's people throughout human history. Another writer, A. Daniel Frankforter aptly captures this, that "A new wine is an old juice." And what God pours into us is what God has always poured into the people of faith. So, in the Gospel account we see that Jesus trusts that those who experienced his miracles would be prepared for the subsequently mundane and would maintain faith.

See in the text, that when the disciples were in the boat, doing what Jesus wanted them to do, the were "making headway painfully." Sometimes making headway painfully means that we "confront the evidences of doubt, the arguments for despair, and the temptations to pseudo-fulfillments" of popular Christianity. Listen again to Daniel Frankforter:

"Faith is a continuous struggle with doubt, and the worship that celebrates faith is composed of many kinds of experiences. It aspires to a level of awareness of God that is constantly pursued, sporadically realized, but never brought under control....Faith implies the acceptance of the dark feelings of abandonment that have afflicted even the saints, and it demands that we open ourselves to the frightening, humbling possibility of awe."

In a humorous pseudo-health advice column this week I read this question: "What are some of the advantages of participating in a regular exercise program?" The answer will startle you, "Can't think of a single one, sorry. My philosophy is 'No pain?...Good!'" But the reality is that pain is a part of health and part of healthy spirituality as well. Making headway painfully, remember, clearly tells us that we are making headway! It beats the option - going nowhere. Someone has said that those who go with the flow, end up down the drain!

Finally, the text indicates that even those who are closest to Jesus never completely get it. Some are terrified at the presence of Jesus, and they should be. Jesus doesn't come to us at our bidding and on our agenda. There is an agenda bigger than our own and it is far superior than puny human pop psycho-spirituality. I remember when Oral Roberts' TV show would sign on with a wonderful little jingle, "Something good is going to happen to you..." Yea, right. And Norman Vincent Peale assured us that Positive Thinking would bring us through, but sometimes we were too beaten up to think at all. And Robert Schuller followed on the heels with Possibility Thinking, which is all well and good if you can posit the possibility of thinking in the first place. Sometimes it is just simply the fact that when God appears, we will fear, and we may be utterly astounded and without understanding.

For me, perhaps, it is interesting to watch a professor who has taught Bible and theology for over forty years and who is incapable of understanding the ways of God. He fears doctrinal impurities; retreats from getting too friendly with other Christians; eschews the thought that an Episcopalian (me) is a Dean in his college; and is utterly astonished when Holy Spirit does something like bless someone he is sure doesn't deserve it. He is most to be pitied.

The ordinary time lesson is a theological one. God is God; we are human. Anything we are, anything we have, anything we do, anything we might become, is because God in Christ has graced us with the ability and ultimately trusts us to get where God - not we - purpose us to be. A fearful, yet good thought. Amen!

CHAPTER 59
THE EIGHTH SUNDAY AFTER PENTECOST

St. Gregory's Church, Woodstock, New York
Exodus 16:2-4, 9-11; Psalm 78:1-25;
Ephesians 4:17-25; John 6:24-35

In ordinary life change is inevitable. Someone once said that, "The only thing that doesn't change is the fact that things change." Some change is inevitable and we have little or no control over it [i.e. aging]. Other change we initiate out of fear or desire. Still other change is forced on us and we must change to conform, or stand beyond the change and be prophetic or rebellious to it. But change happens. Just two years ago I was asked to return to a large parish where I had been the Associate Rector for five years. I had been away for five years and now the invitation to return was given. The first statement made to me was, "Lots of things have changed, you won't recognize the place." It was my cue to NOT return. You can't go back because of change.

The Gospel of the morning shows the need for mind change. Allow me to set the stage. Jesus is confronted by followers who had been happy to get their stomachs filled and who wanted what Jesus had to fulfill natural and material cravings. "You seek me," said Jesus, "not because of the signs, but because your natural cravings for food were fulfilled."

Jesus continues with the directive that our efforts must be placed in laboring for nourishment for the soul and not the body and its desires. [These things, Jesus says elsewhere, will be cared for.] "Labor for food...that endures unto eternal life." And those hearing him, miss the key word, the primary focus, and take attention to the secondary word in his statement. Jesus wants a focus on eternal life, they want to focus on labor. Their next questions gives the whole thing away: "What must we do to be doing the works of God?" The human emphasis on "do" is predominant here. We all want to do something for God. It is damnable in the New Testament; it is all the more terrible in our Western society that evaluates us on what we do. Jesus will have none of it and says if you want to do the works of God, be something. Note the words, "This is the work of God, that you believe..." To believe is not to do anything, but to be a believer. It is a major paradigm shift (sorry) for those who had been led to believe they must do much to receive much. God's work is seldom cause and effect (though there is something of this afterward for the believer) but it is essentially all effect. God provides - we become.

Those listening to Jesus want bread for the stomach, he gives bread for life in its entirety. The Exodus passage of the morning recounts for us the tendency of God's people, be they Israel or the Church, to murmur or complain that they do not have the reward they think they should have for doing what they thought they were doing. Moses reminds them (and us) that, "It is the bread which the Lord has given you to eat." And Paul, in his epistle to the Ephesians, tells them to "put off the old nature and be renewed in your mind." It is a thinking thing. A conversion of the mind, if you will. Suddenly we are confronted with the need to think with the logic of redemption. To think and to be assured that we are called to be before we are ever called to do anything. One of the greatest frustrations I confront in counseling is the situation where a person is trying to do the Christian thing without being the Christian person.

I teach a course called "Person in Ministry." It is a seminary course meant for those who are moving toward ordained ministry. I spend the first two weeks trying to convince doers that they must first be. Often ministry takes place because of who you are and not because of what you do. And this is precisely the emphasis Jesus makes in the Gospel record of today. Be. Notice the final words of the Gospel: "I am the bread of life; he who comes to me shall not hunger, and he who believes in me shall never thirst." Jesus doesn't even say anything about eating the bread. It is a coming to Jesus and a believing. It is the being a person of integrity in the presence of who Christ is to us.

So the question becomes, who are you? Who am I?

I am reminded of an old Rector in a church who was known for being the best hospital visitor in the city. Everyone of his parish and in the city knew that he spent long hours every day in the hospital. This happened for over thirty years. Yet even those who appreciate this ministry were happy, even elated when the church finally ridded itself of his leadership. To this day people will tell you, "He was great at visitation, but you never knew who *he* was." Unfortunately that is so often true of us - known for what we do in the church; questioned for who we really are in the church (and outside the church).

So, beloved, are we dealing with a deep Biblical doctrine here? Yes. It is the doctrine of grace. Grace calls us to be. Meritorious justice demands that we do. Unfortunately the church often subscribes to the latter rather than to the former. It is a major shift from what we have often been taught. We've been challenged to go and do the will and work of God. I challenge us on the basis of today's texts to go and be God's people. It calls for a change of mind.

George Bernard Shaw wrote: "He who cannot change his mind cannot change anything." So today, let us change our minds. God has provided that we might. Let us *be,* for out of our being will come health, and strength, and nourishment for the world we live in. Amen!

CHAPTER 60
THE TENTH SUNDAY AFTER PENTECOST

St. Gregory's Church, Woodstock, New York
Proverbs 9:1-6; Psalm 147; Ephesians 5:15-20
John 6:53-59

Wisdom. Among the missing elements of contemporary life, we could certainly put wisdom.
Knowledge seems to abound; we know more and more
about so many things. Someone jokingly said that we
are learning more and more about less and less and soon
we will know everything about nothing at all!

Wisdom enters largely into the Scriptures of the
day as well as into the lives in which we live. Wisdom
is the sewing together of the insightful, the common,
and the revealed into a decisive whole which becomes
our worldview.

"Wisdom has built her house," is the way in which
the writer of this proverb in its linguistic and cultural
surrounding would have *invited humanity to become
wise*. Feasting, drinking are involved as metaphors for
the pleasure of wisdom. The invitation to the simple
and to those who otherwise have no sense make quick

work of the fact that wisdom is for anyone who will have it. The results are two-fold. The first is in today's lectionary segued by the words, "Leave simpleness, and live, and walk in the way of insight," where the result is a walk.

Paul in Ephesians picks up on this. The believer is one who walks the commitment of one's life. There are some true things about a believing walk:

- First, a walk confirms integrity;
- Second, a walk manifests internality;
- Third, a walk characterizes intent;
- Fourth, a walk defines individuality;
- Fifth, a walk betrays divine intimacy;
- Sixth, a walk proves illustrious to the watching world.

Wisdom as a walk is that we live out the Christian life in an explicable way - "I'm following Jesus..." It would certainly put the Gospel life before the doctrinal, the ethical, the social, the any-other-"adjectived" life. To live the Gospel is wisdom. It is available; it is God's gift; it is God's invitation. And the walk that proceeds from it is natural, in that it is supernatural. It doesn't make temporal sense all the time. Up is down; in is out; first is last; give and it shall be given! These things are nuts to the world. [And Dr. Leonard Sweet of Drew University says that "Christians are people who are n-u-t-s" in that they should, "Never Underestimate The Spirit." Walking this way becomes our witness.

Wisdom confers a goal on every direction, a purpose on every movement, a lesson on every experience, a liturgy on every feeling, a building block on every thought, and a relationship to every breath. Wisdom wraps the believer in the cloak of God.

The second result of wisdom is worship, and worship in the Eucharist expressly. The Gospel places the eating of the flesh of Jesus into central importance in the life of the believer. Worship is the highest and best of humanity, and to worship by receiving is the highest and best of worship.

Unfortunately in the West we have reduced worship to an hour of those things that make us feel good, when wisdom will instruct us that how we feel about worship is of little importance when the worship is real. Archbishop William Temple said it best when he defined worship:

"To worship is to quicken the conscience by the holiness of God, to feed the mind with the truth of God, to purge the imaginations by the beauty of God, to open the heart to the love of God, to devote the will to the purpose of God." Such worship is the result of insightful and Biblical wisdom.

And so, Christians are delivered from knowing it all - gaining knowledge puts us under guilt [right where the church has wanted us these 2,000 years]. Wisdom frees us to experience God and then walk with God and worship with God's people. Amen!

CHAPTER 61
THE ELEVENTH
SUNDAY AFTER
PENTECOST

St. Gregory's Church, Woodstock, New York
Joshua 24:1-2a,14-25; Psalm 16; Ephesians 5:21-33
John 6:60-69

We have been walking through a serial reading of
the Letter of St. Paul to the Ephesians. Parallel with this has been the several-week emphasis on
Jesus as the "Bread of life." There is a stark, and often
overlooked, foundation to the two which relate them
inseparably, and that is the oneness of the bread and
the unity of the church. With all of the world-wide
successes of Christianity, we must sadly admit that the
state of affairs, even in "Christian nations," is anything
but as it should be. The church's witness has been a sad
state of affairs. Most conversion to Christianity takes
places because of individual witness, not because of the
church's corporate witness.

The "one bread" of Jesus' teachings is more like a
scattering of crumbs. It was Gandhi who said that he
would be a Christian but for Christians. The corporate
witness militated against the witness of Christ himself,

who was seeking those (corporately) in whom his very life would be lived out - not an ethic - but a life.

Modernity, that time of history which began with the Enlightenment and spread through the late 1980s is the mentality in which you and I have grown. In Western society it forced Christianity into a merely ethical system, and as such it grossly failed. The arguments currently on the table in Alabama over the Ten Commandments in the courthouse are arguments for an ethical framework. We all have known people who can say with the rich young ruler of the Gospels, "All of these I have kept from my youth," and unfortunately miss the fact that Jesus followed this with the saying "There is one more thing..." The Christ life is not the ethical life; it is precisely the Christ-life: one bread, one body.

One writer aptly puts it this way: "Being members of Christ's body, we are each called to perform the gospel, literally the Good News, with what I would like to call Christly gestures. Performing gestures of faith in Christ's name is to follow, imitate, and participate in the 'Jesus-life' in which every one of our words and deeds is an action of our bodies, hearts, and minds, as we are infused with the power of the Holy Spirit to love one another as we love and serve God in Christ." [Webb-Mitchell]

He continues by quoting Karl Barth: "'Jesus Christ insists upon being enunciated by the choir of primary witnesses. The community represents the secondary witness, the society of men called to believe in, and simultaneously to testify to, the Word in the world.'"

And this leads us to the texts: Joshua calls the people as a people - no individuals here. They are the people of God - a mighty challenge for us who are nurtured in a society which has, up until recently, celebrated the "me-only, me-first" type of life. Closely on the heels of this is Paul's directive to "be subject one to the other," and Jesus' "hard saying" that He is the "living bread which came down from heaven." There is only one bread as there is only one Christ, and the manifestation of this has two goals: the Pauline, "for the sake of Christ," and the "No one can come to me unless it is granted him by the Father." Jesus' own words are a challenge that others know because of our participation in ingesting this bread. It is for the world.

The great Archbishop of Canterbury, William Temple reminded his flock that, "The Christian Church is the only organization in the world that exists purely for the benefit of non-members."

The watching ones demand something to watch that they, themselves cannot reproduce with effectiveness. And those who hear Jesus' own words are troubled by the implications of this "one bread, come down from heaven." Their own plans for delivering Israel from the hands of Rome had not included such personal compromise. Martyrdom is one thing, sacramental unity is quite another. It is much easier to die for a cause than to live for another person - one takes a relatively brief time, the other is a life-long commitment. Jesus' words, according to Simon Peter are words of eternal life - not temporal success. Eternal life, though free, is costly. It costs the sacrifice of self to the body of Christ. Hence Paul will elsewhere write, "you are bought with a price, therefore glorify God in your body."

The church began on the foundation of faith; it has existed for 2,000 years in hope; and that which will make it glorify God and witness to the world is love. And this love is from enlarged hearts - hearts with the capacity for the Kingdom of God. Some continue to follow; others leave. Such divisions have ever been thus, and the world still watches and waits. Amen!

CHAPTER 62
THE TWELFTH
SUNDAY AFTER
PENTECOST

St. Gregory's Church, Woodstock, New York
Deuteronomy 4:1-9; Psalm 15; Ephesians 6:10-20
Mark 7:1-8,14-15,21-23

Why would the Church introduce the theme of sin into the Ordinary Time calendar? Isn't Lent the time for that? Isn't there are time and a place for everything, and Ordinary Time should be given over to growth and development? Yes, and that is precisely why the concept is introduced here - a reminder, that in the midst of redemption accomplished and applied, there is still the vestigial remains of sin in the world, the flesh, and the Satan.

The great man of letters, Alexander Solzeneitzyn captured the reality of sin when he said, "The line that divides good from evil runs through the heart of every person." That is a statement of personal sin - sin for which God has made complete provision and from which we have been delivered in Christ. But there is another, and, I believe more insidious reality of evil and sin, and that is the precise theme of today's lections.

It is no surprise that Paul, in the Ephesian letter, tells of the true enemy of the church when he writes, "We struggle not against enemies of flesh and blood, but against the rulers, against the wickedness, against the cosmic powers of this present darkness, against the spiritual forces of evil in heavenly places." These ungodly rulers of evil are anticipated by the writer of Deuteronomy when his readers were told to not add to or delete from the law of God. There is a sufficiency in the law and a deficiency in laws. And it has been adding to and deleting from the Law of God, which has been the vocation of principalities and powers since the creation of the world. Think of governments, boards, committees, corporations, taskforces, denominations, dioceses, provinces, all of which tend toward their own personality. They become their own power, and people who are members thereof will say and do things they would never say and do individually. Think of the organizations to which you have belonged. These powers add requirements God does not sanction. God's requirements were met in Jesus Christ. God's posture toward us is grace, not legalism.

Now the Gospel account, where would this fit in? Precisely at this point. Jesus is not anti-Semitic, Jesus is anti-bureaucracy. It is the Pharisees as a principality and it is the scribes as a power that Jesus attacks and confronts. [A corollary to this is the fact that "the Jews" did not kill Jesus, the system did, and the implications of this are immense!] Jesus quotes Isaiah who wrote against the hypocrites - plural, systemic, evil, anti-Christ. It is not an individual attack; it is a systemic attack.

Bishop Joe Morris Doss of our Church writes, "Victor Hugo identified the corporate nature of sin in a heart-stopping insight quoted by Martin Luther King, just before his assassination. 'Whenever there is a soul in darkness, there will be sin. The guilt is not with the one who sins, but with those who create the darkness.' One of my favorite novels is *Handling Sin* by Michael Malone. The antagonist is an uptight yuppie trying to live the American dream of small town suburbia by relying on a morally and socially rigid rule of life, a modern version of the age-old effort to justify one's life through the law without the complications and human ambiguity, the earthy messiness of gospel freedom and grace. This yuppie's father, a deposed Episcopal priest, manages to send his unwitting son on an adventurous and hilarious journey, an unsuspecting if heroic journey of an ordinary contemporary in search of his own soul. It is no accident that the story ends during worship on Easter. The whole point of the book is that sin is corporate and that one learns to handle it only by coming to accept the lack of control we may wish to enjoy over it, embracing the reality of the sinfulness handed to us, and thus the forgiveness which is there for all of us, individually and together."

So what is the therefore, now that we have painted this somewhat gloomy picture of the corporate nature of sin. I think the means of living with the corporate sin of humanity is easily delineated. If God is going to judge the nations at the great judgment, then we need not be the final arbiters of systemic right and wrong.

So, I find these lessons from the Scriptures:

1) Pass the acts of judgment off onto God. The last phrases of today's Deuteronomy passage deliver us into only remembering who we are and who God is.

2) Put on the whole armor of God with the result that you will stand in the evil day. Our seeking to rid everything of sin is futile - the Church is called to be a witness in the midst of unbelief.

3) Don't identify yourself as a member of the systemic or corporate [i.e. Pharisees or scribes] for seeking identity in movements is to become the hypocrite. Nicodemus in John 3 shows that his identity would be defined in a relationship to the Christ, not the Pharisees. It made all the difference.

4) Finally, stand tall against the tendency to become systematized - incorporated in anything that is not the Church! The armor is a metaphor for truth, righteousness, peace, faith, and salvation. These are from God - and seldom explain the system - but always define the believer. It is no wonder Paul says, "Persevere!" Amen!

CHAPTER 63
THE THIRTEENTH SUNDAY AFTER PENTECOST

St. Gregory's Episcopal Church, Woodstock, NY
Isaiah 35:4-7a; Psalm 146; James 1:17-27
Mark 7:31-37

The texts today represent and respect the goodness of God. Often throughout the history of the Church God has been celebrated as angry with humanity. Many of us in high school were made to read Jonathan Edwards' sermon, "Sinners in the Hands of an Angry God." It is a grossly off-sided picture of the Biblical God.

Our problem is often that we read the Gospels through the lenses of the Old Testament prophets or of the skewed modernly - interpreted Apostle Paul. To approach the Gospels from either of these perspectives is to miss Jesus and his intent. Here in the wisdom of the collectors of the Lectionary we see the victory, the beneficence, and the grace of God.

Today we are baptizing a young lady. It is not a work we produce or a merit we accrue. There are two major heresies of baptism that the Church has succumbed to over the centuries. First is the far off tendency to see baptism as a "Christening," a time for family gathering, a party, a nice time to let an infant wear great-grandma's "Christening gown." It trivializes baptism.

The second heresy is that perpetrated by those who wish to earn their salvation through good works, the first of which is baptism. A baby is born and we must get that baby baptized lest it die and be committed to eternal damnation by an all-loving God. And so we earn our way out of hell by baptism. This, too, is a heresy of the highest degree.

And so we come to Biblical baptism. It is an act of the Church bestowing God's approval through grace, the *sacrament* of the new birth. It is precisely this, a sacrament, an act of God on our behalf which celebrates God, not us.

Baptism is also subversive. In the time of Christ it put one at odds with the religious and political leadership. In history, persons who declare their ultimate loyalty to the Lord Jesus Christ put themselves at odds with others claiming such loyalty - in this, baptism is subversive. In Orthodox Jewish and Islamic cultures, to be baptized Christian is to end your life with your family and culture. Your funeral is held. There is no middle ground (and though much of this is based on wrong Christian emphases, it is still a fact).

Finally, baptism is successive. We all, today, reaffirm our baptismal vows. And baptism is not an arrival at a destination but being faced in the right direction for a journey.

William Willimon tells of a student at Duke University who attended chapel to fulfill a promise to his mother. He really didn't subscribe to Christianity consciously, but was baptized. Dr. Willimon, over and over, would speak to this student and remind him, "You are baptized." After many months, the student, for all intents and purposes, said to Dr. Willemon, "Okay, I'm baptized, now what?" And so today, we are baptized, and we turn to God and ask, "Now what?" Amen!

CHAPTER 64
ANNIVERSARY - TEN YEARS A PRIEST

Feast of the Holy Cross - September 14, 2003

I saiah the prophet declared that he possessed the tongue of a teacher so that he might have appropriate words for the weary. Don't we all wish we had teachers who made their discipline pertinent to life? So often what we hear taught or preached is theoretical and lacks the "rubber-hits-the-road" matters of the life we necessarily live. Often I am asked by people who hear me preach, "You didn't learn to preach in an Episcopal seminary, did you?" My answer is "No, I did not." And I really didn't learn to preach in school at all. I learned to preach by listening to preachers and teachers. Others have asked, "What is your secret to preaching?" I usually respond that I preach so as to keep myself interested.

Today I am taking a turn from the homily to address my call to ministry. Historically, each priest would spend a week in personal retreat during the week before major anniversaries. Ten years ago today I was ordained a priest in the Episcopal Church. It was one of the best days of my life. And because of this, I believe I should reflect, and I invite you into my reflections.

It was in 1970 that I entered Nyack College as a student in Biblical studies and Christian education. By 1971 I had been called as pastor of a Congregational Church, and upon graduation in 1974 was firmly entrenched in the ministry of the small missionary denomination, The Christian & Missionary Alliance. Pastorates took me to the country hills of Western New York, and Central Pennsylvania, and to the major urban centers of inner-city Philadelphia and Birmingham, Alabama. Ordained on May 10, 1974, I will celebrate thirty years of ordination next year {and I have directed my family that the party is to be one of the largest and best Ulster County has ever had]!

After five years of pastoring a large and growing modern congregation just outside of Utica, New York, in Spring 1991, The Very Rev'd James J. Cardone, Rector, invited me to become his assistant at historic Grace Church in Utica. It would mean a move from the suburbs to the inner city and from being a Senior Pastor with a staff to becoming staff. I accepted within minutes of his offering. I called LaVonne on the phone and said, "Guess what? We're going to be Episcopalians!" And we did. On November 10, 1991 I became the Assistant to the Rector of one of the largest churches in the Diocese of Central New York. The

Bishop and Grace Church helped pay my way to The General Seminary in New York City, where I arrived every Sunday evening (by train) and did one-on-one mentored study for an entire year. In February 1993 I was ordained a Deacon in our Church and on September 14, 1993 (ten years ago today) on Holy Cross Day, I was ordained a priest. Father Cardone made me his Associate Rector and I continued five of the happiest years of my life.

Each of our three sons became Episcopalians, one at a time in his own time. And now, even the thought that my oldest son is a priest is beyond anything we might have dreamed. (I even urged him to run from that vocation if he could; he obviously couldn't and is a successful rector in Mansfield, Louisiana). And so these ten of thirty years demand reflection.

First, ministry has challenged me to continue in the midst of discouragement. Ministry is one of the few callings where you do not see immediate results. Only eternity will reveal whether or not there has been any success at all.

Second, ministry has demanded that I love BOTH the lovely and the unlovely. Ministry is something done to all or it is not effectively done to any. I could delineate literally dozens of unlovely people I have encountered, and how, in dealing with them, I may not have grown to love them, but I was stretched to minister.

Third, the priesthood has taught me to see myself as one among the many. Apostle Paul tells us we are a kingdom of priests - my ordained priesthood is nothing more than a sacramental presence of what we all possess. If you note the Prayerbook you will find that the first order of minister is laity, then bishops, priests, and deacons. You are the people of God that I merely represent.

Finally, the priesthood reminds me daily of the craziness of trying to be anything more than who I am. The best thing I can be for others is myself. To "be there" is greater than to do anything. As a matter of fact, often when we try as clergy to "do something," we find that it hits a dead end, simply because every person needs to do their own something. It was found that to preach against racism in the South was to make people more racist; to preach "love one another" often makes persons more self-loving and self-serving; and to preach forgiveness is to make people more resentful. The best a clergyperson can do is to hold up the model of the perfect life of Christ and the universal provisions of salvation, and say as Christ said, "Follow."

When I was a young adult, Paul Simon made one of his songs quite popular. It had a haunting phrase which is the refrain of every continuing clergyperson. He sang, "Still crazy after all these years." I am convinced that my only sanity is my craziness which has become mine, not through anything I have earned, but through the gracious, though sometimes painful, experiences Holy Spirit has led me through.

So, beloved friends of Woodstock's St. Gregory's, let's continue to be crazy together, until God places another crazy clergyperson here. Amen!

CHAPTER 65
THE FIFTEENTH
SUNDAY AFTER
PENTECOST

St. Gregory's Episcopal Church, Woodstock, NY
Wisdom 1:16-21 (6-11) 12 -22; Psalm 54;
James 3:16-4:6; Mark 9:30-37

C hildren are so sweet and innocent and darling. It is
  no doubt that Jesus employs a child as his model of
kingdom reception. One writer says, "Let's face it: when
life does not run smoothly, or evil rears its ugly head, or
prideful behavior gets the best of us adult types, there
are always children to turn to for rejuvenating the human spirit and restoring confidence in the human race."
But Jesus is not celebrating childhood in this passage. It
is a passage of indictment of earthy values as over and
against eternal values. "Whereas adults possess all sorts
of abilities to give, to rank, and to control, children have
none of these."

Note there are several lessons that surface as we allow this recounting to envelop us:

First, there is the presence of an unheard of declaration. "The Son of Man (a title of divinity and messiahship from the Hebrew Scriptures) is to be betrayed into

human hands, and they will kill him, and three days after being killed, he will rise again." This declaration is unheard of because it declared the vulnerability of the God-man and the reality of the resurrection. Jesus' followers had seen no such things - a leader who serves and a dead man who comes to life. These do not happen, and yet Jesus declares them as factual prophecy.

Second, we find an uncanny selfishness. Missing the redemptive aspect of what Jesus is saying, his zealot-like disciples focus on leadership. (This all too often sounds like the church.) Christian history is littered with the arguments of the who of leadership and, all too often, devoid of the declarations of servanthood. The very thing we are warned to avoid, the Disciples model for us. Who is the greatest? What audacity! What blindness! What a typical human desire! We try to be the greatest because we don't want to suffer under the greatness of another, always thinking ourselves the most benevolent. And it is all a delusion.

Then we find the un-welcomed question. They are asked about their deepest, secretive conversations. What were they talking about? Caught in the act they realize that the All-knowing One knows. They are not so much ashamed of their conversation as they are the fact that He knows. We are never so uncomfortable as when we judge ourselves without a word from God. I love Edgar Allen Poe's *The Tell-tale Heart*, where the main character is haunted by the supposed beating of his murdered victim's heart while police quietly question him about the incident. There is no accusation except his own guilt.

But the lessons are not complete - not yet. There is the unfathomable presentation of a new value system and quality of existence: the greatest must serve; the kingdom is entered like a trusting child; God is welcomed, not appeased! This cuts disturbingly across everything we are raised to believe. It is disconcerting and challenging and often rejected. It is difficult. The great man of letters, G. K. Chesterton said that, "Christianity has not been tried and found wanting, but it has been found difficult and therefore left untried."

The delight that comes from this revaluation is then what is modeled by the Christ and celebrated in all of the Gospel calls to follow Him. It is a servanthood of fulfillment; a placing of oneself last so as to be the first recipients of Grace's distributions.

Dr. Ravi Zacharis in his new book, *Recapture the Wonder,* recounts this historical vignette:

"President Theodore Roosevelt had a routine habit, almost a ritual. Every now and then with the naturalist William Beebe, he would step outside at dark, look into the night sky, find the faint spot of light at the lower left-hand corner of Pegasus, and one of them would recite: 'That is the Spiral Galaxy of Andromeda. It is as large as our Milky Way. It is one of a hundred million galaxies. It is seven hundred and fifty thousand light years away. It consists of one hundred billion suns, each larger than our own sun.' There would be a pause and then Roosevelt would grin and say, 'Now I think we feel small enough! Let's go to bed!'"

If we only feel small, we are much to be pitied. But when we can feel small and subsequently peacefully go to bed, confident in the bigness of our Creator, we are beginning to understand Christ's revaluation of reality. "Now I think we feel small enough! Let's approach the table of the Lord!" Amen!

CHAPTER 66
THE SIXTEENTH SUNDAY AFTER PENTECOST

St. Gregory's Church, Woodstock, New York
Numbers 11:4-6, 10-16, 24-29; Psalm19;
James 4:7-5:6; Mark 9:38 - 48

An evangelist friend of mine sent this account in his October letter to his prayer partners, and I paraphrase:

"The last night we were in Mozambique, my colleague, my son, and I went to a small roadside restaurant for dinner. A twin-lobster dinner for six dollars we just could not resist. We got talking with our waiter, a pleasant, kind, and chatty young African names Ernest, who was so pleased to be serving us. He had no shoes. My son watched this for a few meals, and then looking at his own shoes (he has more than one pair) said, "Dad I want to give him my shoes." They evidently were a perfect fit and the deed was done. It was received with grace. The lessons are manifold.

See with me, the humility of true belief - "Submit yourself to God." Only we can humble ourselves; others might humiliate us, we alone can be the motivation to humility... The James record is one of honest evaluation of the self...

Be proactive to release control. Moses has little worry about those over whom he has no responsibility. There is a wonderful little gem in the last chapter of the Gospel of John, where Jesus says to Peter, "What is that to you...you follow me..." There is a deliverance that comes in releasing others into the care of God.

Finally, consciously negate judgment. In spite of the fact that every factual statement is a judgment, Jesus is telling his disciples to not judge. He reverses the normal statement which says, "He who is not for me is against me," with the intriguing statement, "He who is not against me is for me." He opens the door for myriads to be doing the work of God. The disciples needed to learn that "He who reproves the lame must walk upright" [Samuel Daniel]. Jesus reminded his disciples that their saintliness did not depend on the sinfulness of others.

I love the sarcasm of Arnold Bennet when he writes, "It is well, when one is judging a friend, to remember that he is judging you with the same godlike and superior impartiality."

In this Gospel, "Jesus is stretching the language to the breaking point to make an emphatic point: the kingdom of God is bizarre, paradoxical, weird. Jesus understands the deepest paradox of all: by losing your life for Christ's sake, you receive it. The problem is, too many of us wait until death to lose our life.

Perhaps C. S. Lewis hit it correctly when he said, "Die before you die, you'll have no chance thereafter." Amen!

CHAPTER 67
FEAST OF ST. FRANCIS OF ASSISI [TRANSFERRED]

Galatians 6:14-18; Psalm 121
Matthew 11:25-30

October 4th is the day set for the celebration of the Feast of St. Francis of Assisi. We have transferred the feast to today for a special celebration [and because the Propers set for today in their sum total are basically, senselessly gathered]. We are not gathering the animals and pets for blessing today because of the Woodstock Cycle that will need this space after worship to set up for the second performance at 3 o'clock. So we will content ourselves with a wee homily on the life of Francis.

During the second presentation at last night's Woodstock Cycle, it was mentioned that God might possibly be amused with us as a parent is with a child, even when they fall flat on their back and conk their head! It is a wonderful image and an acceptable metaphor when we posit God as parent.

Francis appears to us to be one of those blundering children. There are several captivating remembrances of him that have endeared him to millions for centuries, and I would like to scratch the surface this morning.

Certainly when we look with believing Christian eyes at a model saint (usually a contradiction in terms), we find that there is the character exhibited, the call manifested, and the coalescing remembered. Each of these will encourage us from the life of Francis.

The character of Francis after his conscious conversion is never questioned. He is solidly converted, soundly committed, and singularly purposed. There is the goal of monastic life and community and the fervent and continual preaching of the Gospel of Christ. One day he called his monks together (upward to 5,000 of them) and challenged them to, "Go forth preaching the Gospel, if you must, use words." He understood the Word made flesh, and was committed to fleshing it out through his brothers and sisters. There is this Christ who defined his character, keeping his mind focused, his heart warm, and his body obedient. And so we are challenged to follow the model.

Then we are captivated by the call he manifested. A call is not a call unless acted upon. Just as there is no Hebrew equivalent of the word "faith" without its corresponding necessity of "faithfulness," so with love in the New Testament there is no such thing as love without the necessary corollary of its being an action verb. Love as a noun is stale and vacuous. Francis embodies this action under the call of Christ. He is considered insane by his father with whom he breaks all ties; a pope calls him a "madman;" and people find him eccentric and unpredictable in the ways in which Christian charity may manifest itself next. He is Church history's extreme example of the person who hears and heeds the call of God in inexplicable abandon. He is, as a called person, for all intents and purposes indescribably unique. His eccentricities serve as a promise of our acceptance by God with all the accompanying accouterments. To be called a madman because one is Christian can be, and often is, a compliment.

Finally, Francis saw all of reality as complete, coalesced, and unified in the risen Christ. Humans, animals, and the inanimate world are redeemed in Christ and taken up into the praise of God.

One of the wonderful teachings of Francis was that when one's pets died, they would be found waiting in the hereafter, anxiously anticipating the arrival of their owners after death. True or not, it is a theology of valuing the entire world created by God.

Little was outside of Francis' theology, and often he was known for extremes and once in a while for flippancies and seeming light-heartedness. And why not? God was in the heavens, and all was right with the universe. He proclaimed an unconditional love of God, and though viewed by many as the strangest of human beings, he was still ordained and given full authority over his order by the very pope who called him a "madman." Brothers and sisters, I am convinced that God is not waiting for our perfections to serve him, but precisely our idiosyncrasies, our uniqueness, and even our madness. If God can use a Francis, and God did, God will use us as well in the eternal work of the kingdom. Amen!

CHAPTER 68
THE EIGHTEENTH SUNDAY AFTER PENTECOST

St. Gregory's Church, Woodstock, New York
Amos 5:6-7, 10-15; Psalm 90; Hebrews 3:1-6
Mark 10:17-31

There are so very many levels of meaning in the Gospels, that we often get off on the wrong foot by not looking at more than one of those levels. The earthy encounters remind us of the Hebrew nature of the foundations of Christianity. Christianity is not the spiritual religion of the Greeks, it is a physical religion of the Hebrews. So when we come to the encounter in today's Gospel account, we see a real man, with a real question, querying a real Messiah and getting a real, earthy answer. The entire encounter revolves around numerous themes: eternity, time, and grace.

Jesus is encountered by a meaningful question misdirected. "What must I do to inherit eternal life?" The questioner is unquestionably self-centered. Wanting eternal life is a human thing; doing something to merit inheritance is something entirely a different thing. The first is a commendable goal; the second is a condemnable means. But lest we condemn this fellow too severely, we must be honest that we live in a world of meritorious beneficence. What I do, I expect reward for. I am capable, and therefore am reward worthy. The self-sufficiency betrays this man's incapacity to receive. The Judeo-Christian lesson is one of receiving, not earning.

Jesus responds with the need to keep the law and he begins delineating it. But the young man stops Jesus mid-list. The requirements are the factual answer to a misguided question. If you want merit, you get merit. Keep everything God has said. And the response is that all these listed have been kept through this man's entire life.

Jesus is not taken in, thankfully.

Listen as Fr. Robert Farrar Capon describes the encounter:

"'Jesus looked at him and loved him.' You poor, amiable sap, he thinks to himself. I like you a lot, Harry. More than you'll ever know. But it just doesn't work that way. You try to save your life like that, you'll only lose it. You have to lose, l-o-s-e, lose your life to save it. Still, I'll give you a shot at what I mean, just to prove it to you.

"And so with consummate understatement, Jesus gently breaks the good news to him. 'You only have to do one simple little thing, Harry: sell everything you have and give it to the poor. That will take care of getting your treasury of merits off your back. Then come and follow me to my death.' And at that saying, Mark says, the young man got very gloomy in the face and went off in a deep depression because 'he had great possessions'-because, that is, he just couldn't bear the thought of being a loser.

"The saddest part of the whole thing, though, is that he turned his back on the only really good piece of news he would ever hear, because in something under threescore years and ten, all that great stuff of his-all those *ktemata polla,* those many good, worldly or spiritual or intellectual-would betaken from him anyway. And so would all the terrible stuff as well: the whole pile of his unacknowledged failures, the ratty tissue of his irretrievable relationships and second-rate loves. *All* of his achievements-his successful virtues as well as his success-loving vices-would someday go whistling into the ultimate no-win situation, the final, redeeming un-success of death. And the next saddest part of it is that in spite of Jesus' clear insistence that no winner will ever do anything but lose-you and I go on blithely trying to win. If it is not financial success that keeps us from the saving emptiness of Jesus on the cross, it is moral success, intellectual success, emotional success, or spiritual success. We simply will not lose; and without losing, we will never, ever, win."

Finally, Jesus uses true Oriental hyperbole to teach his disciples that it will be impossible for those who bring things in their hands to enter into the kingdom. There is no reference here to a door called the "Eye of the Needle." Jesus is not showing that it is difficult to earn your way into the kingdom, he is teaching that it is impossible to earn your way into the kingdom.

It is a declaration of human impossibility countered magnificently by the divine possibility. God does it all - everything that is needed to have the human inherit eternal life has been done.

It is in this that Jesus is the great leveler. Everyone is placed in the posture of receiver. The gift is made available and all that can thwart this receiving is the obstacle of self.

Thomas Aquinas puts it this way, "Divine care supplies everyone with the means necessary for salvation <u>so long as they do not put up any obstacles</u>." And Jesus' encounter with this rich young man is recorded for us precisely because the man had obstacles.

One school of spiritual thought is that God redeems and nurtures us by subtraction and not by addition. Certainly the lessons of the day justify this position. "Nothing in my hand I bring, simply to Thy cross I cling," wrote the hymn-writer.

Perhaps the great G. K. Chesterton captures the lesson best: "We are perpetually being told that what is wanted is a strong men who will do things. What is really wanted is a strong men who will undo things; and that will be the real test of strength."

As we move to the confession this morning, we may need to confess both our vices and our virtues to find a place in grace. Amen!

CHAPTER 69
THE TWENTY-SECOND SUNDAY AFTER PENTECOST

St. Gregory's Church, Woodstock, New York
1 Kings 17:8-16; Psalm 146; Hebrews 9:24-28
Mark 12:38-44

Easy interpretations are often nicely applicable, but often incomplete. So with this text. It is used during October/November in many parishes to deal with stewardship. And we could and maybe should do that this morning. St. Gregory's is now at a crossroads; needing to attract a new permanent priest, it needs to bolster its financial picture to make things appealing. We are currently many thousands of dollars behind in our budget, and as we enter this time of stewardship, our needs are many. Some will give much and some little, but all must give for the ministry here to continue. There must come that day when we can remove ourselves from the Congregational Support Plan of the Diocese of New York. And this emphasis is important.

But it is not the emphasis of the Gospel this morning. The Gospel account has several intensive lessons for us and it is imperative that we gaze into this historical account. We are first confronted with the fact that there is a diversity and hierarchy of motives. The self-serving Scribes were motivated by a sense of receiving recognition; the poor widow motivated by faithfulness. One needed to be seen; the other had nothing really to see. One is indicted; one is commended as a model of motivational integrity. There are the haunting suggestions of Jesus that we question our own motivations in the doing of the right, for it is entirely possible to do the right thing out of the wrong motivation and thus be "condemned" (Jesus' word).

The motivation that is pure and honest and well-intentioned is the rewarded element. The amount mattered little while the motive mattered most!

Keeping the thought flowing, Jesus clearly concludes that there are two types of giving - one from abundance, the other from poverty; and somehow the giving from poverty is the commendable giving. We often think that we have nothing to give of self, substance, effort; yet it is precisely when there is poverty that giving takes its ultimate significance. It is at the exact moment when we think we have nothing to offer that we have everything to offer, and it is likely that when we think we have the most to give that we must recognize that God may not need it. It is one of those healthy humility matters. [I always struggle writing a resume for a Christian position on how to appear the best qualified for the position while all the time maintaining my humility!] The Elijah account of the morning shows that the widow of Zeraphath was in the exact position of having nothing with nothing to give, and that was what she gave. In return, it was a gift received and it is in the receiving that reward is found. This doesn't mean that we give God the left overs; it means we give God everything!

The system to which the Scribes gave and the system to which this poor widow gave is corrupt. As a matter of fact the widow was giving to the very system that "devour widows' houses." Her estate was a result of the system to which she pledge solidarity. And Jesus did as well. He was well willing to pay the tax to Caesar and to the temple, and as such helped to support those who crucified him. It was those who support the system who have the sole right of criticizing the system: Jesus, the widow, the scribe. The issue comes when some, such as the scribes, will not judge the system, but become part of it. Let's face the fact that those who are in the work should best know it and should be in the place of self-judgment. It is the meaning of the prophet's words: "It is time for judgment to begin in the house of God." Just as Socrates stated, "The unexamined life is not worth living," so "The unquestioned system is not worth sustaining." Jesus and the widow and the scribes qualify to do just that. The scribes abdicated their watchmen's role. Only those who "buy in" should have say in the work they are giving to. It is a different kind of lesson from this text, but it is Gospel. It is none other than those who have left all to follow Christ in discipleship who have the right to question the work of Christ in the world. Others have only the right to look on expectantly.

The lesson is relatively easy: give, weigh, beware.

The story is told of a man who awoke amidst great heart palpitations and sweat, recalling a terrifying nightmare. His wife said, "Honey are you alright?" He said, "No! It was the most awful thing you could imagine. I was in church, and dreamed that I fell into the offering plate." God help us all! Amen!

CHAPTER 70
THE FIRST SUNDAY
OF ADVENT

St. John's Episcopal Church, Kingston, NY
Zechariah 14:4-9; I Thessalonians 3:9-13; Psalm 50
Luke 21:25-31

We live in a day of frustration, ambivalence, and agnosticism. Often there is doubt. Just this week, in light of the election questions, two lawyers were in the same elevator with me at the college building in Manhattan. One said to the other, "If Bush is elected President, our nation is doomed.!" One of my bold students broke into the conversation saying, "I thought King Jesus was ultimately on the throne?" Touché.

If we are at the mercy of the American electoral system, we are of all humanity most to be pitied. There must be more.

There is. And Advent I teaches us that God has something to say from the Canon of Holy Scripture. In the Gospel record of the morning, we are given a *preparatory prophecy.* "Look, the kingdom of God is near." Kingdom is a metaphor for the actualized reign of King Jesus. This truth gives us anticipation – something for which to hope. It grants believers expectation. There is a culmination of all life and all history toward which we hopefully and excitedly move. The Apostle writes, "He (God) who began a good work in you will perform it…" Advent celebrates that we are not left clueless concerning the future. God's kingdom, which is near, can only be benevolent.

Then, the prophecy of the morning opens to us a *valuable vision*. Finally, evil is judged and good is rewarded. Wrongs are made right. Righteousness reigns. The text tells us that there will be continuous day – meaning that time is irrelevant if not non-existent. Government as we know it is eradicated and there is God reigning over His people. This is not the drunken vision of a riotous visionary, but the sane vision of a prophet of Israel.

Finally, in our Epistle reading, we are provided with a *purposeful present*. Now matters. It is in the now that God is tying together the past and the future. We have a history, a heritage, and a hope – and we are in the midst of its all being done, right now. It is now that we may be increasing in our love for one another; holiness and Christian maturity can be becoming a reality now; and all of this is to prepare us for a glorious end or goal.

Advent, Christ's second coming is mirrored and prefigured in his first Advent.

So what are the "therefores?"

First, we are people of promise. There is something to believe. Second, the vision extends beyond our human limitations. Third, we have an end (a purpose) before the end (the finality).

The song-writer put it this way:

But just think of stepping on shore, and finding it heaven;
Of touching a hand, and finding it's God's;
Of breathing new air, and finding it celestial –
Of waking up in glory, and finding you are home.

CHAPTER 71
FOURTH SUNDAY OF ADVENT

St. John's Episcopal Church, Kingston, New York
Micah 5:2-4; Hebrews 10:5-10; Psalm 80
Luke 1:39-56

Pastor Joan has asked me to have a brief homily this morning as we say morning prayer together on this fourth Sunday of Advent. Tonight is our Christmas Eve celebration of the birth of Incarnate Jesus Christ.

Advent prepares us for an inversion of values. The historic record shakes what we esteem.

The Old Testament reading mentions the "little town of Bethlehem," a town of the tribe of Judah, and it is not a very prestigious place. There is little known of it; it is small (still is) and there is nothing of much import that happens there. It is a revelation of the *irrelevance of place*.

God's activities are not place-defined. God works where He will; when He will; and with whom He wills. The place is inconsequential when it comes to the work of the Lord. Remember that there are no little places. Wherever you are God is at work, and it is not less of a work than God is working elsewhere. If God can do it in Bethlehem, and He did, God can do it in Kingston, and He does!

In the Epistle we are told that a body has been prepared for this intrusive God. This benign invasion is to happen in the flesh – in the body; hence, the word *Incarnation*. This is God's proclamation of the elevation of the value of the body. Two-thousand years of Church history have deprecated the body, much in contrariness to the teachings of the New Testament. God in the kenosis, the self-emptying which He does to enter the human race, is celebrating that He will work in and through a physical body then, and God continues to so work today. (Later, the Apostle Paul will even tell us in II Corinthians that it is the body that is the temple of the Holy Spirit).

Finally, the Gospel tells us of Mary's response. "Mary said," is significant. It is an affirmation of an unknown, a trust in God. On top of all of this, this is a Biblical celebration of woman. Do you even begin to realize what this means in a patriarchal society such as the Hebrews had? It is scandalous at best.

All three of these truths flow against the culture of the day and what the Church has often taught. Power, maleness, possession, spirituality, location – all of these are lauded as having value; and, in one Sunday's Scriptures, God wipes them from the scale of eternal valuation.

Today we anticipate the coming of the second person of the eternal Trinity as a human infant. The implications are innumerable. Join the upset! Amen!

CHAPTER 72
FIRST SUNDAY AFTER CHRISTMAS

St. John's Episcopal Church, Cornwall, New York
Isaiah 61:10-62:3; Galatians 3:23-4:7; Psalm 147
John 1:1-18

Today we gather, a few of us in the chancel, due to the severe snow-storm of last evening. My notes are in the pulpit, and so we will weigh in heavily on the Lord, and the Spirit to guide our few words this morning. Most of you need to return home for shoveling and clearing ways for continuing the living we are called to do, so we will hear from the Lord and move on to His table.

The Gospel text of the morning tells us of the wonder and the glory of this Jesus of Nazareth. We are told of the beholding of his glory, unparalleled in human experience. John saw this (no doubt a reference to the Transfiguration), but he speaks as if we all can experience the transfigured glory of Christ.

Allow me to tie this with an Old Testament precedent, the tabernacle of Moses. This is not a stretch at all, since John writes that "the Word became flesh and *tabernacled* among us." All that the tabernacle and the temple stood for in Hebrew worship and approach to God, Jesus is for us today.

The tabernacle of Moses was a tent in the wilderness, a traveling place of worship. It was covered with four coverings, one seen from the outside, one from the inside, and two sandwiched between the others and not seen normally. It is these two outward coverings with which we will interest ourselves these few moments. They are pertinent to our life in Christ.

The outer covering of the Tabernacle was for the purpose protection from the elements. It was made of tough badger's skins, and it shed water. It was not known for its aesthetics, but for its utilitarian purpose. It was, quite frankly, quite ugly from the outside. There was nothing attractive or attracting about the outward appearance.

Now the inside was something else. Here were ten widths of the finest linen made in the known world. It was pure white, with some dyed to red, some blue, some royal purple. The bands of linen were held together with solid gold clasps, and embroidered on the linen were gold cherubim to remind those inside the tabernacle that they were in godly care.

The contrast between the outside ugliness and plainness and the inside beauty was stark. Now this tabernacle is a type of Jesus Christ.

As with the tabernacle, so with Jesus — from the outside there is nothing particularly drawing. Isaiah wrote, "he had no form nor comeliness that we should desire him." There is nothing other than normal humanness to those outside of Jesus. But once "in Christ" we can say with John, "we beheld his glory, the glory as of the only begotten of the Father, full of grace and truth." The incarnation places us in Christ beholding his beauty, appreciating his person. We are thus privileged as we celebrate the incarnational feast of Christmas. Enjoy being "in Christ!" Amen!

CHAPTER 73
THE SECOND
SUNDAY AFTER THE
EPIPHANY

Resurrection Church [Episcopal],
Hopewell Junction, NY
Isaiah 62:1-5; I Corinthians 12:1-11; Psalm 96
John 2:1-11

Epiphany is that season of the Christian calendar that turns our attention to things we are to know about God through Jesus Christ. An epiphany is an insight, a revelation, an opening. And so we are confronted with things we would not naturally conclude without such an enlightening. We learn about who Jesus really is. He is more than the little baby in the manger - much more. He is a radically different Messiah than Judaism had sought.

In this familiar Gospel record of the marriage feast at Cana of Galilee, several important realities instruct us in the type of person Jesus really is. The text in the Gospel of John 2:1-11 is our focus.

First, in the response to his mother Mary, Jesus has the servants of the house use the jars which were normally used for temple preparation and purification. These, upwards to 50 gallon jars, were used for ritual cleansing. These celebrating people had it right. The rite preceded their delight.

It is only after recognizing the content of Christian ritual that we can find the contentment of Christian reality; it is only in the context of Christian ritual that we can find the common-place become uncommon; and it is only a consequence of ritual that we can find water becoming wine.

Note secondly, that in the working of this wine-making miracle, there are six stone jars. If seven is the perfect number, the seventh vessel is Jesus himself. Jesus the corner-STONE is the seventh stone jar. It is the presence of Jesus that takes the emptiness of stone jars and gives them beneficial powers.

Finally, the head steward of the house serves the wine and the guests are taken aback to notice that the best was served last. This is often the perspective of God. At the opposite end of what we expect comes the best; at the end of what we can produce, comes the best; at the end of what we can store up in earthen vessels, comes the best God has to offer.

Dr. A. B. Simpson, a nineteenth century New York City pastor and evangelist wrote these wonderful words:

> God has his best things for the few
> That dare to stand the test;
> God has his second best for those
> Who will not have his best.

It is not always open ill
    That risks the promised rest;
The better often is the foe
    That keeps us from the best.

Give me O Lord the best things
    Let others take the rest.
I do not want your good things
    For I have got the best.

-1897-

But, alas, what are the "therefores?" Is there a lesson to take away from this text? Of course. God is a miracle working God. But wait, it is not that simple.

Certainly we must see that God delights in our delight. G. K. Chesterton surmised that Jesus hid his mirth while on the earth as God incarnate. And it is certainly possible from this text to see that we get a glimpse of the mirth and merriment of God in Christ. Take a long look at the revelation, the epiphany that Jesus is God's message of delight in you and in me.

Then note that Jesus, who is elsewhere revealed as the water of life, is also our wine of celebration. He takes mere water and makes it more than water. He is man, but more than man, he is the God-man.

And finally, to our benefit and the glory of God, when we come to the end of ourselves, we find miraculous provision. When we may be at loss or embarrassed by our limitation and lack, there we will find Christ who came that we might have life and that more abundantly. Amen!

CHAPTER 74
THE FOURTH
SUNDAY AFTER THE
EPIPHANY

St. John's Episcopal Church, Kingston, New York
Jeremiah 1:4-10; I Corinthians 14:12b-20;
Psalm 71:1-17; Luke 4:21-32

I think it is safe to say, on the authority of the New Testament, that the Christian faith is a no-wimp faith. There is something dynamically life-changing in committing oneself to the following of Jesus of Nazareth, who was called the Christ. After all, they crucified him. He would have been unwelcome in comfortable American Christianity. There are demands of the faith; demands that do not negate our salvation by grace through faith.

Even though the Scriptures reveal to us that the just shall live by faith, it is nonetheless true that there is a certain life subsequent to conversion that shows itself worthy of God.

Now, I know I must stand clear of becoming a preacher of ethics or moral thought, but there are applications of our Christian creed and confession which must be made manifest in our lives.

The Epiphany blessing given by many priests following the post-communion prayer says, "May Christ the Son of God be manifest in you, that your lives may be a light unto the world." This is significant. A central element of Epiphany, the opening or revealing of who Jesus is, is the fact that as believers in this Jesus Christ, we become little epiphanies, making Him known to the world. This is awesomely essential to understand. Hence the texts of this Lord's Day.

The Old Testament lessons direct our attention to speaking. Our speaking is to be proscribed by truth, conspicuous by kindness, and thirst-inducing as salt. Scripture elsewhere tells us to allow our speech to be seasoned with salt. Salt makes thirsty; it preserves; and it melts frozen hardness. The Scripture is calling us to be a people, who, in Jesus Christ preserve the integrity of common speech, of conversation.

Then the epistle indicates that the Christian life is one of a process, a journey of maturation. Growing in the grace and knowledge of the Lord Jesus Christ, the Christian becomes more him or herself by becoming more Christ-like. We are all urged on to maturity in Christ - better than we were yesterday; manifesting the fruit of the Spirit more than before, yet still pressing on to a more glorious tomorrow. This will keep us from false guilt over our lack of spiritual perfection. Do not expect it; merely grow in grace.

Finally the Gospel record is clear that ours is a precipitous salvation. Christians often are not popular; they are often not accepted; their faith is ridiculed in art and culture; and they are not in the majority - never have been. There is a real tenuousness to true Christian faith because we are ordained to stand when all else falls.

Epiphany reminds us in Jesus, himself, that it can be done by his grace and enablement.

Amy Carmichael, a life-long missionary to India during the early part of the twentieth century, wrote and often prayed this prayer:

From prayer that asks that I may be
Sheltered from winds that beat on Thee;
From fearing when I should aspire,
From faltering when I should climb higher,
From silken self O captain free
Thy soldier who would follow Thee.

From subtle love of softening things
From easy choices, weakenings,
(Not thus are spirits fortified,
Not this way went the Crucified);
From all that dims Thy Calvary,
O Lamb of God deliver me.

Give me a love that leads the way,
A faith that nothing can dismay;
The hope no disappointments tire,
The passion that will burn like fire.
Let me not sink to be a clod-
Make me Thy fuel, flame of God.

May we, this Epiphany, make this our prayer as well. Amen!

CHAPTER 75
FIFTH SUNDAY
AFTER THE EPIPHANY

St. John's Episcopal Church, Cornwall, New York
Judges 6:11-24a; I Corinthians 15:1-11; Psalm 85
Luke 5:1-11

The Luke 5:1-11 Gospel text is a record of Jesus telling his disciples that they will continue in their habitual work of catching, but that their catch will change. Catching is something we can all understand: some catch fish; we can catch a cold; some catch the flu. If I am speaking correctly you can catch my drift; in sports we often catch the ball; and when we sum everything up we hope to have a catch phrase.

To catch something is to make it yours. You, as the one who catches, now determine what you will do with what you caught. Therefore, when Jesus says, "From now on you will catch people," he is directing his disciples to understand that there will be a certain determinant in their relationship to those they evangelize.

First of all, such catching is a Christian given. You have no choice. As a Christian you will catch people. Now whether you are good at it or not, whether you

413

do what you should with those you catch or not, these are the questions; but you will catch people. You cannot, as a Christian, not have a witness. Your decision is whether or not your witness is one of integrity or dis-integrity. This choice is ours to make, but we will catch people.

This leads to the next insight: what we catch them with we will catch them to. The fact is that these called by Jesus left all to follow Him. This is a record of history that is a model of radical discipleship. No one leaves all without counting the cost.. The questions raised confront us with our approach to Christianity. Is it casual or committed? Is Christ an addition to all that we are and possess or a replacement? Is our faith Christ-centered or self-centered? These questions are meant to haunt the serious believer.

Finally, there is a consequential act of following. The leaving of all things is finalized by a following. This is, in the original text, indicating that it is a continuous and constant following. There is no intermittence here. We are confronted with the fact that Jesus is our model; that it is he who gives direction; that it is he who is our companion on the journey; that it is he who grants us continuity; and that ultimately it is Jesus Christ of Nazareth who is the Way!

We dare not miss the seriousness of the call. Amen!

CHAPTER 76
THE SIXTH SUNDAY
AFTER THE EPIPHANY

St. John's Episcopal Church, Cornwall, New York
Jeremiah 17:1-10; I Corinthians 15:12-20; Psalm 1
Luke 6:17-26

After nineteen years as a clergyman in another denomination (the Christian & Missionary Alliance), I was ordained a deacon and priest in the Episcopal Church in 1993. At my first wedding, I had everything planned to the smallest detail. Nothing would go wrong; I had the rubrics down perfectly. In the absence of a deacon, when it was time to read the Gospel, the congregation and I stood, and I walked the long chancel aisle to the altar to take the Gospel book and read the Beatitudes. The book was not there; someone had forgotten to place it on the altar. Quickly, I grabbed my black leather prayerbook/hymnal combination, turned to something, and recited the Beatitudes by memory (having memorized them in fourth grade Sunday School). Thank God for Mrs. Haines who forced us so to memorize. It saved me many years later.

However, the Beatitudes often are left unplumbed in their magnificence. God gets a bum wrap. He is blamed for curses and circumstances, and he is often forgotten or ignored during blessings and bounty.

Gary Larsen, the creator of the Far Side comic strip, was probably the most theological of all comic strip writers. His cartoons would often give us a raw glimpse of what true thinking of God is like. In one particularly wonderful comic, in one frame he has an unsuspecting fellow walking nonchalantly down the street oblivious of the fact that a piano hung precariously above his head, held in place by a moving company block and tackle. God views all this through his video surveillance monitor, with his finger poised pensively over the SMITE button. Larsen is right; we often think that God is out to get us.

But this is the furthest thing from the truth of the Holy Scriptures. One more example to force this into our thinking. In Umberto Eco's outstanding book, *The Name of the Rose,* and in the film of the same title, the plot is for a Franciscan monk to look into deaths and murders at Mediaeval Benedictine monastery. In the film, Sean Connery plays the Franciscan who discovers that people die and are murdered because they have discovered Aristotle's lost work on laughter and mirth. And of course we all know that the church should have nothing to do with mirth and levity, and so the faithful librarian sees to it that the book is kept away from all but prying eyes. The plot is intriguing.

Our Scripture texts of the day give us epiphanies into the facts of curses and blessings.

First, what is a curse? It is nothing more or less than an abandonment by God to the results of our wrong choices. It is the presence of God shrouded. To be cursed is to be unable to recognize blessings when they are present. In essence a curse is the darkness of having my own way.

Then what is a blessing? (The term beatitude means blessing.) It is the presence of God, even when God seems absent; it is the affirmation of living a life of belief, even when despair is a momentary reality; it is the promise of God, when all appears just the opposite of his promise; it is grace made applicable in less than gracious circumstances; it is nothing less than God consciousness.

Early in the decade of the 1980s, I had a wonderful youth pastor named Stan Hotalen. Stan and his wife, Connie, had two wonderful little girls, and soon upon leaving for Africa as missionaries had a son. One evening we received a wire that the son had succumbed to a rare West African disease and may not live the night through. Before we could rally the church to pray, the announcement came that the son had died. Of course we continued to pray for Stan, Connie, and the family. Some weeks letter a prayer letter was sent to all their prayer partners in the United States, and the letter began this way:

God has blessed us with a very great sorrow...

Without blaming God for what had happened, they were blessed because they were conscious of God through it all.

The end, the purpose, the goal, men and women, is in being and not necessarily doing anything. It is in being blessed and being a blessing even when the body politic is ruptured and hemorrhaging; being blessed and being a blessing when all around appears anything but what God would ordain. You may be in such a depth of frustration, fear, or despair today. The news is good. You are blessed. Will you see it?

William Blake penned some poignant words which are applicable to our situations this day:

> Life's dim windows of the soul
> > Distort the world from pole to pole;
> And goad us to believe a life
> > When we see with, not through the eye.

The eye of flesh will fail, the vision of the believer is clear. Will you see through your eyes with your spirit today - see that God desires to bless and not curse?

An old hymn sung in the little Methodist Church, when I was a youngster, comes to mind again and again:

Bane and blessing, pain and pleasure
    By the cross are sanctified.
Peace is there that knows no measure,
    Joy that through all time abides.

May it be so with us. Amen!

CHAPTER 77
SEVENTH SUNDAY
AFTER THE EPIPHANY

St. John's Episcopal Church, Kingston, New York
The Gill Chapel, Samsonville, New York
Genesis 45:3-28; I Corinthians 15:35-50; Psalm 37:1-18
Luke 6:27-38

Unfortunately, mainline Christianity of the post-World War II era and fundamentalistic Christianity have both served up the same unpalatable offering of Jesus as a great ethical teacher. If we would just be like Jesus, obedient and nice, we would get along with everyone and never get in trouble. The one problem is that Jesus got himself in big trouble – trouble that ended in a cruciform way.

The Epiphany emphasis of the day is that there is a Christian ethic, but that it grows out of and is not the sum total of Christian life. It is entirely possible, according to the New Testament, to do everything right, and end up dead!

The ethic of Jesus is not salvific; it does not bring salvation. It is diametrically opposed to the systemic; it *is* meant to be evangelistic; and it is not intended for me to come off looking good to God, but rather that, through me, God comes off looking good to others. What people think of me reflects on what people think of my God!

The Old Testament lesson of the morning is recorded so that we will come to the irrefutable Judeo-Christian conclusion that God works through circumstances. Life is going somewhere; it means something. Archbishop William Temple went so far as to say that in every co-incidence, God is working incognito! So if God works through the circumstantial, I must re-valuate how I am treated.

Joseph was sold into slavery by his brothers and went through a series of hellish encounters in Egypt; and when he sees his brothers after many many years, his response is, "You meant it to me for evil, God meant it for good." When we have been mistreated, it is the natural tendency to mistreat in return; but as we see God at work, we will be forced to conclude: "God meant it for good."

In Paul's first letter to the Corinthians, chapter fifteen, he gives an irrefutable argument for the bodily resurrection of Jesus from the dead. And this will certainly be a thematic focus for Eastertide. So why is it our reading for today? Precisely because we are called to live in resurrection perspective at all times. This is a new way of seeing. We, as Christian believers, do not see things locked in temporal turmoil, but rather in resurrection life. The perspective is wider, broader, deeper, and fuller. My life is more that three score and ten; it is in Christ, eternal. How I see reality must transcend the temporal.

One writer caught this truth in a cute quip: "If a tree falls in the jungle with nobody there to hear it, does it make a noise? One of Britain's bishops answered in lyric form:

> "There was a young man who thought God
> would find it exceedingly odd
> when he sees that this tree continues to be
> when there's no one about in the quad.
> Young man, your astonishment soars!
> I'm always about in the quad,
> and that's why this tree will continue to be
> since observed by yours faithfully, God."

A resurrection perspective sees God "about in the quad."

The Gospel record of the morning shows us in stark relief, the love ethic of Jesus. We receive what we don't deserve: therefore, we must give beyond what we can produce. It is a principle of life that you can only love once you have been loved, and you will only love to the degree to which you have been loved. So allow God to wrap his loving arms around you so that you in turn can love as he loves you.

This Jesus ethic, then, is not to impress God, but rather to be like him. You are the only Bible some people will read, the only representative of God they may ever know. Be like him!

The hymn-writer challenges us with warm words:

> Could we with ink, the ocean fill,
> And were the sky of parchment made.
> Were every stalk on earth a quill
> And every man a scribe by trade.
> To tell the love, of God above,
> Would drain the ocean dry.
> Nor could the scroll contain the whole
> Though stretched from sky to sky.

Being like Jesus is not an option, but to be like him we must know him, and not some modernistic or fundamentalist interpretation of him. "Take my yoke upon you and learn of me," says Jesus. Let's start our lessons! Amen!

CHAPTER 78
THE SEVENTH
SUNDAY AFTER THE
EPIPHANY

St. John's Episcopal Church, Kingston, New York
Genesis 43:3-11, 21-28; Psalm 37:1-18
I Corinthians 15:35-50; Luke 6:27-38

[On occasion, and thankfully not often, when the current author stands to preach, there is a sense in which the Holy Spirit directs a move in a direction not hitherto planned. This was the case at St. John's on the Seventh Sunday after The Epiphany. The following reworking of the previous sermon was done extemporaneously at both services on that Lord's Day.]

This week's Gospel record is one many of us would rather delete or at least pass over, looking for another more comfortable one. I, for one, and I suspect you, too, are guilty of not living up to the spiritual ethic demanded by Jesus here. We are confronted with the fact that we are sinful in these regards. So be it. Jesus has perfectly kept these. In regard to our eternal salvation, we stand in His righteousness, not our own.

But it isn't all that easy. The fact that these texts are before us, written under the guidance of the Holy Spirit, considered inspired by the church, and therefore preserved for our good, tells us they are important. They are the ideal Jesus sets before his people. They are the manifestation of the Spirit-filled life. They are pertinent, applicable, and certainly God-glorifying when we are faithful to them.

Just because we haven't yet arrived is no excuse to keep us from moving in the direction he gives us. These are therefore road maps, showing the direction when we are lost in situations where the texts would be applicable. Their overarching definitiveness is love, and love is that gift of God that drives us toward Christ-likeness.

We begin to understand these "requirements" and the means of meeting them, when we realize the lessons of the Old Testament and the Epistle today.

First, the entire story of Joseph, loved by his father, hated by his brothers, sold into Egyptian slavery, with an up and down life of prison to palace, is a story of the providence and care of God. Elsewhere in the Genesis record, Joseph tells his brothers, "You meant it against me for evil, but God meant it for good." There is here, a conviction that whatever the circumstance, God has purposed it (even though He may not have planned it) and He is present with us in it. Jesus' promise to His disciples was to be with them "always, even to the end of the world." There is no place, time, situation, or circumstance where God is absent. Even when you sense his absence, He is present.

A cute little poem was composed by a British Bishop in answer to the skeptic who kept asking, "If a tree falls in the forest and there is no one there, does it make a sound?" The Bishop wrote:

> There was a young man who thought God
> Would find it exceedingly odd
> When he sees that this tree continues to be
> When there's no one about in the quad.
> Young man, your astonishment soars!
> I'm always about in the quad.
> And that's why this tree continues to be
> Since observed by yours faithfully, God.

That's why we continue to be – God is about. He is here – that assurance is a motivation to keep on the journey toward the ideal Jesus sets forth in this morning's Gospel.

But there is a second matter of perspective, and that is, not only is God with us, there is a future for us. We do what we do, because there is hope. The Epistle reading is from Paul's impeccable argument for the physical resurrection of Jesus (which we will celebrate now, only weeks away). Based on the resurrection of Jesus of Nazareth, Paul is assuring the Corinthian believers that they too will have an eternal future. This is resurrection perspective. It sees God about in the quad, now and always. It makes turning the other cheek and loving the unlovely part of a long term plan.

We are not a time-locked people, but a people proscribed by the resurrection from the dead. It makes living worthwhile and radically different than what the world expects.

Many of us grew up without unconditional love in our homes. Many have unlovely circumstances now, but God loves unconditionally. You can only love when you have been loved, and then you will only love to the degree that you have been loved. So as Lloyd John Ogilvie writes, "Let God love you." Then we will understand the indescribability of God's love.

The song-writer put it this way:

> Could we with ink, the ocean fill,
> And were the sky of parchment made;
> Were every stalk on earth a quill,
> And every man a scribe by trade,
> To write the love of God above,
> Would drain the ocean dry,
> Nor could the scroll contain the whole,
> Though stretched from sky to sky.

Being like Jesus is not an option, and in being like him, we must be assured of His presence now, and confident of His plans and purposes for a long term future. When we have these, we may bless more, and turn more cheeks, and therefore more heads toward Christ. Amen!

CHAPTER 79
THE LAST SUNDAY
AFTER THE EPIPHANY

St. John's Episcopal Church, Kingston, New York
Exodus 34:29-35; I Corinthians 12:27-13:13; Psalm 99
Luke 9:28-38

Today is the last day I will be privileged to be at St. John's for ten weeks. I had been asked by Father James Heron many months ago to supply for him during a large part of his sabbatical, and I had agreed. Pastor Joan had known this before our mutual agreement, and now I ask you, my home church, to pray for me while I usher a congregation through Lent and Easter. I need your prayers to be effective to a group I have never met. Pray for me. LaVonne and I will return the first of May for all of the late Spring and most of the Summer. I thank you in advance, and pledge my continued prayers for all of you.

To the texts of the day, and the wonderment of their being brought together by the lectionary editors. The Old Testament record of Moses' face shining on his descent from Mount Sinai is paralleled with Jesus' transfigured face shining on Mount Tabor at the event

431

we call Transfiguration. These are type and ante-type for sure, but we are left with the little portion from I Corinthians 12 and 13 in the middle. What would you make of it?

Initially, I think we need to see the uniqueness of the Law as represented by Moses. This is what distinguished the Hebrews, the Jews, from all other nations, they had one God, and He had revealed his spiritual, ethical will to them. We Christians are inheritors of this tradition. What we have for a spiritual law is unique and wonderful. And Moses is held in an outstanding regard by Jews and Christians alike. He was an ancient history super hero. Read his life sometime. [Or watch Charleston Heston play the role.]

Then on Mount Tabor, at the Transfiguration, this Jesus of Nazareth is changed in the presence of Moses, Elijah, and Peter, James and John. He is affirmed again by the Father to be His chosen Son, the vessel through whom truth would be revealed and redemption accomplished and applied. His uniqueness is unquestioned, and the supernaturalness of his work is celebrated. [This is done so much so that impetuous Peter wants to build three structures to just stay there and say, "the heck with the rest of the world…']

And then there is you and there is me. We are not on par with the Savior Jesus. After all, the New Testament and two-thousand years of church history tell us that He is the second person of the Holy Trinity. We are not. As good as some of you might be, you are still lousy at being God. And we probably don't even approach the stature of a Moses. But, alas, do not despair – Paul to the rescue.

These verses tell us that we are still God's people. And that is what makes us special.

It is as if Moses and Jesus are book ends, and we are the volumes in between. Moses and Jesus are chosen to lead the people, and in their faces, there is a glory that shines forth from seeing God and living.

And between them, we find Paul's admonition that we see the face of God in others.

And that has always intrigued me when I have heard it, for exactly how do we do that?

By doing ministry in the gifts of the Holy Spirit, and by allowing the Holy Spirit to work in others as well. C. S. Lewis said it always amazed him to see people who thought so highly of what the Holy Spirit said to them, and so little of what the Holy Spirit said to others. You will see God in yourself and others, when you work for God according to your gifts. My gifts are teaching and preaching; my wife's are service and pastoring. We've learned to expect from each other what God has gifted us with.

Then there is a life committed to love. I Corinthians 13 is often called the love chapter; but, in essence, if the gifts God gives me are what I do, then love is how I do them – how I practice who I am.

There follows faith in Paul's overall scheme of things. And faith is the power in which I do what I do; faith that God will takes my efforts and make them effective; faith that God will make use of me as He made use of Moses and Jesus.

The promise here is that, in the Church, there are no little people and no little places. Faith says, I count.

This is all wrapped up in hope. Hope is the anticipation with which I do what I do. I am expecting that there is purpose and plan and fulfillment and wonder and reward. What I do counts to the glory of God. This is why elsewhere, the Apostle Paul writes, "whether therefore you eat or drink or whatsoever you do, do all to the glory of God." God is making use of those He created.

Many have called this the glory of the ordinary. You and I are honored that God has called us, gifted us, and filled us with faith, hope, and love – the three graces which abide.

John Oxenham writes this wonderful little poem:

Is your place a small place?
Tend it with care;—
He set you there.

Is your place a large place?
Guard it with care; —
He set you there.

Whate'er your place, it is
Not yours alone, but His
Who set you there.

1852-1941

CHAPTER 80
ASH WEDNESDAY

Trinity Church, Fishkill, New York
Joel 2:1-2,12-17; II Corinthians 5:20b-6:10; Psalm 103;
Matthew 6:1-6,16-21

Society doesn't care for Lent. It isn't supposed to. Lent is an intensely personal time, an individualistic interlude in the calendar of a year's events where everything we're told in the church setting deals with how we live with others – how we do things together and how we accomplish things for God – in other words, how to be the church. Even last Sunday's texts dealt with the exercise of spiritual gifts in the body of Christ. But Lent is different; it takes the spotlight from the masses and makes it intensely personal.

But even in making Lent personal, we find that self likes Lent no more than society does! Since most of us have been Christian for some time, we are adversely tuned to reflecting on our sinfulness and its needs. And that is precisely why we are confronted with the Gospel record for today. It begins with a warning:

437

"Beware!" Exegetically, this word in its current context would mean to "take heed in the light of an impending danger." There is something dangerous on the prowl for those who "practice piety." Note that the practicing of piety, i.e. the doing of Godly and spiritual things, is not wrong, it is the audience before whom it is done that defines its significance. Jesus' warning is apropos to our Lenten disciplines, because it refocuses our performance.

We should perform piety, godliness, holiness. This is the distinct behavior of those who claim Christianity. But for whom and before whom it is done will determine whether or not it is either real or genuine. Piety practiced for the sake of fellow human recognition is vacuous at best and is condemned by Jesus as its own reward. Piety and godliness practiced for the sake of God is genuine and is accruable for great reward.

Our spiritual disciplines are precisely that, ours. We cannot trumpet our own, nor can we deprecate others. There is only one person we need to impress and He is none other than God. What we do here today, and over these next forty days, makes little sense to the world, particularly in our Western cultures. But it makes infinite sense to the God behind the discipline. Who, after all, are we endeavoring to impress?

If "piety" comes from "pious," it is therefore God-oriented. This is the position we hold before God.

Then "humility" comes from "humanity" and is therefore our position before our fellow creatures.

Lent therefore does two things for us (and it does this year after year, because we need this repeated tweaking). Lent teaches us:

First, see the God-centered orientation of our piety. If God is not the center of what I am doing this morning (evening), then I have my reward, and there is nothing for which I may look forward. But if God is the center of my piety, then I am absolutely and completely delivered from having to impress anyone else. I do not need to care at all what others think! I am, in essence, free. So it is into His secret presence I go, and if you happen to be around – welcome – I'm busy...

In the secret of His presence, how my soul delights to hide;
Oh how precious are the lessons which I learn at Jesus' side;
Earthly cares can never vex me, neither trials lay me low,
For when evil comes to tempt me to the secret place I go.

When the soul is faint and thirsty 'neath the shadow of His wing,
There is cool and pleasant shelter, and a fresh and crystal spring

*And my Savior rests beside me, as we hold communion
sweet,*
*If I tried, I could not utter what He says when thus
we meet.*

*Only this I know, I tell Him all my doubts and griefs
and fears,*
*Oh how patiently He listens, and my drooping soul
He cheers!*
*Do you think He ne'er reproves me? What a false friend
he would be;*
*If he never, never, told me of the sins which He must
see.*

*Would you like to know the sweetness of the secret of
the Lord?*
*Go and hide beneath His shadow, this shall then be
your reward.*
*And whenever you leave the silence of that happy meet-
ing-place*
*You must mind, and bear the image of the Master on
your face.*

Notice in our Gospel text that Jesus mentions three
disciplines: prayer, fasting, and giving. It is interesting
that all three begin with me and are oriented in three
directions:

Prayer is God-ward – keeping me right with God;
Fasting is self-ward – keeping me right with myself;
Giving is other-centered - keeping me right with others.

These are not for others' applause, but for my personal audience, God, to be delighted and impressed with my disciplines.

Then, too, Lent teaches the transcendent nature of true value. It invites us to the re-valuation of all that we place worth upon. It turns things upside down. We stress one set of values; God says, free yourself from these and embrace my values.

Mahatma Gandhi, concerned with the encroachment of the Enlightenment-gone-wild Western cultures, wrote that we are guilty of "seven blunders." They are:

Wealth without work;
Pleasure without conscience;
Knowledge without character;
Commerce without morality;
Science without humanity;
Worship without sacrifice;
Politics without principle.

Whatever you might think of Gandhi, he is right on target with the teaching of Jesus. It is the second reality of each line that is the believer's focus. And Lent brings us to the values that matter most.

We now have forty days to lift up the things that have eternal worth, and to extricate ourselves from those, which, though they give us place in the world, keep us from the things of God. Amen!

CHAPTER 81
FIRST SUNDAY IN LENT

Trinity Episcopal Church, Fishkill, NY
Deuteronomy 26:1-11; Romans 10:5-13; Psalm 91
Luke 4:1-13

There is an apocryphal story told of a chap who was without work for a long, long time. After trying every possible avenue to secure employment, one morning in the newspaper he saw an ad for help at the local zoo. He immediately went to the zoo, applied, and was hired on the spot. He job was to don a guerrilla suit and play the part of said animal for the whole day. It seems that the guerrilla had died the day before, and may school children were coming that day to see the display.

For the entire day, he swung back and forth on the vines, and ate all of the bananas thrown into him. About four o'clock in the afternoon he had had enough of bananas and prodding school children so he climbed into the tree and fell fast asleep in its branches. Rolling over in his sleep he fell into the lion's cage.

Soon the lion began his approach – closer and closer. The chap in the guerrilla suit kept yelling "Get me out of here! Now!" But to no avail. Soon the lion was right up at his side and said "Keep quiet buddy before you get us both fired!"

It seems that these two chaps were in something together. And that is how Lent is – we are in this together. All experiencing those things the Scriptures call "common to humanity...."

Our Gospel record of the morning is evidence that Jesus of Nazareth was in the same situations as we, since he, too, faced temptations. Elsewhere the Scriptures tell us that He was "tempted in all points like we are, yet without sin."

I propose that the temptations of Jesus, and His means of handling them are lessons for us in the Lenten season, so let's look more closely at the Gospel account:

First, there is a temptation to side-step responsibility. It is one thing to turn stones into bread; it is an entirely different thing to feed the hungry. It is one thing to "do this to the least of these my brothers and sisters;" it is an entirely different thing to sidestep the work involved in so doing.

The temptation Jesus faces is to move outside of the mandated role of facing and fulfilling the needs of the needy. It is so easy to circumvent the process to get to a desired end, when often the end includes the process. A quick fix to social needs and ills may be quick, but it is not the modus operandi of the God of Jews and

Christians. Jesus recognizes the temptation and knows the work ahead of Him on behalf of others.

At the college where I teach and am Academic Dean, I have several students each semester who have been raised under fundamentalistic presuppositions, and appear, at least, to others as being super pious (self-righteous is more like it). One student commenting on something I said in an Old Testament class, claimed, "Before we feed people we ought to preach the Gospel to them." An astute colleague in class responded without missing a beat: "Sometimes people are so hungry they can't hear the Gospel." Amen. Jesus recognized this and withstood the temptation.

The second temptation is to live by exceptions. Do the miracle. Avoid the work. Cast yourself down and let angels keep you from harm. This is a temptation we have to which we must not succumb. Many like to live from spiritual high to spiritual high not recognizing that most Christian growth takes place in the valleys of life. Hurricanes don't always veer away; accidents are not always avoided; cancers don't always disappear. More often than not the Christian life is one of plodding rather than soaring.

A. B. Simpson, a late nineteenth century clergyman of New York City insightfully penned this poem on the subject of the temptation to avoid:

There's a sweet and lowly pathway, leading up to
God
Four short letters mark its milestone, P-L-O-D,
plod.
If with wrecks of early promise, many a path is
strawed,
'Tis because some ardent dreamer, would not learn
to plod.
When of old the hosts of Joshua, round the ramparts
trod,
Victory crowned their seven-fold circuit, when they
learned to plod
Are you waiting for a promise – trusting in your
God?
Though He tarry He is coming, faith must learn
to plod.
Are you suffering in affliction, or 'neath the chasten-
ing rod?
God is working, wait upon Him – wait and pray
and plod.
Let us plod, steadily plod – all along life's way.
Zeal may fire and hope inspire, but plod will win
the day!

1897

Finally, and closely related is the temptation to
shortcut the path to glory. The goals and ends for
which the believer is destined are those that take us
through rather than deliver us from. There is little to be
gained from gain-less endeavors. Jesus faces the temp-

tation and fixes his eyes on the Jerusalem encounter three years hence. Ours, too, must become the vision that transcends the immediate, or we will succumb to an insidious temptation which makes the immediate dominate our spiritual lives.

Just how them, do we face and overcome these temptations?

First and foremost is the realization that Jesus did this for us. He faced temptations without succumbing. He is tempted in all points yet without sin. Thus He won over these insidious temptations for us.

[Our closing hymn celebrates this reality]:

O love, how deep, how broad, how high;
How passing thought and fantasy,
That God, the Son of God should take,
Our mortal form for mortals' sake.

For us baptized, for us he bore
His holy fast and hungered sore;
For us temptation sharp he knew,
For us the tempter overthrew!

Finally, it is of note to see that Jesus resists and the "tempter overthrew" by quoting the Old Testament in each situation. There is a power in the Scriptures, and I propose that we spend this Lent immersing ourselves in this written foundation of our faith.

You and I may not be great at memorizing Scripture, but there is something to the efforts. They come to mind at just the right time.

An illustration makes the point. When someone says they cannot memorize the Scriptures, they are directed to take a wicker basket and hold it under running water for ten minutes. "Why, it won't hold water." "No, you are correct, but please go do it anyway."

Ten minutes later they return, confidently confirming that they have a basket that holds no water. They are correct – almost.

First, it may not hold water, but it is much cleaner than it was previously, "You are clean through the word which I have spoken unto you," the Scriptures teach. And then second, since the basket is wicker, it has imperceptibly absorbed water. And so too, our efforts at getting at the Word of God.

May we this Lent be people who stand firm on Jesus' own victory over the temptations common to all of us, and may we commit to practice the lessons of the Word that it will be in our hearts and on our tongues as we need it in our regular Christian lives!

Amen!

CHAPTER 82
THE SECOND
SUNDAY IN LENT

Trinity Church, Fishkill, New York
Genesis 15:1-12, 17-18; Psalm 27; Philippians 3:17-4:1
Luke 13:22-35

I went to my psychiatrist to be psychoanalyzed;
To find out why I killed the cat and blackened my
wife's eyes.

He put me on a downy couch to see what he could
find;
And this is what he dredged up from my subcon-
scious mind:

When I was one, my mommy hid my dolly in a
trunk
And so it follows naturally that I am always drunk;

When I was two I saw my father kiss the maid one
day
And so that is why I suffer, from kleptomania.

When I was three I suffered from ambivalence toward
    my brothers;
And so it follows naturally, I poisoned all my
    lovers.

I'm so glad that I have learned the lesson it has
    taught,
That everything I do that's wrong is someone else's
    fault.

Selected

My apologies. But I just had to use this to introduce our subject of the morning. Our attention is drawn by our texts to our responsibilities as those who belong to God – the recognition that we are the center of the decisive issues which make for godliness.

G. K. Chesterton was following a series of article and letters in the *London Times* many years ago. The title of the series was "What's Wrong With the World?" Chesterton wrote a letter to the editor: *"Dear Sir, what's wrong with the world? I am. Yours truly. G. K. Chesterton."*

Every human being shares the same three basic problems in life. Our three problems are delineated this way, your past, your present, and your future.

Lent is the tithe of the year – 1/10th of the 365 days we have been given each year. And in this tithe of time, we deal with time. How do I spend it? Where do I go in it?

Notice first, that in the Old Testament lesson we are reminded of the covenant [the *berith*] that God and Abraham had between them. Now a covenant, a *berith*, is a yoke to hold two or more animals together so they go in the same direction. We are, during Lent, called on to Reflect on the Covenant. Our baptismal covenant is based on the New Covenant in Christ's blood.

We confirm this, because we believe something. The Christian is precisely Christian in this world because we point beyond ourselves to the covenant of God. To be a Christian is to live in such a way that our lives make no sense without God.

The New Testament lesson directs us to Respond with the Body. Elsewhere, the Apostle Paul, tells us that our bodies are the temples of the Holy Spirit. It is no mistake, that in Romans 12:1,2 that Paul says "Present your bodies, a living sacrifice..." Respond in Lent with who you really are. This is why abstinence, "giving up something for Lent," and the like are part of Lenten discipline – to bring the body along with the mind and the heart.

Finally, the Gospel challenges us to Reorient Ourselves Toward the Cross. There is an essential cruciform nature to Christian nurture, life, and maturity. We have that wonderful collect which reads: "He stretched out his arms on the hard wood of the cross that the whole world might know his embrace."

The famous preacher of the middle of the 20th century, A. W. Tozer tells us three compelling things about a crucified person:

A crucified person is only facing one directon;
A crucified person has no further plans of his own;
A crucified person has made up his mind that he
is not going back.

In light of this, Paul exemplifies our Lenten testimony, "I am crucified with Christ…"

C. S. Lewis wrote, "I believe in Christianity as I believe that the sun has risen not because I see it but because by it I see everything else." Lent shines the necessary Christian light by which we see our need and God's provision.

"In the heart of man a cry;
In the heart of God, supply."

Amen!

CHAPTER 83
THE FOURTH
SUNDAY IN LENT

Trinity Church, Fishkill, New York
Joshua 4:19-24, 5:9-12; Psalm 34; II Corinthians 5:17-21
Luke 15:11-32

It was a delight to hear Deacon Vivian expound the lections for us last Lord's Day. It is, for every preacher, a needed time to listen to others, to feed his or her own soul; and last Sunday did just that for me.

Today is "Mothering Sunday." Halfway through Lent we welcome the day of flowers and happiness, that though we are penitential, deliverance is sure. Easter is not far away, even though it leads us through the Passion.

Several lessons belong to this day. First is to recognize the titles the Church has given to the Sundays during Lent. They are not Sundays of Lent – a feast day cannot belong to penitential order. Rather, they are Sundays *in* Lent. The Church in her wisdom placed the Resurrection celebrations of each Sunday within the Lenten season, as well as other seasons of the Church Year, but delivered them from being defined totally by the Lenten aura. This is a serious thing to see. It is acceptable to be hopeful on the Sundays in Lent. They are not created by Lent but by Easter.

Then there is the lightness of being that is celebrated on this Mothering Sunday. Grace is the theme and grace is something that lightens burdens and grants abilities.

My father, far from being a religious man, a non-active Episcopalian all his life, used to pray one prayer when faced by people he could not abide. He would close his eyes, clench his teeth and pray to God: "God give me grace!" His theology of grace was correct. Grace is the ability to grasp truth and to make it applicable in our lives.

It was this Mothering Sunday's grace-filled emphasis which brought Percy Dearmer to pen these wonderful words of the hymn on page 145 of your hymnal:

Now quit your care and anxious fear and worry;
For schemes are vain and fretting brings no gain.
Lent calls to prayer, to trust and dedication;
God brings new beauty nigh;
Reply, Reply, Reply with love to Love so high;
Reply, Reply, Reply with love to Love so high.

To bow the head in sackcloth and in ashes,
Or rend the soul, such grief is not Lent's goal;
But to be led where God's glory flashes,
His beauty to come near;
Make clear, make clear, make clear where truth and
    light appear.
Make clear, make clear, make clear where truth and
    light appear.

For is not this the fast that I have chosen?
(The prophets spoke) To shatter every yoke,
Of wickedness the grievous bands to loosen,
Oppression put to flight,
To fight, to fight, to fight till every wrong's set
    right;
To fight, to fight, to fight till every wrong's set
    right.

For righteousness and peace will show their faces
To those who feed the hungry in their need,
And wrongs redress, who build the old waste
    places,
And in the darkness shine.
Divine, divine, divine it is when all combine.
Divine, divine, divine it is when all combine.

> Then shall your light break forth as doth the
> morning;
> Your health shall spring, the friends you make shall
> bring
> God's glory bright, your way through life
> adorning;
> And love shall be the prize.
> Arise, arise, arise! And make a paradise!
> Arise, arise, arise! And make a paradise!

I did not know that hymn for the first forty years of my life, and now I cannot get enough of it. It is so utterly grace-filled. And thus it brings us to the lections of the Day and particularly the Gospel record of what is generally known as the parable of the Prodigal Son.

Now lest we become too comfortable with our Mothering Day in Lent – too "off the hook" to be troubled by something we have not done – we are confronted with a parable that is most often misinterpreted.

Usually this parable is seen as a repentance and salvation parable, that one who is lost and away from the Father comes in utter repentance and submission asking for forgiveness. But this is not the interpretation that gave Jesus trouble with the Pharisees, you see.

This was as political a parable as any Jesus taught. There is here an important focus on three realities:

First, the youngest Son is a Son, part of the family before he takes his inheritance and goes away to a far country. He is in before he is out, before he is back in.

Second, the Father is entirely grace-filled and does not act on the basis of justice but of flagrant mercy.

Third, the elder Son is more of a prodigal than the younger, and this elder Son is Jesus' way of speaking of the Pharisees.

And so the Gospel is about grace: grace offered; grace received; grace rejected. Let's take a closer look.

So often the youngest son is the focus – even the printed sermon helps, that some preachers use, call today's emphasis "The Lost is Found." And yet, if we read this parable slowly and exactly, we find that the lost is never even sought. He is not found, he returns. There are some specifics we should look at in this Gospel record:

- The youngest son leaves, but he is still a son;
- The youngest son is in complete possession of the inheritance until he squanders it;
- He is never sought by father or brother;
- He returns of his own volition understanding that servants of home fare better than a child away.

Certainly this youngest son is a lesson for us anyone today who is not at home with the Father. He or she may be, if they will only return.

The Rev'd Albert B. Simpson, a preacher at the turn of the last century wrote this apt hymn upon preaching on the prodigal son:

Oh how easy it is to be saved,
If to Jesus you only will come;
He is waiting to welcome you just as you are
And there's nothing to do but to come.

He has said he'll in no wise cast out,
The soul that to Jesus will come;
Only come at his word and his promise believe
For there's nothing to do but to come.

His forgiveness will cover the past
If to Jesus you only will come
And his love and his grace for the future provide,
Till at last to his glory you come.

Do not struggle for feeling or faith,
There is nothing to do but to come.
He is willing to fill you with all you require,
From the moment to Jesus you come.

It is not the coming that saves,
But the Christ to whose mercy you come,
Then come unto Him, He is waiting for you,
And there's nothing to do but to come.

No doubt the father is a lesson for us in this Lenten period. He is more than understanding, and overtly and unconditionally loving. There are aspects of the father (who I believe represents God in this parable) that we often overlook:

- To be asked for an inheritance before you are dead is to be reckoned dead by the one making the request;
- The father gives;
- The father releases (freedom for the child);
- The father risks;
- The father receives and rejoices;
- The father reprimands.

And this leads us to the Lenten focus on the elder brother in this family. He is reprimanded by his father because of his refusal to be related to his brother.

- They are both still brothers;
- They are now in the same home;
- Older rejects younger, though he has not lost anything because of the younger;
- Older confesses he has not entered into the whole range of what was his;
- Older is reprimanded and reminded of his position.

What a phenomenal parable. Often its truths are missed; and the reason the parable was told in the first place was to rouse the complacent and self-righteous Jewish leadership. You have no choice but to welcome the returning.

The fact of our presence in this place makes the statement we desire to be right with the accepting parent – God. That means each is in the same homeward movement and we dare not shun any.

> To live above with saints we love,
> Oh say, that will be glory.
> But to live below with saints we know,
> Well, that's another story.

Lent calls us to rejoice. Many are coming home! That does not in any way detract from our abundant inheritance; it rather enriches the family festivities.

On this fourth Sunday of Lent, let's commit to celebrating – that which was lost has returned and we get to welcome them!

CHAPTER 84
THE FIFTH
SUNDAY IN LENT

Trinity Church, Fishkill, New York
Isaiah 43:16-21; Psalm 126; Philippians 3:8-14
Luke 20:9-19

On this fifth Sunday in Lent, the week before Palm/ Passion Sunday, we are reminded that there is so much that has been done for us in the finished work of Christ. We are today prepared to look with clear vision at the events of our upcoming Holy Week. God has done and is doing a new thing in His creation and we are invited into the party.

The lessons are strange in many ways, yet there is abundant evidence that their 2000 plus years of existence have not only stood the test of time, but have defined time's best elements.

The text seems to begin to define Jesus for us, and in defining Jesus, defines discipleship. Christianity is not a religion to make us nice, it is a relationship to make us real. And the starkest reality is that which we will begin to face in a week's time.

Two thousand years of church history have almost obliterated the biblical Jesus and given us a smiling, soft, and gentle Jesus, devoid of conviction and with every manly characteristic removed with the slick surgery of political correctness.

Notice in the Gospel record of the morning the final verses. "They perceived that he told the parable against them!" Right on. We are a people who not only need a cradle, we are maturing saints who must reckon with the cross.

Allow me a lengthy poem by Dr. John David Burton, one time Poet-in-Residence at Princeton Seminary. John David and I completed our doctoral work together.

What have we done to You, Jesus,
Proud son of Joseph's clan?
We have cut the balls from Your belly
And made you less than a man.

We have softened in sanctuaries
The voice which could crack like a whip,
We have made flabby the carpenter muscle
Which could fashion the frame of a ship.

We have shadowed the look of eagles
Which hard men could see in your eyes,
Which called them to leave every safety
For mission beneath Roman skies.

How vanished the manly compassion
You showed for a harlot's pain,
When You stood against her accusers
And called her to live again?

What happened to what Mary and Martha
Saw in You which brought them such joy?
It was more than a motherly interest
For You were more than a boy.

Who took from You the courage
Which could tame demon wild?
Whence went the strength so certain
That it could take time for a child?

The Master must have back His manhood,
That hard men may follow Him still,
And set themselves in their bellies
To know and to do His will.

What have we done to You, Jesus,
Proud son of Israel's race?
We have curled your hair like a lady's
And given You a weakling face.

We have hidden in hymns old and musty
The joy of a man in His prime
And made the hours in Your company
A solemn and dreary time.

Who will give back to You, Jesus,
That which drew men to Your side,
That we may find You in Your manhood
And in Your strength, and ours, abide?

Getting Jesus back means wrestling with the Scriptures before us.

The Gospel tells us he must be received, accepted, believed, followed. The consequence of rejection is rejection itself. God obliges his creatures by abandoning them to the results of their choices. If you don't want Jesus Christ, you need not have him.

The Epistle reading from Philippians assures us of the absolute abundant life which comes by knowing Christ. The Christian life is fuller, richer, higher, deeper than a life outside of Christ. It is, according to Paul "surpassing worth." Our life with Christ is not therefore only chosen, it is valued. More than anything, worth suffering the loss of many things.

Therefore we accept Jesus Christ; we value Jesus Christ, and the result is found in the Old Testament lesson - we know that we too are so valued and accepted. "...The people I have formed for myself that they might declare my praise." What an assignment. Our mission in life is to praise God.

"Whether therefore you eat, or drink, or whatsoever you do, do all to the glory of God." I often tell my students, that if they will see themselves in school to the glory of God, they can be delivered from pupil excessive compulsive disorder. School is school, not the judgment seat of Christ. Average is good if you know you are average to the glory of God.

In 1992 this was brought home to me by a dear little friend of mine named Tommy. At the time, Tommy was twelve or thirteen and was in my confirmation class. Tommy was the Rector's eldest son. I was the associate rector. Tommy, at birth, was a spina-biffeta baby. Along with this, because of physician error, he lost oxygen and the result was Tommy becoming a child who suffered from cerebral palsy. He is brilliant, but often frustrated because he cannot do what other children can do. He plays no sports, and what you and I would say in two minutes, sometimes takes Tommy twenty.

Tommy is my friend. One day he told me that his gift of Holy Spirit was martyrdom, and that he expected someday to have to die for his faith. And he added, "When I get to heaven, I will be able to ride a bicycle!"

There are two requirements in my confirmation classes. The first one is honesty. If at the end of the course you do not wish to be confirmed because you do not believe and therefore do not wish to be a hypocrite, I will take your position over and against your parents many times. And secondly, if you do wish to confirm your faith before the Bishop, I must have a fifteen minute conference with you when you articulate that faith to me.

Our class of fourteen had finished, and I had interviewed ten and Tommy was number eleven. He came into my study at the church and after pleasantries, I said, "Tommy, tell we what it means to be a Christian." Tommy thought for a few moments and then began a very brief metaphorical story, which took him almost a half-an-hour to tell:

"Well, Father Mackey, it is like this, we are at a baseball game (remember Tommy can be involved in no sports at all and is from a non-sports oriented family). At that game, God the Father is on pitcher's mound. Jesus is up to bat, and the Holy Spirit is the bat."

I chimed in, "But where does that put you?"

"Just give me a minute, Father…."

"God, the Pitcher, pitches me, and Jesus and the Holy Spirit can hit me anywhere they want me to go. That's what it means to be a Christian."

Well, when he finished his sentence, I needed to hurry him from my office as my eyes welled up with tears. He had it. Better than most adults I know. Tommy had it right.

Here we are on the doorstep of Holy Week. I can only think God is winding up for the pitch, and where we are hit by Jesus and the Holy Spirit, is entirely up to them, if we will only allow God to make the throw. Amen!

CHAPTER 85
THE SUNDAY OF
THE PASSION:
PALM SUNDAY

Trinity Church, Fishkill, New York
Isaiah 45:21-25; Psalm 22; Philippians 2:5-11
Luke 22:39-23:56

On this special day in the life of the Christian and of the Church, I wish to lift a brief portion of a verse from the last verse of the Gospel our good Deacon read at the Liturgy of the Palms. It effectively sums up the thrust of a week of Christian witness upon whose threshold we now stand. The verse is from the Gospel of St. Luke, chapter nineteen and verse 40: *"I tell you, if these were silent, the very stones would cry out."*

There is, within Christianity, always the tendency to keep it to ourselves, and to listen to the Pharisaic among us who think that witness is to proselytize and that this Jesus thing is so intensely personal that any public display is forbidden.

Jesus seems to deem otherwise. And the response Jesus makes to the command of the temple leaders is noteworthy.

First, there is an affirmation: "I tell you…" Jesus makes the paradigm and we are called to fit in. Christianity is nothing less than the life of Christ and our privileged status to participate. We do not make it up as we go along. It has been made up, worked out, completed, and offered to us by the one who came to "seek and to save that which was lost." Jesus never rebukes praise; rather Jesus rebukes Phariseeism. It is hypocritical to serve God and not say so; to put on the front and not to own up to the fact; Jesus is calling for, allowing, and accepting the integrity of a people who have been squashed by the hypocrisy of the systemic evil of Hebrew leadership. [And lest we get too hard on the Jews, the Church has just as great a tendency toward systemic evil in its bureaucracy].

Then Jesus deals with the impossible: "If these were silent…" He takes for granted that those singing his praises cannot be silenced. There is a song and a cry and a praise which is characteristically Christian. There is nothing like it in any faith in the world.

A great evangelist tells of his first crusade in Russia when the country was still strongly and fearlessly Communist. One of his close associates was walking (watchfully) down a Moscow street when he caught himself whistling a Christian hymn. Upon realizing this, he wanted to stop, but just then a man approached in the opposite direction. The man, dressed all in black, approached, and the associate became quite fearful; but not wishing to make a sudden change in behavior, kept whistling. As the man passed, without a nod or word, the associate heard a very intent and purposeful echo of the very song he was whistling from the stranger. They turned, looked at each other and pointed to heaven, returning on their separate ways.

There is no song like the Savior's song. The songwriter put it this way,

> Keep silent, ye mountains, ye fields and ye
>   fountains,
> For this is the time I must sing.
> It is time to sing praises, to the rock of all ages,
> And this is the time I must sing.

Scripture is replete with the songs of the believer. From the delights of Moses east of the Red Sea, through the Psalms, to the Magnificat of Mary, the early hymns quoted by the Apostle Paul, and the celestial hymns of heaven recorded by John in the Revelation. "If these are silent…" they never become silent by choice.

Finally, Jesus indicates that He will receive praise, if not from persons, then from the very creation itself. "…these stones will cry out…" And in the historic scheme of things, Jesus' disciples are in many ways silenced, and the stones become the silent testimony to the Savior.

Note the stones which do the praising:

First there is the stone rolled in front of and then away from the tomb. It bears silent testimony that He whom the system thought was dead is alive and the tomb is empty.

Then there are the stones of the Via Dolorosa – the "way of sorrows" in Jerusalem. It has borne silent testimony for two-thousand years to the Galilaean peasant rabbi, Jesus who carried a cross there two-thousand years ago.

There is the stone pavement of the Antonia Fortress in Jerusalem where, carved in stone is "the king's game," where someone would be elected king and then crowned with a crown of thorns in mockery of systemic monarchical reign – a testimony that Jesus was there.

There are stones of parish churches, cathedrals, the catacombs in Rome and elsewhere giving silent testimony to the life of Christ. Tombstones of the centuries celebrate lives lived to the glory of Christ. These stones cry out!

Finally, there are the stones of idols which in silence cannot speak. They have eyes that do not see; ears that do not hear; and mouths that cannot utter a sound. I experienced this first hand in 1985 when touring the great country of India. On an early morning trip to the Ganges River to see the funeral pyres and the witness the faithful taking their ceremonial bathes, I watched something that has haunted me ever since.

There in the middle of a small city was a life-size stone and cement elephant. It was painted bright orange and was covered with food and flowers, evidence of the previous day's offerings and sacrifices. A Hindu holy man was washing the orange elephant with a bucket of soap and water and a hose.

I asked my tour guide, "What is this man doing." His reply was confident and quick, "He is washing his god." This elephant was one of the three hundred and thirty million Hindu deities. And I was struck with the fact that the stones cry out: "Hosanna in the highest, blessed is He, Jesus, who comes in the name of the Lord." For in the Christian message, we do not wash our gods, our God washes us. As our baptismal act reads [BCP, page 307]: "Now sanctify this water, we pray you, by the power of your Holy Spirit, that those who are cleansed from sin and born again, may continue forever in the risen life of Jesus Christ our Savior..."

The stones cry out, inviting us to join their chorus in heaven storming melodies. "Blessed is He who comes in the name of the Lord." Amen!

CHAPTER 86
WEDNESDAY IN
HOLY WEEK

Trinity Church, Fishkill, New York
Isaiah 50:4-9a; Psalm 69:7-15, 22-23; Hebrews 9:11-28
John 13:21-35

After we had announced the addition of this healing
holy eucharistic service on Sunday, I spoke with
my son about the timing of the service. Liturgical scholar
that he is, he informed me that the Eastern Orthodox
churches always set aside the Wednesday of Holy Week
for an emphasis on the sacrament of unction, or anointing for healing.

The foundation of the practice is based upon much
use of olive oil in Hebrew sacred ritual for centuries,
and then more firmly on the Epistle reading of the evening from the fifth chapter of the book of James. James
in essence gives us the steps to be taken when "any are
sick among you."

The step is one of obedience, as is the approach
to any sacrament, and as in all sacraments, there is
something objectively powerful and grace-giving in the
work that is accomplished there in the believer. "If any

among you is sick…and they shall be…" There is a causal relationship between the doing what we are told to do and the receiving what God wants us to receive. It is not an earning of grace, it is the avenue through which grace travels.

Even evangelical believers who eschew the use of sacramental language saw in the Epistle of James an objective directive to do what must be done to receive God's touch in body, mind, and spirit. [i.e. A. B. Simpson; Keith Bailey; A. J. Gordon; et. al.].

This is the action step of the process of divine healing. There is also an attitude step, and this is found in the Gospel record of the healing of the ten lepers. Jesus encounters ten lepers imploring him to heal them. He does, and directs them to the Temple Priests to be declared clean so that they might re-enter society. All ten go on their way, but one turns back, encounters Jesus a second time, and does so with an attitude of thanks.

Gratitude is the attitude of healing, for not only is this leper healed, Jesus declares, "Go your way, your faith has made you whole." There is a significant difference between healing and wholeness, and the sacrament of anointing and prayer calls us to wholeness. This cannot be missed.

To vacillate at this point is to miss the posture by which we may successfully experience the next three days. The Triduum is not a time of self-reflection - that ends tonight - rather it is a time of Christological reflection when whole persons (cleansed through the wonderful disciplines of Lent) now stand (or kneel) in awe at the Christ of God.

Come tonight, be anointed, be made whole. Amen!

Let us name before God, those for whom we offer our prayers this evening....

CHAPTER 87
MAUNDY
THURSDAY

Trinity Church, Fishkill, New York
Exodus 12:1-14a; Psalm 78:14-25;
I Corinthians 11:23-32; John 13:1-15

That Jesus knows where he is going cannot be missed when reading the entire tenor of the Gospel record. There is in his mind the thought that he will soon cross the systemic line and will suffer the consequences. Even the disciples know that the danger looms and they urge him not to go to Jerusalem just now. "But the Son of Man must suffer many things and die…" This is Jesus' prediction as they trek the dusty roads toward Judah's capital.

There is little laughter as there might have been in previous days when deliverances were many; when the oppressed were freed and when the demonized were delivered. There is no levity now. It is Passover and the history and heritage of the Hebrew nation was almost not enough to sustain hope in light of the looming disaster every disciple predicted.

This was a human night. One writer put it this way: "Jesus' awareness of his impending death permeates his actions and can be compared, I believe, to the knowledge held today by the terminally ill…Jesus… may be likened to a cancer patient who celebrates an anniversary - fully aware of the 'lastness' of it all, yet celebrating nonetheless." (Lucy Bregman)

Jesus is no less human on this night, and I would ask that you follow him, with me, as he leaves the last supper with the disciples and descends into the Kidron Valley and to the Garden of Gethsemane. Here, unlike the somewhat perfected saints of two-thousand years, Jesus is starkly human – an indelible declaration of the total Incarnation of the second person of the Holy Trinity.

Jesus first says, "Let this cup pass from me…" This is his prayer for removal. There is no innate desire to drink the cup of death at this time, in this place, in this fashion. This thirty-three year old rabbi is wanting to continue on; to confront more of the systemic evils of his day; to preach and proclaim the good news that God lives with humankind, and so he pleads, "If it be your will, let this cup pass…" It is the normal, expected human step of *Removal…*

But, in prayer, Jesus moved to the second step of discipleship, to the next level of anticipation when in the second set of recorded prayers he states to the Father, "Nevertheless, not my will but yours be done…" This is the necessary step of *Resignation*. Often our wills can only get to this level as we are called by God to do the un-doable. Often this is the only humanly motivated way we can do the God-thing God calls us to do; to perform the distasteful; to love the unlovely; to go the extra mile. Sometimes the only way to bear the cross is through resignation. Jesus also moves to this step.

Finally, however, Jesus in the encounter with the authorities at his arrest states to his "willing-to-fight" disciples, "Nothing will keep me from this mission..." This is the faithful step of *Resolve*. This is the goal of our Lenten walk and mission, our discipleship and dis-cipline. Resolved to do the work of Christ. Resolved that resurrection can only come through crucifixion. That the new person can only rise when the old person is dead.

And so we stand here on this human night – re-move this cup; resigned to drink it; resolved that it will be drunk completely dry.

This is our night of resolve....

Thy will be done. No greater words than these
Can pass from human lips, than these which rent
Their way through agony and bloody sweat,
And broke the silence of Gethsemane
To save the world from sin.

G. A. Studdert-Kennedy

CHAPTER 88
GOOD FRIDAY

Trinity Church, Fishkill, New York
Isaiah 52:13-53:12; Psalm 22; Hebrews 10:1-25
John 19:1-37

B eing the right brain person that I am, I am not quite
proficient in mathematics and science. But on the
elementary level, I do somehow remember being told in
geometry and physics that the shortest distance between
two points is a straight line. I also remember when we
began cursive writing, that I was told over and over to
"write in a straight line." Coloring was always a delight
to me, and more than once I was ordered "color within
the lines!" And so I, along with many others grew up
coloring in the lines, writing in straight lines, and drawing lines by which to measure distance.

Good Friday (its name giving a hint to its paradox)
breaks into the line of what believers for ages have held,
and that is that God is linearly doing something in this
world. Smack into this line of God's acts, comes an
act that has to it a distasteful odor; an act that is best

understood by the Jew as a stumbling block and by the Gentile mind as foolishness at best.

The death of the Incarnate Son of God, which is what the church says happened this day, is as oxymoronic as opposites can be. Spending time venerating a symbol of death, and receiving the body and blood of Jesus is peculiar at best.

Good Friday. Note the paradox - we call this Friday 'Good;' Note that an emblem of death brings life; note that the crucified reigns.

The story is told of a cocky young lad who marched egoistically into the National Gallery of Art in Washington, DC. After several hours he emerged, engaged the guard in conversation and said, "I'm not impressed with your art." To which the wise guard replied, "It wasn't the art that was on trial here, it was the viewer!"

On the cross the crucified reigns; the observers are the judged.

Hear what Fr. Robert Farrar Capon writes so stunningly: "Consider the scene in church on a Sunday. Here are a bunch of people, more or less dressed to the nines; in an expensive building, with maybe very spectacular music, and even a paid choir, *deliberately celebrating the worst thing the human race-which includes them-has ever done: the murder of God Incarnate.*

"Do you see the point? They've taken the rottenest thing that ever happened and reinstalled it in their lives as a joyful remembrance. They haven't run away from the evil; they've actually made it the centerpiece of their celebration. They've taken what should have only caused alienation, and by the pardon that flows from it to them, they've turned it into a festival of reconciliation."

This is the giant contract with which we are confronted on this Good Friday. That God's straight lines are defined differently than yours and mine.

Many of us have lived through foggy times, crooked times, confused times this past year since last we celebrated Good Friday. The word is that God, in Christ, has been there before you and has been there with you.

"Where was God when my child was killed in a car accident?" cried the grief-stricken mother. The wise answer was, "Right where he was when his own son was brutally murdered, standing as near as he can be."

Senator Jeremiah Denton of Alabama was a prisoner of war in Viet Nam in the early 1970s. On what he thought was Easter Sunday he penned these words, and they sum up this day with no further comment:

The soldiers stare; then drift away;
Young John finds nothing he can say.
The veil is rent, the deed is done;
And Mary holds her only son.
His limbs grow stiff, the night grows cold,

But naught can loose that mother's hold.
Her gentle, anguished eyes seem blind,
Who knows what thoughts run through her mind?
Perhaps she thinks of last week's palms,
With cheering thousands off'ring alms.
Or dreams of Cana on that day
She nagged him till she got her way.
Her face shows grief but not despair,
Her head though bowed has faith to spare.
For even now she could suppose
His thorns might somehow yield a rose.
Her life with him was full of signs
That God writes straight with crooked lines.
Dark clouds can hide the shining sun,
And all seem lost, when all be won!

                                        Amen!

CHAPTER 89
EASTER VIGIL

Trinity Church, Fishkill, New York
Romans 6:3-11; Psalm 114; Matthew 28:1-10

A preacher stood in the pulpit one morning and held up a "victory" sign with one hand. He then preached his sermon, and then held up a victory sign with the other hand. Following the service, his warden confronted him and said, "Father don't you think that a bit presumptuous to announce that your own sermon is so victorious?" The priest replied, those weren't victory signs, they were quotation marks!

And so tonight, I will not quote someone else's sermon, but I will confess at the beginning that I have stolen a great outline from Dr. Emmanuel Scott, a favorite black Southern preacher of mine.

You and I have been raised, taught, and trained in the thinking of Enlightenment modernism and scientism. Such a presuppositional system tells us that dead people do not come back to life. Dead people stay dead.

Hidden Mirth: The Grace Behind the Goodness

John David Burton wrote:

When Heaven heard on Friday
That he had died,
Did angels plan a funeral for Jesus?
Those bright spirits had sung his birth,
Watched over him as he grew.
Surely they would want to do what many a
Family of earth has done, grieve a beloved Son
Fallen on a distant field.

Did the Father and the Spirit, broken-hearted
Leave arrangements to the archangels,
Michael to plan a litany and eulogy,
Gabriel to rehearse celestial choirs in Psalms
Of sorrow, this to tell of grief so great
That it must be expressed in song?

Were seraphim sent out to take the terrible
Word to distant stars,
That creatures of every galaxy
Could come posting in on wings of the wind?
Monday, at the earliest,
Would be a time for the whole Creation
To meet in lamentation for Him Who, even as a
Boy, had been Heaven's joy, so bright with promise.

So it was done.
They would meet to memorialize the Son,
Perhaps to embrace as earthlings do when
Caught by grief too great to bear alone.

Then, the morning before the day they
Marked for mourning,
Comes the word seeming too good to be true,
That He is alive again!
Oh, He had died, but some how, some way, He
Has taken up His Life again and will, they
Say, soon be coming home.
No! No! Do not cancel the plans for
Heaven's hosts to gather. Rather, let now
The trumpets tell that what seemed the
Hell of sorrow had become Heaven's joy,
Our Son thought lost is safe and sound
And coming home!
Change the selections for the choirs, that what
The morning stars sang together at Creation's
Dawn shall be sung anew,
"Our joy that hath no end!"

So it is done, and the victory won over sin
And death and hell is marked in songs the notes
Of which have been sung forever by those
Who have ears to hear, minds to understand,
And hearts to believe.
Still, it is worth a wonder whether angels
Planned a funeral for Jesus
When they heard on Friday that He had died.

Yes, he had died. But the news of the morning
is that he has been raised, "Just as he said." The Jews

understood that there would be a resurrection at the end of time, and Jesus merely announces it early as "the first-fruits."

But in what sense is he alive?

Jesus is alive in the Context in which he has always been alive!

- "I am he who came down from heaven…"
- "Before Abraham was, I am…"
- "I and the Father are one…"
- "Glorify me with the glory I had before the earth was made…" (John 17)

The crucifixion and descent into Hell were mere blips on the screen of God's consciousness. He died, but is alive in the context in which he has always been alive.

Jesus is alive in the Constitution of things. The creation is imbued with the life of the risen Christ. He is in persons dynamically and in the balance of creation statically. If, as the church has declared for two-thousand years, he is omnipresent, then he is omnipresent. Everywhere – in everything. He has "made the whole creation new…" according to Eucharistic Prayers "C". There is nothing which is outside the presence and purpose of Christ.

- "For by him, and in him, and to him, all things exist…"
- "For in him we live and move and have our being…"
- "In him all things consist…"

We find thirdly that he is alive in the Church of his founding. I know, I know, there is a question about this when you read the antics of the church for two-thousand years. (I could add to the litany of imbeciles, hypocrites, demons, and despicable creatures who parade themselves as members and even leaders of the church.) But he is alive in the church of his founding.

- "I will build my church and the gates of hell shall not prevail against it…"
- "To the church at Corinth (or any other abnormal city or place in the world …)"

This is the Jesus who is alive. If you want to find him, look in the church. [And this is a challenge for those of us in the church to manifest him and not ourselves!]

Finally, he is alive in the Continuity of his personality. There has been a several century move to make God the "ground of all being, "the unmoved mover," that which no higher can be thought of. But in Jesus we are told that "The one who has seen me has seen the Father...

- "I am..." – a declaration of personhood;
- "Jesus wept," – a declaration of emotion;
- "Jesus taught..." – a declaration of intelligence;
- "Nevertheless not my will but thine be done..." a declaration of will, volition.

It is these constituent parts that make a person: emotion, intellect and will. And Jesus possessed all three. It is why the writer of the Epistle to the Hebrews would declare with confidence to a discouraged and dispersed Christian community, "Jesus Christ, the same yesterday, today, and forever..." He is alive in the continuity of his personality. We do not have a God who is untouched with the feelings of our infirmities. Rather we have a God, who in Christ, knows where we live and empathizes and sympathizes with us, even today as the God-man at God the Father's right hand.

"Alleluia, Christ is risen!"
"The Lord is risen indeed. Alleluia!"

Amen!

CHAPTER 90
EASTER DAY

Trinity Church, Fishkill, New York
Acts 10:34-43; Psalm 118:14-29; Colossians 3:1-4
Luke 24:1-10

Miracles don't sit well with the modernist, scientific age which we are, thankfully, leaving. Entering into post-modernity with the help of the New Age Movement, Christianity has much to gain as we again welcome mystery, miracle, and wonder.

On a particular Easter season a child was visiting a large and prestigious church in Manhattan – a church known for its liberal theological stand. In Sunday school he was taught that the Hebrews left Egypt through the Sea of Reeds which was only 6 inches deep with water, and that there was no miracle involved. The little lad took the teacher by surprise when he countered her saying, "What a wonderful miracle that was – for all those Egyptians to drown in just six inches of water!"

Well, we won't get into the specifics of the Exodus this morning, but I would like us to view the limitations we put on Easter's miracle when we put God in a scientific, Enlightenment box.

First, let's take the fundamentalists on. They constantly harp on the facts of the resurrection past. There are, they say, (rightly I might add) irrefutable arguments for the physical resurrection of Jesus from the tomb. The arguments fall into many categories and are clear, concise, persuasive, and compelling. There are arguments made through jurisprudence by Simon Greenleaf, one of the greatest evidential lawyers ever. There are arguments from history with people like William Lane Craig and N. T. Wright, two of the greatest historians alive today. There are arguments from psychology, that the motley crew of eleven disciples could not have done what they did without having seen the risen Christ. And the arguments from philosophy, the changed calendar, the extra-biblical sources, and on and on can be added. All to say that early on a Sunday morning sometime around 30 AD a relatively unknown Galilean Rabbi walked bodily from his tomb to the amazement of all who knew and followed him. That is the focus of the fundamentalist.

Then there is the focus of the existentialist, represented by the theological liberal. What happened two thousand years ago is at best irrelevant, but we all know that the dead do not come back to life, so Jesus is alive in his spirit and lives to encourage us to live good lives. The new flowers, the Spring air, the feeling of freedom that comes after forty days of Lent, all of this is the risen Christ in our midst.

Whereas the fundamentalist puts Jesus in a past-tense box, the theological liberal puts Jesus in a present-tense box. One has evidence with no experience; the other has experience with no foundation.

And then there is the theological New-Ager. It will all work out in the end. Somehow that wonder that Jesus of Nazareth created around him two thousand years ago will again be created around the world and we'll all be one. It's Woodstock baptized into the church. Jesus, the mere name is niceness and hope. There is little, if any, of history; and there is nothing of experience of Jesus Christ, just the kind and gentle following of selected parts of the example he set. These folk put Jesus in the box of the future.

But where would we put Jesus if we would free him from the systemic-induced boxes that we often erect around him?

- We would need the Jesus of the Garden tomb and the Jesus who walked from the tomb, for this gives us a *history*.
- We would need the Jesus of experience so that we might know him personally rather than only by hearsay. This gives us a *heritage*.
- And we must know the Jesus who will bring everything to fruition because he is alive and has promised a finality to the future. This gives us *hope*.

A number of years ago I was preaching at an old folks home on a day near Easter. I knew that few people were grasping anything I had said. But every time I spoke of the historic fact of Jesus rising from the dead an old Baptist preacher in the back would struggle out a feeble "Amen!" Then I would talk about hope for the future, and a dear little old organist in the front row would repeat over and over, "Someday soon I will see Him face to face." But there was one fellow who was bed ridden – rolled into the meeting lying flat on his back. He could not speak even one word. He would not respond to his name and gave no sign of any consciousness. Frustrated that I could not reach him, I walked over to the piano and began to play an old chestnut of a hymn. Its words go like this:

> I come to the Garden alone,
> While the dew is still on the roses,
> And the voice I hear, as I tarry there,
> The Son of God discloses.
>
> And He walks with me,
> And He talks with me.
> And He tells me I am his own.
> And the joy we share as we tarry there
> None other has ever known!

When I got to the refrain, the man on the bed lifted himself on one elbow and sang every word by heart – in tune, clear and crisp. The old Baptist preacher got his historically resurrected Jesus that day; the little old organist was reminded that there is a future with Jesus Christ; and the bed ridden man who could not communicate assured us all that "He walks with me and he talks with me."

Luke chapter twenty-four reveals to us the following account, *"In the morning...two...in shining garments said, 'He is risen!'"*

What a waste!
What a useless, wretched waste, to have a
Man as fair as He crucified at Calvary,
Then taken away to a cave for a grave
With only a few to remember his Name.
And then...the morning came.

Ah! If only He had listened as we
Begged Him to,
He could have gone on with the work the
World needed Him to do.
No! He was drawn to Jerusalem
As the moth is drawn to the flame,
There to die as the moth dies,
And then...the morning came.

Pilate could have saved Him
When the priests made charge,
"This Jew brings disorder within our border,"
But the Procurator wanted no blame

So Caesar's man just washed his hands
And still...the morning came.

Even those who loved Him
Thought they had lost the game.
The women wept, Peter went fishing,
And then...the morning came.

As He died, so we die.
That body, however you tend it,
Against age and disease defend it,
Will one day decay and time have
Its way with your and my mortal frame.
Our hope is still in a Man on a hill
For whom our morning came.

Come to think of it,
Only fools will believe it.
In a world where power and wisdom are
Counted on for lasting fame,
Who would believe Death vanquished
For me, for you, because of a Jew
For Whom the morning came?

John David Burton

Alleluia! Christ is Risen!
The Lord is risen indeed! Alleluia!

CHAPTER 91
SECOND SUNDAY
OF EASTER

Trinity Church, Fishkill, New York
Acts 5:12a, 17-22,25-29; Psalm 111; Revelation 1:1-19
John 20:19-31

"Coincidences are God working incognito," said famed Archbishop of Canterbury William Temple sometime around World War II. And the Gospel of the morning is shot through and through with what the natural mind would claim as coincidences – when in actuality they are God's providences. The right people, the right place, the right circumstances, the right humanity, the right deity are all in place and the dynamic is captivating.

Afraid of the Jews, the disciples hid behind closed doors. They were being charged with stealing the body of the one who called himself "Messiah," and the disciples knew the penalty could be stiff. But there is a real sense in which each need of the disciples is met in a definitive and tangible way as the risen Jesus stands among them.

[Note that John uses the words "risen Jesus" rather than the "risen Christ," directing us to the living humanity of this one he knew so intimately.]

When the disciples were under duress, the risen Jesus offered them peace. Note that they were still behind closed doors for fear of the Jews [the systemic leadership of a flawed system], but they were at peace. Peace is not the absence of conflict, but rather, peace is the knowledge of the adequacy of one's resources. These disciples now had a risen Jesus. This was an adequacy they could not produce on their own. "Peace be unto you," is a declaration that you have the resources available to live the life to which Christ calls you.

When the disciples were under direction, the risen Jesus offered them power. "As the Father sent me," says the risen Jesus, "so I send you." This is direction. And to move in this direction, the disciples needed power, and Jesus grants them Holy Spirit. Power is from the Greek word *dunamis* from which we get our word dynamite. Holy Spirit gives us dynamic to be the sent ones of God.

When the disciples are under doubt, the risen Jesus offered them proof. Some merely saw him; Thomas needed to touch him; many ate with him; and whatever their level of proof needed, Jesus grants that level to them. He does not condemn Thomas, but shows him, bids him touch, and challenges his future doubts.

They just happened to be together – coincidence or providence? They were visited by Jesus – coincidence or providence? They were met at the point of each of their needs – coincidence or providence? It is quite uncanny that the focus of the entire pericope is on Jesus and yet the beneficiaries are the disciples. This is paradigmatic. This is how God works – while always remaining the center of everything – everyone is to receive blessing and benefit.

I wonder if Jesus ever once wished
That these eleven might rise to the task?
Could they ever be counted on to keep the message
    alive?
What will happen when he goes to heaven soon?

I wonder if Jesus ever once wished
That they would believe without proof?
Could faith be true and might they act the part
Of what a disciple was to be and do?

I wonder on that day after Thomas felt the scars
If Jesus thought – "There – that's over."
Or did he know that we would spend centuries
Asking to see the scars – show us hands and side.

I wonder if Jesus thought that day – or thinks to-
    day
I guess I'll just be faithful – grant them peace

And give them power and – well – show them
   hands
And side – so that in faith they will abide.

I wonder if, at eucharistic meal, Jesus is not there
   with
Words again – peace – power – proof –
And without missing a century's beat
Stands among his locked-away disciples once
   again.

                              Source unknown

Amy Carmichael spent her entire life as a single
missionary in the country of India. This was her life
prayer:

From prayer that asks that I may be
Sheltered from winds that beat on Thee;
From fearing when I should aspire,
From faltering when I should climb higher;
From silken self O captain free
Thy soldier who would follow Thee.

From subtle love of softening things
From easy choices, weakenings.
(Not thus are spirits fortified,
Not this way went the crucified).
From all that dims Thy calvary,
O Lamb of God, deliver me.

Give me a love that leads the way
A faith that nothing can dismay;
A hope no disappointments tire,
The passion that will burn like fire.
Let me not sink to be a clod,
Make me Thy fuel, flame of God.

Jesus, stand among us - as the risen, reigning Lord.

Amen!

CHAPTER 92
THIRD SUNDAY OF
EASTER

Trinity Church, Fishkill, New York
Acts 9:1-19a; Psalm 33; Revelation 5:6-14
John 21:1-14

All three texts of the day show us important provisions that Jesus Christ makes for his creatures. They are poignant and deep, as well as simple, everyday, and mundane at times. Jesus is the confinement of God to human flesh so that we might be recipients of his manifold provisions.

John David Burton, one time Poet-in-Residence at Princeton University writes:

God was before anything was,
By Him/Her all things were made which are made.
The Might and Mind which formed the earth
  from
Nothingness and fixed the stars in the sky,
Galaxy on galaxy, universes past all counting,
All of This was limited once to the rounded
Belly of a peasant girl, gossiped about by

Villagers, nearly set aside by proper Joseph.
This Creator comes to be held by swaddling
Cloths, later by the limited shop of the
Village carpenter, later still held by spikes
To a Roman cross, then confined to a darkened
Tomb.
From that prison grace He is loosed, that
You and I – by the world confined – might be
Through him forever free,
God confined and we are free.

There is an captivating sense in which Burton is right – God is confined for Jesus continues today at the right hand of the Father as the God-man, interceding on our behalf.

Let's approach the texts and allow them to speak to us. First from Acts 9, the encounter of Saul of Tarsus with Jesus on the Damascus Road shows us that Jesus makes converts. He takes what we are and makes us Christian believers – related to God – standing in Christ for all of time and eternity.

Dr. Gerald Kennedy of Methodist fame tells the story of a bishop in their church who spoke to a large gathering. When the gathering was over a cocky college student confronted him during the discussion and accused him of speaking only of Jesus Christ. "You never mentioned Buddha, you never mentioned the Islamic people and Mohammed, you never mentioned the Hindus." The insightful bishop replied, "You are correct my boy. Are you a Christian?" The student's reply fed the bishop's direction, "Kind-of a Christian."

"Ah," said the bishop. "I have never met kind-of a Buddhist, or kind-of an Islamic, or kind-of a Hindu. Your problem is clear. Your problem is Jesus Christ, and until you find that Jesus Christ is your problem and your answer, you will be stuck as a kind-of."

Jesus makes converts. It is expected, anticipated, empowered, that we say "Jesus is Lord. Jesus is my Lord."

Then in the second reading (omitted at the early service but still referred to), we see the wonderful worship experience around the throne in heaven from John the revelator's text, and we see that Jesus makes meaning. Our postmodern world is looking for meaning more than proof, reasons, or answers. Meaning can only be found ultimately in Jesus Christ.

Jesus gives us God which delivers us from being locked into humanity alone.

Jesus gives us worship which delivers us from valuing only the creature and not the creator.

Jesus gives us sacraments which deliver us from stuff having no purpose.

Jesus gives us wonder which allows us to know that we are part of something immense. The great writer Dorothy Sayers wrote that the "doctrine or dogma is the drama," and Jesus gives us a dramatic life centered on the wonder of who he is and who we are because of Him.

Finally in the Gospel record, we find something that I am sure on the surface you will find funny. But lest you think me frivolous, I hasten to deal with the reality of the record before us.

Whereas in Acts we see that Jesus makes converts, and in Revelation we find that Jesus makes meaning, here in the Gospel we find that Jesus makes breakfast.

Here is Jesus concerned for the disciples' morning meal. He is not only the God of conversion, the Christ of meaning, he is the Lord of the menial, the mundane, the material. Everyday, in every way, the living Christ is present in our little experiences as well as our large ones. He watches our desires and often fulfills them; He makes appearances in the lives of those we love and in circumstances where we are sure He is absent. He gives us little blessings in the midst of curses, and meets us at points where we know we cannot go on. [On Easter Day at the 10:00AM service LaVonne and I had the wonderful experience of seeing friends of many years, unchurched people, sit here at Trinity and worship with us. It was one of those "breakfast blessings" which are the specialty of the risen Jesus.].

So what do we do with this? We find that there is much for which to be thankful – the blessings are real. Jesus makes big changes in our lives; He gives meaning and purpose to our living; and He is present in the little things as well.

Soon after the completion of the Verazzano Narrows Bridge over New York Harbor, a pastor was decorating his church on Christmas Eve afternoon for the midnight service. He looked up and noticed that a major roof leak had made a terrible stain behind the alter and drew attention away from everything else. Frustrated, he went for a walk, and during his walk he passed a pawn shop, where, in the window was this lovely hand-embroidered brocade tablecloth. It looked like the right size to cover the stain, so he entered the shop, negotiated the price and left with the lovely table cloth.

Proud of his purchase, he immediately went to the church to hang it. It did the trick - looking wonderfully liturgical and new for the Christmas Eve celebration. Just then, he turned and noticed an older lady sitting in the front pew praying. When he approached, she said to him, "Father, were did you ever get such a lovely piece of hand embroidered fabric?" He told her the story. She replied, "May I approach it?" "Why certainly," said the priest. As she did, he noticed that she lifted the corner and looked intently on what she saw there. "What is it?" he asked. "These are my initials, I embroidered this tablecloth many years ago in Germany before the War."

Absolutely taken aback, the priest offered to take the cloth down and give it to her. She assured him that using it in the Lord's service was far superior to anything she could use it for, and so it was left.

The priest asked her where she lived and she replied, "Across the bridge in Staten Island, I only do housekeeping here in Brooklyn." He offered to drive her home and she accepted.

The service that night was glorious. Wonderful attendance, great singing, a moving homily - all was blessed. As the priest and the altar guild were cleaning up following the service, the priest noticed an older gentleman sitting in the front pew. When the priest approached, the old man commented on the loveliness of the hanging behind the altar. "My wife embroidered a table cloth much like that back in Germany many, many years ago. But we were separated during the War and I have not seen her in many years. Is there any chance that there are three initials in the lower corner?"

The priest, completely undone by this story assured the man that the initials were there; and sure enough, when they approached the tapestry there were the initials he predicted. The priest compelled the old gent to take a ride with him across the bridge to Staten Island. It was now one o'clock in the morning, but the man, having no family and nothing to do went gladly along for the company.

When they arrived at the home where hours ago the priest had dropped off the housekeeper, they approached the door, where - well, you can guess the rest of the story- husband and wife separated by war and many years were re-united as an indescribable Christmas present.

My question is this, was it merely a leaky roof, a resourceful pastor, a coincidental service? Was it any of these frivolous little things, or did Christ hang afresh on the wall of that little parish church that Christmas Eve? Amen!

CHAPTER 93
SIXTH SUNDAY OF EASTER

St. John's Episcopal Church, Kingston, New York
Acts 14:8-18; Psalm 67; Revelation 21:22-22:5
John 14:23-29

E aster is a wonderful story and only a story if there is no experience of Easter with which the human race can identify. And since we are still in this celebrative Eastertide, I would like to challenge us to see in the Gospel record of the morning, that there is a marvelous meeting of human need in the provisions of the risen Lord.

The cultural analysts tell us that we are in an age of paradox. We have more money and less value, more toys and less time to play with them, bigger houses with less time at home, more experience and less heritage, more titles and less opportunity to express their meanings. We are in an age of bigger is better, faster is greater, and sooner is better than later. There is a head-long rush to fulfill our lusts for prestige, empowerment, and affluence.

Each of these are goals of the Western world and goals that we have exported to third world countries as well. The loftiness of unique appointment, the authoritative manner, and the living better than the Jones' or our parents are all the purposes many have.

Along comes the risen Christ and confronts the church and takes these human lusts and longings, turns them into legitimate desires, and in Himself fulfills them.

First, note with me that the Gospel record indicates that Jesus speaks to Judas (not Iscariot) and tells him that there is the reality of love between God and His followers. There is a *position in Christ*. This is the declaration that those "in Christ" have a treasured position in which to stand. It is a position of being God's possession. We have the knowledge that we are loved by God and that God is interested in our loving God in return. We are invited to keep His word and produce a life which is blessed – God conscious.

The story is told of St. Francis of Assisi sending his monks out with the command, "Go forth preaching the Gospel. If you must, use words." We are the privileged to allow our lives to proclaim the truth of a living Christ.

The second thing Jesus says is that in order to do what God has ordained for you to do, in order to accomplish what God wants us to be, we have the *power of the Holy Spirit*. In reality, Holy Spirit is not a cloud that hovers over the church when incense is used; rather Holy Spirit is a person who is sent to be the comforter, the aid, the goad, of the Christian believer. Comforter essentially means goad – one who eggs us on....

There is much that calls for this type of power – a power unlike the power sought by the world. A hymn which was sung in the West Hurley Methodist Church when I was growing up went this way:

Be strong! We are not here to play
To dream; to drift.
We have hard work to do and loads to lift!
Shun not the struggle. Face it!
'Tis God's gift. Be strong! Be Strong!

Maltby Babcock

Even in struggles, which are the gift of God, there is the presence and power of Holy Spirit to make us be strong. Just when you think you cannot do it – you and Holy Spirit can, and will!

Finally, there is the real reaction to the seeking for security, such as the seeking for personal affluence in our culture. Jesus bids his disciples *peace*.

Peace is not the absence of conflict or you and I would never, never know peace. There is too much conflict in and outside the church, family, employment, and on and on to think that peace would ever be possible. So peace must mean something other than the lack of conflict. And so it does.

I think of the slaves of the eighteenth and nineteenth centuries in America who knew more peace than did their slave holders; I think of prisoners of war who know more peace than their captors; I think of those who suffer in multiple ways yet know more peace that those who seem to suffer not at all, and I ask what is peace?

One of my heroes is former Senator Jeremiah Denton. A Vietcong prisoner of war he tells the following story:

"In the spring of 1968 we celebrated Easter weeks ahead of the rest of the world. We didn't know when it was to fall (April 14 as I discovered many years later), so we guessed, and chose a Sunday in March. I said that we should pray for a sign that would deliver us from our long ordeal.

"I composed a poem in three stanzas. One stanza I "recited" on Holy Thursday, the second one on Good Friday, and the third on Holy Saturday. Almost all of us in Alcatraz (the name they had given this POW prison) had a deep belief in God. Thus, each stanza was eagerly awaited, and the following morning the others would scrape back their comments on my efforts.

"The poem was titled "The Great Sign." It represented a conversation on Holy Saturday night, about thirty hours after Christ was crucified, among the three women who found the stone rolled away from Christ's tomb on Easter morning.

"I made up the first stanza for Joanna, one of the holy women. It went:

His manger birth drew kings in awe,
His smile the former blind man saw,
In Him divine and mortal merged,
Yet He's the one the soldiers scourged.

"The second stanza I composed for Mary, the mother of James:

He praised the humble and the meek,
The grateful deaf mute heard Him speak,
His face was love personified,
Yet He's the one they crucified.

"The third was spoken by Mary Magdalene:

Now our tears and doubts combine,
How could He die yet be divine?
We must dispel this faithless gloom,
Let's pray at dawn beside the tomb.

The poem illustrated as well as anything the desperate hopefulness of the prisoners in our dark and lonely cells as we looked for a 'Great Sign.'"

Their sign came the next days as they were told that bombing had ended in their part of the country. The rejoicing began.

Peace, men and women, is therefore, the knowledge of the adequacy of our resources. And in Christ, you can know peace anywhere, any time.

I'm not much into bumper sticker religion, but there was one which caught my attention a number of years ago. It read:

NO CHRIST: NO PEACE
KNOW CHRIST: KNOW PEACE.

So in the midst of the search for prestige, authority, and affluence, we find in the risen Christ, possession, power, and peace. Amen!

CHAPTER 94
THE FIFTH SUNDAY AFTER PENTECOST

St. John's Episcopal Church, Kingston, New York
Isaiah 66:10-16; Psalm 66; Galatians 6:1-18
Luke 10:1-24

You are I live in a century, a society, a nation, and a time when what we do is the most important thing about us. We have been raised in a Western culture which makes demands on our persons: demands that we produce, that we succeed, that we arrive. And many of us have become fully baptized into that thinking, so that we are convinced that more is greater, bigger is better, richer is finer, and that if a little is good a lot should be far superior. We are a people of superlatives which eschew anything lacking much less normal. Normal is the enemy of special.

I have students who are ready to drop out of school because they are average; and regularly counsel people who are not sure they should go on living because they are not popular, famous, well-recognized, honored, or some other superlative position of standing.

Then along comes Jesus – usually cutting across the demands of the culture by devaluing them and recreating the true values of the reality of life.

The Gospel writer, Luke, records for us an encounter between Jesus and seventy disciples. In this encounter, Jesus instructs the disciples in three areas: he grants a commission; he guarantees an assurance; and he guards with a caution.

First, Jesus commissions these seventy to go and to be laborers in Jesus' harvest. He assures them in their going that what they are is fundamentally more important than what they do in God's eyes. He instructs them on insecurity and risk, and tells them they should not be known by the baggage they carry [a disturbing but necessary lesson for the church in the 21st century].

Could it be that we want to do rather than to be because people can see our baggage and recognize our greatness?

- We have the baggage of position;
- We have the baggage of power;
- We have the baggage of prestige;
- We have the baggage of education;
- Ad infinitum…

Second, Jesus grants these seventy the assurance of intermittent success. He assures them that sometimes their Christian witness will find results and they may stay and minister, and sometimes they will be met with failure and they are to move on. This is a strong indication that we are not to be looking for perfection in our Christian walk. [What a relief – and can you believe you heard a priest of the church say that?]. Jesus is not looking for perfection but for faithfulness, and his assurance is that perfection is unattainable.

Finally, Jesus cautions his seventy that they should not get too elated when they do have success. To pin one's spiritual security on high points of success is to set oneself up for sure failure and shattered expectations. Rather, Jesus points the seventy to the position they have in "heaven" with their names written in the book of life; in other words, in the objective realities of Christian faith. There is security – outside of this is the possibility of existential success (or failure).

Victories are worthy of rejoicing and rightly so; such as when we succeed in a Christian virtue against all odds, or some other minor class-B miracle. But this is not to be our spiritual anchor. Rather, our spiritual anchor is in relationship, a relationship which invests us with the dignity to _be_.

> People are unreasonable,
> illogical, and self-centered.
> Love them anyway.

Hidden Mirth: The Grace Behind the Goodness

If you do good, people will accuse you
of selfish ulterior motives.
Be good anyway.

If you are successful, you will win
false friends and true enemies.
Succeed in being anyway.

Honesty and frankness make
you vulnerable.
Be honest and frank anyway.

The good you do today will
be forgotten tomorrow.
Do good anyway.

The biggest people with the biggest
ideas can be shot down by the smallest people
with the smallest minds.
Be big anyway.

People favor underdogs but
Follow only top dogs.
Fight for some underdogs today.

What you spend years building may be
destroyed overnight.
Build anyway.

Give the world the best you have and you'll
get kicked in the teeth.
Give the world the best you've got anyway.

Selected and edited

CHAPTER 95
THE SIXTH SUNDAY
AFTER PENTECOST

St. John's Episcopal Church, Kingston, New York
Deuteronomy 30:9-14; Psalm 25; Colossians 1:1-14
Luke 10:25-36

The parable of the "Good Samaritan" is probably one of the most known of Christian scriptures in the whole world. The story is challenging and calls otherwise selfish and self-centered persons into life for others.

But the parable is not this simple. There is a context in which this parable is spoken by Jesus, and there are some key elements we need to see before we can pass a judgment on the text and apply it to our situations.

First, the parable is told in answer to the query of a lawyer. This person was a religious attorney who would fight before Jewish and secular authorities for the rights of the privileged classes of Judaism. He was a "company man," for all intents and purposes. He is a man with an agenda, and is owned by the system that gives him his purpose for living. He is one of "the Jews," referred to in the New Testament – not your everyday

Jew of the street, but one who is a true Jew, unlike those around him.

The second fact that must be reckoned with is that the parable is told by Jesus in the context of Jesus revealing truth to the "babes" (Luke 10:21) and keeping riveting truth from the "wise and intelligent." Jesus has very little space in his kingdom for those who have no space for others in the kingdom. This must be borne in mind as we approach this parable.

Finally, we need to be convinced that parables were plentiful in Palestine in Jesus' own day. They were often used to get a point across which otherwise might be grossly offensive spoken in pure logical prose. The parable lent itself to the hearer returning home thinking, "Now what did he mean by that?" And Jesus employs the parables as his methodology in repeated fashion to keep the Jewish leaders on their edge. He purpose is to deconstruct their false religions and show them the true God. In light of this, we come to the story.

Initially, we must see that those who pass by are known by the system to which they owe allegiance. A priest and a Levite pass by on the other side. Priests and Levites are to be people or person-centered. But these proved that the system to which they owed allegiance and from which they took their identity was systemically evil. It precluded them doing what they were ordained to do.

Any application of my life to actions counter to its purpose is evil; it is anti-neighbor and anti-Christ. Jesus was saying that as human ministers of God, the priest and the Levite proved they were neither priest nor Levite, in actuality. [Remember, we established last week that it is what one is that is fundamentally more important than what one does in God's eyes, and so, it is applied here as well].

Notice then, that the one who does help the needful person is unidentified systemically. He lifts his neighbor; he commits his neighbor to careful hands; and he commits himself to the continued benefit of the neighbor. His business is persons and he is only identified by who he is, "a Samaritan." This is an essential part of understanding what Jesus is doing in this parable. He is answering the question of a person who's life was interpreting the laws of Moses – a Jewish lawyer – known by what he did – now challenged by Jesus to be who he ought to be.

Finally, the text is plain that Jesus emphasizes that it is a Samaritan who helps the needy, and it is a Samaritan who gets the medal for setting the example of what Jesus himself means to teach. This was quite upsetting to any Jew, especially to those of the systemic Jewish model. Jesus not only puts the knife in, he turns it a bit adding that the model neighbor was a half-breed Jew – usually written off, discredited, ignored at best. This one, precisely, this one, is the carrier of the message of the parable.

The lessons are, of course, manifold. We are necessarily invited into the scene where one's allegiance is to personal integrity not to political and systemic institutions. To miss this, is to miss that which Jesus teaches, and that which ultimately gets him crucified. Jesus is endeavoring to free his seekers from finding their purpose in anything less than in God. The lessons for systemic Judaism were powerful and quite harsh two-thousand years ago. They are just as harsh today to a systemic church in systemic America torn apart by systemic racism and class-ism.

It is the person who must make the change of commitment and it is in the Epistle reading where we find the foundation upon which to make that change. Notice Colossians 1:13 & 14 from this morning's reading:

"He has delivered us from the dominion of darkness and transferred us to the kingdom of his beloved Son, in whom we have redemption, the forgiveness of sins."

The dominion of darkness is nothing less than the arena of systemic evil which is most inviting for all of us. It seeks our participation. The systemic makes us something important; all the while Jesus is coming to make us someone!

The question of the Jewish lawyer, then, *"Who is my neighbor?"* answers itself. Anyone who is a "who" is my neighbor. All definitions and divisions are null and void. Take a stand like that and it might get you crucified. Amen.

CHAPTER 96
THE SEVENTH
SUNDAY AFTER
PENTECOST

St. John's Episcopal Church, Kingston, New York
Genesis 18:1-14; Psalm 15; Colossians 1:21-29
Luke 10:38-42

I am grateful that there were no calls to me from the Vestry this week asking me not to preach after last Sunday's heavy exegesis of St. Luke's Gospel. I am not sorry for the extraordinary difficulty of that homily, and I assure you that it flows in the center of these three messages I have been privileged to preach while Pastor Joan is on holiday.

Two weeks ago we saw that what we are is fundamentally more important than what we do in God's eyes. Some accept the Christian message, some reject it, we are only called on to be faithful.

Then last week we saw that the Levite and the Priest both rejected the implications of who they were and became the opposite of their calling. They rejected being God's person in a crisis and a Samaritan took their place.

Today we are confronted with the familiar story of Martha and Mary and we find that everyone is not always right, and that we need to correct course when our way gets confusing rather than clear, complex rather than simple, aggressive rather than calm, compulsive rather than trusting.

Martha often gets the short end of the stick in interpretations of this encounter; but alas, she deserves it. Not because Jesus cares for Mary more than Martha, but because Jesus cares equally as much for Martha as he does Mary.

Martha invites Jesus; Martha ignores Jesus; Martha implicates Jesus. Jesus never confronted Martha with her compulsive behavior until Martha confronts Jesus for his allowing Mary not to be compulsive. Martha's is an "idol of efficiency," as one commentator puts it. She is into everything so heavily that everything is in her and there is no place for Jesus to be Jesus, Mary to be Mary, or Martha to be Martha. Martha had to do something to be somebody, while Jesus and Mary [and the disciples by implication] were simply busy being.

We return to Martha's actions: Jesus enters Martha's home; Jesus engages others; Jesus enlightens those who will listen. This includes Martha. Jesus uses a Hebrew oral tradition which interpreters today call the "double knock." If something is said once it is important, if it is said twice you had better listen. Jesus says, "Martha, Martha, you are troubled about many things…" In other words he wants to enlighten her into a way not of doing, but of being. The greatest Christian gift is the gift of Christ to humanity to merely be. We have nothing to earn and nothing to prove. Jesus merely says, "Be."

Many have seen the active versus the contemplative life taught here. I am not sure that is the case. If everyone were contemplative, who would do the work. What Jesus is doing is precisely drawing the conclusion that any action we perform must come from simplicity, singularity, and a life of satisfaction. We don't compare ourselves to others, nor do we compare our relationship to Jesus with others' relationships to Jesus.

Martha, it seems, did good things. But this goodness kept her from the best, and Jesus marks Mary as the model of the best part. What that was, obviously, was not the sitting and listening and ignoring the making of dinner, but the singularity and simplicity of being Mary. "Martha, be Martha," Jesus seems to say, "and stop trying to do so many things for me."

Dr. Albert B. Simpson, in the early part of the twentieth century wrote a gospel hymn which goes like this:

> God has his best things for the few,
> Who dare to stand the test.
> God has his second best for those
> Who will not have the best.

It is not often open ill
That risks the promised rest.
The better often is the foe
That keeps us from the best.

I want in this short life of mine
As much as can be pressed,
Of service true for God and man
Help me to be my best.

Give me, O Lord, the best things
Let others take the rest.
I do not want their good things,
For I have got the best.

Simpson's may not be the best poetry, but the theology is sound. God's best is that we allow God to do for us so that we can be for Him. Amen!

CHAPTER 97
FEAST OF
ST. DOMINIC

St. John's Episcopal Church, Kingston, New York
August 8, 2001

On this occasion of our second Chapter meeting of the Order of Preachers-Anglican, I am privileged to address the historic issue of preaching. Preaching is Biblical. It is essential to the evangelistic enterprise of the gospel; it is indispensable to the maturation of the church. Preaching – that simple, one-to-many announcement of the person and work of Jesus Christ for the glory of God and the benefit of humanity.

"To preach is to manifest the incarnate word from the written word by the spoken word," according to one preacher. But probably the best orientation of the truth of preaching was stated by James S. Stewart the great Scottish divine and academe:

"Through the apostolic preaching men were still encountering God in Christ. The missionary proclamation of the mighty acts of redemption was in fact a continuation of the divine redeeming activity; it was something more than a religious lecture that was going on; it was God in action to judge and save men [sic] by confrontation with the living Christ. So all down through the centuries."

That which you and I sense as a call of God is something far larger than we ourselves. We have stepped into the flow of that which God began. And let us remember that he calls it "foolishness."

There are two lessons from the Scriptures of the day. Two lessons we must assimilate if we are to be the preachers of the gospel of Christ. First, we are sent people. Sent for a distinct purpose; sent with a defined message; sent with a divine assignment. When one is sent, he or she is sent because of an ability to do that which has been assigned. We should be the best at preaching that the church can find.

Too often the church has taken its good preachers and made them teachers. But Dr. James Montgomery Boice, last Pastor of Tenth Presbyterian Church in Philadelphia speaks eloquently to this:

"Over the years I have developed a number of concerns for which I am nearly always ready to go on crusade. One is the place of scholarship in preaching. We have a pernicious doctrine in contemporary evangelicalism – I do not hesitate to call it that – which says that if a minister is average in his skills and intelligence, he should take an average church. If he is above average, he should take a larger church. If he is really exceptional - if he is keen about books and simply revels in the background, content, and application of the Word of God - he should teach in a seminary. Ugh! I am convinced that those with the very best minds and training belong in the pulpit, and that the pulpit will never have the power it once had (and ought to have) until this happens."

We are forced to agree with Dr. Boice's conclusions. And therefore our minds must continue to stretch and to grow; we must continue in training to warrant our "sent-ness" into the pulpit.

And this being our best applies to our ethics in the pulpit as well. An unknown writer aptly states:

"Given the alternatives of telling more or less of the truth, of appealing to the highest or lowest motives, of offering significant or insignificant choices, surely doing the 'optimistic' thing, the best we possibly can, is our obligation. At the same time, choosing between poor and good rhetoric, better and best homiletics, sufficient or superior persuasion should be no chore. If a preacher wishes to stretch his [sic] mind, sharpen his persuasion, improve his voice, in a word 'develop' he should consistently do his best in any sermon. He may pay a severe penalty if he does not."

A person named Doctor Koller, states, "When a preacher goes into the pulpit with less than his best, he begins to deteriorate. This may account for the loss of momentum occasionally to be seen in the ministry of man who was outstanding at the age of thirty and mediocre at fifty.' Experience has shown that the opposite of the above practice is also true. When a man [sic] goes into the pulpit with his best, he begins to grow and this may account for the truly effective Christian persuaders in our pulpits today."

The second emphasis of the texts of the day show conclusively that preaching is not the possession of the preacher, but of God. Even Jesus did not own his own preaching. The truth was vaster than he alone. Preaching is taking God and making God and his mighty acts able to be assimilated by the human heart and mind. Jesus pictured this as no other, and the men and women of the street followed him in indescribable numbers.

"Every time you present a truth, picture it; if you would persuade, portray; don't argue, imagine; don't define, depict; the quickest way past the ears is through the eyes, and the shortest way to the heart is through the imagination; no one ever possesses a truth until he or she 'sees' it for themselves."

We see this applied in the true story from Baltimore. It happens on a dark and rainy night, sometime in the mid-1930s. A young night club entertainer named Bob stumbled in a hang-over stupor into the back of a seemingly deserted church. He sat down, hiding behind one of the pillars that supported the balcony. When it was time for the service to begin, the pianist and preacher came to the platform. There was no one to sing, so the preacher preached the sermon he had prepared. Bob heard the gospel that night – alone – the only congregation gathered. And that night Bob began seeking the God who had already found him.

Bob was indeed converted, went to school and was ordained a Baptist preacher and became one of the best and most successful evangelists in America in the second half of the twentieth century. Many remember Bob; few remember the faithful preacher who preached to a congregation of one – Bob. And that preacher must have done his best, because even Bob never remembered his name, but his message changed Bob's life and many subsequent lives.

May it be said of us that "truth from his [sic] lips prevailed with double sway; And fools, who came to scoff, remained to pray." Amen!

CHAPTER 98
THE SIXTEENTH SUNDAY AFTER PENTECOST

St. Gregory's Church, Woodstock, New York

Exodus 32:1, 7-14; Psalm 51:1-18;
I Timothy 1:12-17; Luke 15:1-10

This sermon was preached the Sunday after the infamous attacks on the Pentagon, the hills of Pennsylvania, and the World Trade Center in New York City. The date: September 11, 2001.

There is a certain sense in which every preacher today must step outside of their normal approach to sermon-writing and delivery, and to step into the flow of the sorrow and suffering of the people of the United States of America. My personal approach is seriously adjusted today, and I will return to that format next Lord's Day.

At hand is the Biblical support for the Christian believer to continue to believe, even when evidence is lacking. The Biblical history, the history of salvation,

539

is replete with the assurance that God is, and that God can be trusted in the dark times as well as in the light of day.

I was in Manhattan when the absolute seriousness of the day's events began to take root. Along with millions of others, the question "why?" surfaced. Being unable to travel to lower Manhattan where my school is located (just eight blocks from "ground zero") I looked up friends on 44th Street to see if I might stay the night until travel out of the city was again a viable alternative. While there, my friend, the pastor of the large Lamb's Church of Time Square, talked to a panic stricken friend on the phone and quoted Deuteronomy 33:27, "The eternal God is your refuge and underneath you are the everlasting arms." He assured the person on the other end of the line, that when you are free-falling, what you need is to be caught by trustworthy arms.

The people of Israel in our Old Testament lesson of the morning were sure God had abandoned them because Moses delayed in returning from Mount Sinai. And when God delays, the first human response is to replace him with whatever God is at hand. The breakneck speed at which we are endeavoring to reopen Wall Street is an indication that the economy is a viable idol; the patriotic motif which is becoming so prominent (and I am all for patriotism) is an indication that the nation is becoming a viable idol; and that all races and genders are getting along in a renewed brother and sisterhood is indication that unity is a viable idol.

That all of these have their place and are good for the human family, must not displace the fact that it is God who can fill the void left by terrorist hands. Probably the greatest testimony to date is that of Father Michel Judge, the first recorded victim of Tuesday's disaster. It is more than coincidence that God allowed his ambassador to lead the way to death – a way that many hundreds will, no doubt, follow.

Years ago, my pastor at the West Hurley Methodist Church, the Rev'd J. Filson Reid was manning a call-in Christian radio broadcast over WGHQ. A woman called in accusing God of delaying his presence when her daughter was killed by a drunk driver. "Where was your God when my daughter was killed?" she cried. And a calm, faith-filled Pastor Reid responded, "Right where he was when his own son was killed – standing nearby weeping and grieving."

Today, God appears to be delaying. Yet God is present – present in the order of creation, present in the love of persons, present in the work of compassion, present in the counsels of the righteous. And God is weeping and grieving. And it is God's presence which must be recognized to keep us from idolatry.

Centuries ago, Francis Bacon aptly wrote that "four species of idols beset the human mind: idols of the tribe; idols of the den; idols of the market; and idols of the theatre." We must be cautious lest we bow before any of these.

America is God's nation only in the sense that all nations are God's nation – do not worship it.

Christians who were spared death in the disaster were only spared in the way persons of any faith or no faith at all were spared. We dare not worship a triumphalism which is not ours.

The markets of America have been closed for a week, and just because they open on Monday is no guarantee of anything – do not worship them.

News-people are endeavoring to outdo each other in stories and pictures, often passing along lies, innuendo, and error – do not worship their theatrics.

Someone has aptly stated that we each share three common problems: our past, our present, our future. And so we do. Many feel we have lost our past, that we struggle with out present, and they question if we have a future. But we must not forget that Moses comes down in God's time, not at the demands of irritated Israel. And we see that our three common problems are addressed by God:

- God finds us best in our lostness;
- God aids us best in our weakness;
- God teaches us most in our confusion and ignorance.

In post-World War II America, on January 10, 1948, a keen and wonderful thing happened to show the faithfulness of God. The story is true and involves three persons: Marcel Sternberger, Bella Paskin, and Maria Paskin.

It happened one day in the mid-1940s that Marcel Sternberger, who always rode the same Long Island Railroad train to work in New York City decided to stop off and visit a friend in a Brooklyn hospital. After the visit, Sternberger began to board a Brooklyn subway line he had never ridden before to complete the trip into work. As he boarded, he noticed there were no seats, until, just as the doors were to close, a man rushed from the train leaving one seat open. Sternberger sat down and noticed that the man next to him was reading an Hungarian newpaper. Sternberger read Hungarian. He engaged the man in conversation asking if he was looking for employment since he was in the "want ads" of the paper. "No," came the reply, "I am looking for my wife."

And the Hungarian began to tell Sternberger the story of how he was taken away to prison camp during the war, and when he returned his wife was nowhere to be found. Sternberger asked his name. "Bella Paskin," came the reply.

Sternberger asked Mr. Paskin to detrain with him at the next stop. As they left the subway, Marcel Sternberger removed a piece of paper from his wallet. A woman had given it to him at a party the week before. It bore her name and phone number. Sternberger called the number.

"Maria Paskin?" asked Sternberger. "Yes." "Would you tell me your missing husband's name?" "Bella Paskin," was the reply. "And where did you live in Hungary?" And the address was given. The man standing with Sternberger confirmed each answer. Sternberger handed Bella Paskin the phone with the words, "Mr. Paskin, speak with your wife."

The magazine, *Readers' Digest* ends its story this way:

"Even now it is difficult to believe that it happened. We have both suffered so much; I have almost lost the capacity to not be afraid. Each time my husband goes out from the house I ask myself, 'Will anything happen to take Him away from me again?'

"Her husband is confident that no overwhelming misfortune will ever again befall them, 'Providence has brought us together,' he says simply. 'It was meant to be.'

"Skeptical persons would no doubt attribute the events of that memorable afternoon to mere chance.

"But was it chance that made Sternberger suddenly decide to visit his sick friend and hence take a subway line that he had never been on before? Was it chance that caused the young man sitting by the door of the car to rush out just as Sternberger came in? Was it chance that caused Bella Paskin to be sitting beside Sternberger, reading a Hungarian newspaper? Was it chance – or did God ride the Brooklyn subway that afternoon?" [from *The Readers' Digest*]

Chance or God – we can idolize the former, or sink into the providential arms of the latter. And that brings me to the Scripture my friend quoted on the phone, "The everlasting God is your refuge and underneath you are the everlasting arms." A. B. Simpson sings it this way:

Are you sunk in depths of sorrow
　　　Where no arm can reach so low?
There is one whose arms almighty
　　　Reach beyond your deepest woe.
God the Eternal is your refuge,
　　　Let it still your wild alarms,
Underneath your deepest sorrow
　　　Are the everlasting arms.

Other arms grow faint and weary
　　　God's can never faint or fail
Others reach our mounts of blessing
　　　These our lowest, loneliest vale.
Oh that all might know God's friendship
　　　Oh that all might see God's charms
Oh that all might have beneath them
　　　Jesus' everlasting arms.

Underneath us, Oh how easy
    We have not to mount on high
But to sink into God's fullness
    And in trustful weakness lie.
And we find our humbling failures
    Save us from the strength that harms
We may fall, but underneath us
    Are the everlasting arms.

CHAPTER 99
THE SEVENTEENTH SUNDAY AFTER PENTECOST

St. Gregory's Episcopal Church, Woodstock, New York
Amos 8:4-12; Psalm 138; I Timothy 2:1-8 & Luke 16:1-13

Today's gospel record is one of the most familiar in the entire Scriptures. We read of the "rich man and Lazarus." The story is not only familiar, it is often mis-told and remembered amiss. We use the parable to form all kinds of doctrines – a sad commentary on our desire to see those punished who deserve it. The supporting reading, however, may serve to correct our reading of the Gospel and to shed light on the depths of a simple meaning which Jesus intended.

The simple lesson is that *whatever we are, and whatever we have, we receive, we do not merit.* The lesson is the humility of being provided for by God. The key verse in the parable reads this way, "you in your lifetime received your good things…" The key is reception. To forfeit this for meritorious action is to miss both the grace of God toward us and the resulting commonality it makes of us with our fellow human beings.

People often feel that the rich man goes to hell because he didn't treat Lazarus rightly. That is a heretical misreading of the text concluding that we are redeemed by our works. Nothing is farther from Jesus' mind. The whole issue is this: "If they do not hear Moses and the prophets, neither will they be convinced if some one should rise from the dead." It is a declaration that people will not receive what God offers, but would rather live by what they produce.

> What I produce is measurable-
>> What God offers is limitless;
> What I produce I take praise for-
>> What God gives deserves thanksgiving;
> What I produce may become hellish-
>> What God gives is heavenly;
> What I produce is temporal-
>> What God gives is transcendent;
> What I produce is personal-
>> What God gives is inter-personal;
> What I produce may be oblivious of others-
>> What God gives is community.

This is precisely the essence of the parable. The richness of the one and the poverty of the other are coincidental to the central focus of our Lord. The warning of Amos in the Old Testament lesson of the day is a warning against pious smugness which exudes the image, I deserve. The warning of the Epistle reading is that we must consciously remove from ourselves the thought that we are spiritually self-sufficient and self-made. Someone once said, "I could tell he was a self-made man, the workmanship was so poor." We are best made when we are God-made. And so, when we are God-made, according to Paul in his First Letter to Timothy, we find several things are demanded of us.

First, we refocus our aims. Paul tells Timothy to aim at righteousness, godliness, faith, love, steadfastness, gentleness. These sound vaguely familiar to the list of the fruit (singular) of the Holy Spirit in Galatians 5:22,23 where Paul writes, "The fruit of the Spirit is love, joy, peace, longsuffering, kindness, goodness, faithfulness, gentleness, self-control." Paul indicates that people of the Spirit are bearing a differing quality of demeanor and purpose. Refocus our aims, says Apostle Paul. We may not always be right, but we can aim at being Christ-like.

Second, Paul writes, fight the good fight of faith. There is something inherently difficult to the Christian life. Faith, which is related to "eternal life" in Paul's words, may be just the most difficult faith to possess and maintain. It is freely given and, therefore, received only with gratitude and humility. Therefore, the fight of faith is the fight with the self which would claim the glory, the praise, and the merit for what we have done. Again, it is hard to give anything but gratitude to a God who gives everything! Fighting the good fight of faith has no adversary but the old self, and it is a formidable foe!

Third, and finally, Paul directs that we "keep the commandments unstained and free of reproach." The operative word here is "keep." Does Paul mean that we must keep them in the sense of being perfect? If so, it is an impossible injunction. But the essence of the word is "to watch over, or preserve" (Vine). It does not dictate perfect fulfillment of the commandments of God (Jesus alone did that). Rather it is a strong injunction that we not diminish God's standard because we cannot keep it. Rather, we honor the commandments and keep them free of reproach when we manifest the fruit of the Spirit. What is the best testimony to God and the word is not form, but freedom; not conformity, but a heart of flesh. Just because we are redeemed sinners who, this side of glory, will never be perfect, does not indict the commandments as unreasonable or unfathonable. They are a declaration of God's standard, and as such we honor them even in our weakness and sinfulness.

All of this brings us back to the Gospel of the day. We are persons who have received. What are we that we have not been made; what do we have which we have not been given?

Back in the nineteenth century a gospel song-writer put the words to poetry:

What have I gotten but what I received?
Grace has bestowed it, now I believe;
Boasting excluded, pride I abase;
I'm only a sinner, saved by grace.
Adapted from James M. Gray (19th Century)

If we are people of obtainment instead of attainment, we will be delivered from measuring ourselves against others – for there is always someone better than we and we can always find someone worse that we. By God's grace, we are what we are. God has so given. Let us be glad. Amen!

CHAPTER 100
THE EIGHTEENTH
SUNDAY AFTER
PENTECOST

Resurrection Church, Hopewell Junction, New York
Habakkuk 1:1-6, 12, 13, 2:1-4; Psalm 37:1-18
II Timothy 1:1-14; Luke 17:5-10

The great British journalist G. K. Chesterton once said "Anything worth doing was worth doing badly." I believe today's Gospel record would support the Chestertonian statement. The statement could be seen as a brief commentary of the words of Jesus.

As I turned to today's lessons in an old copy of the "C" year lectionary booklet, which I had saved from destruction at the hands of an unwise sexton, someone had written in the margin, "Serving can be thankless...." Amen to that! Any of you who have given of yourself in the service of God, the church, and others, know by experience that much of the service that you do is done without recognition. If you want recognition, don't enter service-oriented professions or avocations.

A number of related thoughts can be drawn from the texts of the day. First, the prophet Habakkuk assures frail and fearful believers who are sure they are not up to the task, that "the righteous ones will live by their faith." It is a faith thing, a mental and spiritual orientation, fixed on the God who keeps promise. There is nothing of perfection, keeping the commandments, doing great exploits for God, or anything of the sort. The "righteous ones will live by faith." The requirements are nil, nada, none at all. Believe.

The hymn-writer of the early twentieth century put it this way:

> Fear not, little flock, from the cross to the throne;
> From death unto life, Jesus went for his own.
> All power on earth, all power above,
> Is given to Him for the flock of God's love.
>
> Fear not, little flock, He goeth ahead,
> Your Shepherd selecteth the path you must tread;
> The waters of Marah he'll sweeten for thee,
> He drank all the bitter in Gethsemane.
>
> Fear not, little flock whatever your lot,
> He enters all rooms, the doors being shut;
> God will never forsake, God never is gone,
> So count on God's presence in darkness and dawn.
>
> Only believe, only believe,
> All things are possible, only believe.
>
> Paul Rader circa 1921

The epistle reading assures us that we must continue by faith in our life of belief. "I know whom I have believed," says Paul, "and am persuaded that he (Jesus) is able to keep that which I have committed unto him, against that day." (The Revised Standard rendering, this author believes is inaccurate).

Paul is saying that we are to entrust ourselves to God's care, and know that what is entrusted to God's care is cared for.

The illustration of this best comes from the airline industry. There are two types of baggage on an airplane. Your carry on which is yours and your checked luggage which becomes theirs until you claim it. If you lose your carry on and ask for reimbursement, you are laughed from the claims office. If they lose your luggage they pay. They will keep that which you commit unto them (more or less – hey it is an illustration!).

Finally our Gospel reading is the simple lesson that we should be a servant by faith. Faith doesn't think about our faith; it does what is necessary. It believes, behaves, and serves.

Oh, back to that Chesterton statement – "Anything worth doing is worth doing badly." Why? Because anything worth doing is simply worthy doing. The value is in the doing of it not in the quality of the doing or in the product produced. These are merely coincidental to the doing.

And so, serving can be thankless – serve anyway. Living by faith can be difficult – live by faith anyway. Continue in faith – but continue. Serve by faith, but serve.

Several years ago a preacher who I cannot track down wrote these words. I have used them with graduating seniors a number of times in the past, and they are appropriate for us today:

"People are unreasonable, illogical, and self-centered.
Love them anyway.
If you do good, people will accuse you of selfish ulterior motives.
Do good anyway.
If you are successful, you will win false friends and true enemies,
Succeed anyway.
Honesty and frankness make you vulnerable.
Be honest and frank anyway.
The biggest people with the biggest ideas can be shot down
By the smallest people with the smallest minds.
Think big anyway.
People favor underdogs but follow top dogs.
Fight for some underdogs anyway.
What you spend years building may be destroyed overnight.
Build anyway.

Give the world the best you have
And you'll get kicked in the teeth.
Give the world the best you've got anyway.

The reason is simple. It is the doing of the gospel of faith. Amen!

CHAPTER 101
THE NINETEENTH SUNDAY AFTER PENTECOST

St. Gregory's Episcopal Church, Woodstock, New York
Ruth 1:1-19a; Psalm 113; II Timothy 1:3-15
Luke 17:11-19

When we find records of Jesus' encounters with people, they are often recorded because they are stark reminders of what truth does when it confronts error. Jesus has a mission, and those who fail to perceive the truth of it are often the recipients of the barbs, which are implicit in the actions and words of the encounters.

This is no less true in the Gospel record of the morning. Everything there is about the story is so very Palestine in the first century. The only place Jews, Gentiles, and Samaritans could be grouped together was in the pathos of this leprosy. It was precisely their morbid estate that allowed them to unite. [The implications of this for the church may be vast since leprosy is often an metaphor for sin in the Bible]. But they were a pathetic group, thrown together by their terrible condition.

Ten lepers approach rabbi Jesus. They know by hearsay that this one heals people, and this is precisely their need. Nothing else much matters; and so they come as close as leprosy allows and they plead. Jesus hears; Jesus heals. End of story.

No. Not so fast. There is something of essential, foundational truth here which dare not be missed – and it is so very needed in the days in which we live.

First, note Jesus' acceptance of the whole group un-qualifiably. There is no standard to meet; no merit to prove; no pedigree to display; no racial or ethic quality to manifest. That they were lepers was enough. They had a need. Jesus meets needs.

This is so very important, precisely because Jesus lived in a day when pedigree was predominant. You and I live in a similar day. The various criteria which we use to evaluate others are multiple, but each one is a bastard standard, illegitimate at best – when Jesus allows anyone to make approach. There is no quality which God finds more appealing than to be, quite simply, unqualified.

The second thought is quite like the first: Jesus heals the ten individuals indiscriminately. There is no appar-ent order of healing that is of any consequence; there is no varying degree of wellness which comes forth in this healing gesture; there is nothing which sets any one apart from the other ten. Need is met by supply. Desire is met by will. A. B. Simpson of the nineteenth century simply put it this way: "In the heart of man a cry; in the hear of God, supply." Nothing more, no improvement, nothing better.

The story is artfully recorded here. Jesus tells them to "go and show yourselves to the priests," in obvious obedience to the Levitical Law of the Hebrew Scriptures. And when they begin to move in obedience to his directive, they were cleansed (a word often employed to describe the healing from leprosy which was considered a "dirty" disease). Simple going is met by thorough cleansing.

Finally, the wholeness of one individual is discovered unpredictably. The one who returns to Jesus does indeed obey the injunction to show himself to the priest. Jesus, unbeknown to this one, is the great high priest, as Scripture will tell us several years hence. But he returns to give thanks, and in giving thanks, he is "made whole."

There is an infinite difference between mere healing and abundant wholeness. Many get the initial healing from the hand of God and then miss the added blessings by forgetting the next step of radical gratitude. When God acts in grace, the only posture is gratitude.

But the focus of the record of this incident in the Gospel is to show that Jesus finds the spiritual wholeness he seeks in a Samaritan, this foreigner. At best he was considered a half-breed – despised and rejected by those of pure Hebrew blood. But Jesus uses the incident to make a good example of the one who returns with abundant thanks. It is the foreigner whose faith has made him whole. And this is the lesson Jesus has been working toward.

Men and women, God wants us to find the lessons of heaven in the least likely places. We think we should find them in church and in the canon of Holy Scripture, but they are often found elsewhere. You would think in this encounter of Jesus with ten lepers, that the most spiritual one was the one who was the best and most faithful Hebrew. It was not; it was a foreigner.

The lesson is stark and should call all of us to note where we find God's communication of grace and truth.

Dr. John David Burton, one time Poet-in-Residence at Princeton University and colleague of mine in our doctoral program, writes convincingly:

> Watch out from Grace and Truth.
> They may appear, so well-disguised it is hard to
> tell just who is there, Incognito God.
>
> Grace and Truth appear as usual much of the time,
> tenor on the high note in the Christmas choir,
> lily-scented ecstasy on Easter morn.
> Then Grace and Truth surprise us all, showing up
> to kick the hell out of Pharisees who prostitute
> women in bondage as savage as that of any pimp.
> Present-day Pharisees do it, of course, in the
> name of the Bible, *a la* Southern Baptists and
> pseudo-

Presbyterians, all unworthy successors to
the Bishop of Paris, saying to Joan of Arc,
"In Nomine Jesu, I light your fire,"
this, of course, after the Maid of Orleans had
won the day for God and France,
Grace and Truth will not hold still for men to
prostitute women, using God as the excuse.

One Philadelphia day, Grace and Truth sat down at
a table with deist Thomas Jefferson and Franklin
the inventor, Grace and Truth joining to scoff
at George the Third and his "Divine Right of
      Kings."

Grace and Truth got shot one day on a Memphis
motel balcony.
Some said a Baptist preacher named Martin Luther
King got what he had coming,
not knowing that Grace and Truth would get up
from that bloody floor to march around the world
to Johannesburg and beyond.

Watch out for Grace and Truth.
They show up as usual most of the time,
tenor on the high note in the Christmas choir,
lily-scented ecstasy on Easter morn.
Other times Grace and Truth appear in such
disguise it is hard to tell just Who is there,
Incognito God.
                    Watch out for Grace and Truth.

In our Gospel story it is the Samaritan leper who shows us Grace and Truth. Keep your discerning eyes open so that we can tell just Who is there. Amen!

CHAPTER 102
THE TWENTIETH SUNDAY AFTER PENTECOST

St. Gregory's Episcopal Church, Woodstock, New York
Genesis 32:3-8, 22-30; Psalm 121; II Timothy 3:14-4:5
Luke 18:1-8a

There is an apocryphal story told of two despicable brothers. As children they were the incarnation of evil; as teens, they terrorized their small town; and as adult men they were the worst of the worst – dishonest, lacking all integrity, lying, and deceitful. They were indescribably bad.

In the course of time, one of the brothers died. The remaining brother went to the priest and offered $10,000 to the priest and $10,000 to the parish, if, at the eulogy, the priest would call his brother a "saint."

The priest was in a terrible dilemma. What would he do? The day of the funeral came, and during the eulogy, the priest waxed truthfully eloquent. "We know that this man before us was one of the most horrible persons who has ever lived on God's earth. Every evil that could be perpetrated he has perpetrated. He had, as best as we all can tell, no redeeming qualities. But compared to his brother, he was a saint!

Naming something is important. It tells us of the character behind the name. Shakespeare, in considering the rose by any other name, concluded that it would smell as sweet, and left the name "rose."

Our encounter with Jacob in the Old Testament lesson this morning is an encounter of identity. If you will remember the last time Jacob is asked what his name is, it is asked by his blind father Isaac as he was intending to give the patriarchal blessing to his eldest son. Jacob lied and said he was Esau, and he has been living with the deceit ever since. Now he asks the angel of God who wrestles with him to give him a blessing, but the blessing is dependent upon Jacob's owning up to who he is. Finally he says, "My name is Jacob," and he receives the blessing. Though he limps away from the encounter, he is a new man, for he now is honest before God and with himself.

The Christian faith calls us to own who we are. Never are we threatened in the Gospel to become someone we are not, nor were ever intended to be.

The pathetic story of the life of Leo Tolstoy is a model and a picture of what we must never be. "He could never achieve the self discipline to abide by his own rules," writes Philip Yancey of Tolstoy. "His desire to reach perfection led him to devise ever new sets of rules." His wife Sonya's diary reads:

"There is so little genuine warmth about him; his kindness does not come from his heart, but merely from his principles.

"His biographers will tell of how he helped the laborers to carry buckets of water, but no one will ever know that he never gave his wife a rest and never – in all these thirty-two years – gave his child a drink of water or spent five minutes by his bedside to give me a chance to rest a little from all my labors.

"'Where is his love?' she demanded after one violent shouting match. 'His nonresistance? His Christianity?' He never showed affection toward the children who consumed so much of her life. The one who professed so much love of humanity had difficulty loving any single individuals, even the members of his own family."[2]

Tolstoy is the infamous example of a person who loved God without identifying who he was so that God could love him. Jacob comes to that place. We are invited also.

And if the Old Testament lesson tells us to claim who we are, the Epistle reading encourages us to read what we are told. Paul instructs Timothy to continue in what he has learned and believed, and leads him to the unquestionable place of Scripture in the life. There is a

---

[2]Taken from Philip Yancey's *Soul Survivor: How My Faith Survived the Church.* I highly recommend this book for believers who have been abused by the churches they have attended and/or served.

deep-seated need for the Christian believer [as there is for the Jew] to read the book which we claim is inspired by God.

The instruction of Paul is that the Scriptures are beneficial. His words are "inspired by God and profitable." And Paul lists four profits we can take away from the Holy Scriptures:

As teaching – it tells us what *is* right;
As reproof – it tells us when we are *not* right;
As correction – it tells us how to *get* right;
As training in righteousness – it tells us how to *stay* right!

This is the applicability of the Holy Scriptures to the life. Jesus has said, "You search the scriptures for in them you think you have eternal life." And he was commending their search. May we, too, read and listen to the Scriptures.

Finally the Gospel is a record of simple instruction, and that is to pray. Jesus' directives here are for those who hear him to bombard God with those things which have import in their lives.

Lawrence Leshan, PhD., an experimental psychologist from New York, established through his research that there was a connection between healing prayer and actual wellness. There was an efficacy to the prayers of those who emotionally established themselves with those for whom they prayed. Simply put, one commentator on today's Gospel says, just PUSH – Pray Until Something Happens.

A true story with which to end our discovery this morning. In the late 1980s a young mother, let us call her Helen, found that she and her husband were expecting their second child. Soon tests showed that the baby would have an external spine if carried to term. Their doctor recommended abortion. But the couple was committed to pro-life values, and they asked if I would pray for them. Each Sunday for six months, the young mother-to-be would kneel at our altar rail and I would anoint her with oil and pray. As the months went by, many in the parish along with me wondered how God would work in this situation. One Sunday morning the call came. Helen had given birth to a perfectly healthy baby girl. Mother and new daughter were completely healthy.

"Simplicity, wholeheartedness, and repetition in prayers, characterized the behavior of the widow with the unjust judge. And she was granted justice."[3] Amen!

---

[3] From *Sythesis*, October 21, 2001.

CHAPTER 103
THE TWENTY-FIRST SUNDAY AFTER PENTECOST

St. Gregory's Episcopal Church, Woodstock, New York
Jeremiah 14:1-10, 19-22; Psalm 84;
II Timothy 4:6-8, 16-18 & Luke 18:9-14

A small boy was in Sunday school one morning when the teacher was teaching the lesson of Lot's wife, who, when she turned to look back at Sodom and Gomorra, turned into a pillar of salt. "That's nothin'," said the little chap, "my mom was driving down the street and she turned to look back at a yard sale and turned into a telephone pole."

The Rev'd Arthur Oudemool, one time pastor of Old Dutch Church in Kingston, New York claimed on his call-in prayer line that we must "watch where you are going, for you will inevitably go where you're watching." The point is that the aim is of fundamental importance. The starting point, facing the right direction makes all the difference to the journey. And this is the foundational lesson of the Scriptures of the morning.

Several phrases from the three lessons of the morning are germane to the central theme:

- "O, Lord, for your name's sake, act..."
- "The Lord...to him be glory for ever and ever. Amen!"
- "Jesus told this parable to some who trusted in themselves that they were righteous and despised others."

Each supports and supposes the truth that God is the central focus of the life of faith, and not we ourselves. And this is difficult medicine to swallow when we live in a culture and a society which deems each of us individually as the purpose for existence.

In the flow of all of this autonomous individualism, God comes to be the center; the still-point, amid the chaos of self and sin.

Friends of mine, The Rev'd Bill and Gracie Cutts served for more than forty years as missionaries to the Doni people of Irian Jaya, Indonesia. They truly took Christianity to these people without taking Western culture to them. In translating the Bible, they wished to translate "Alleluia" for them, but could find no word or words readily available. One day, working with the native interpreter, a particular passage was successfully translated when the interpreter said in his own tongue what was literally, "Make God big!" It was an equivalent to the "Alleluia" which Bill and Gracie had exclaimed. They had their words for Alleluia – "Make God big." That is exactly what the Scriptures of the day teach. That you and I, "humanity," is never more fully human than when it places God on the throne of the universe and "Makes God big!"

And so the Scriptures give us several directions which are taken from the texts.

First, we aim at protecting and affirming the impeccable reputation of God. It is God's reputation that is flawless – not possible to say about the church's. And so to turn attention to God brings success, where bringing attention to the church or to individual Christians may just bring the opposite result.

The prophet Jeremiah, one of Judah's favorites, sought deliverance not for his good or even the good of the nation, but that Jehovah's name be protected. Jeremiah was jealous for God, and the lesson is movingly powerful.

Second, Paul, in sharing the inevitability of his impending death, shares that the glory for any good belongs to God and not to him. [It really is one of Paul's better moments when he seems to forget somewhat about himself, for his besetting sin seemed to be pride]. And here Paul is sure of his faith in God because God will do what fulfills God's own purpose – what is beneficial for the Kingdom. It is a marvelous injunction that leads us to understand that we are part of something marvelously larger than we ourselves.

The great mind, G. K. Chesterton writes:

"We are all creatures through space, clinging to a cannonball....An invisible force holds us in our own armchairs while the earth hurtles like a boomerang; and men still go back to dusty records to prove the mercy of God."

That we continue in the light of human history is nothing less than the outworking of the Kingdom in the midst of chaos. We are, precisely, recipients of abundant mercy.

Finally, the parable of the Gospel account of the morning makes trust in oneself and comparisons with others anathema. It is a non sequitur, a dead end, a cull de sac on the road of life. It takes us nowhere at all. Seeking from God is the antidote to utter selfishness. Placing the focus on the things of the Spirit places other things within the scope of focus and clarity. A Christian world-view results - God on the throne of the universe and humanity basking in the wonder of grace, mercy, and peace. We "go down to our homes justified..." in the words of the parable.

In 1943, in the throws of World War II, the great C. S. Lewis wrote:

"Doctrines are not God: they are only a kind of map. But that map is based on the experience of hundreds of people who really were in touch with God—

experiences compared with which any thrills or pious feelings you and I are likely to get on our own are very elementary and very confused….If you want to go any further, you must use the map….In other words, theology is practical….If you do not listen to theology, that will not mean that you have no ideas about God. It will mean that you have a lot of wrong ones -bad, muddled, out-of-date ideas. For a great many, the ideas about God which are trotted out as novelties today, are simply the ones which real theologians tried centuries ago and rejected.

"Aim at heaven and you will get earth "thrown in"; aim at earth and you will get neither.

"Aim at heaven and get earth thrown in" – that is what the lessons of the day assure us.

Possibly this is said best by Elizabeth Barrett Browning in these words:

"And I smiled to think God's greatness flowed around our incompleteness; 'Round our restlessness, His rest." Amen!

CHAPTER 104
THE TWENTY-SECOND SUNDAY AFTER PENTECOST ALL SAINTS' SUNDAY

St. Gregory's Episcopal Church, Woodstock, New York
Ecclesiasticus 44:1-10,13,14; Psalm 149
Revelation 7:2-4.9-17; Matthew 5:1-12

Two thousand years of church history have served to solidify numerous strong and healthy celebrations, among them the celebration of All Saints' Day. It is wonderfully theological and affirmingly positive and healthy.

In the academic setting where I currently minister [an orthodox Christian liberal arts college in the Tribeca section of Manhattan, New York City], I have some of the keenest scholarly minds in America coupled with the wonderfully Christian spirits of these professors. We have a good time in the work we do. However, several of my colleagues are given to the academic pursuit of Christian truth divorced from the application of it to "rubber-hits-the-road" spiritual day-to-day living. There is a bit of disagreement over the philosophical approach I take as dean, that all theology is practical theology.

There is a basic Biblical conviction that what God reveals, God reveals for the benefit and redemption of humanity. It was Paul Tillich, the great theologian of a generation past who wrote, "Being religious [theological is my term] means asking passionate the question of the meaning of our existence and being willing to receive answers even if the answers hurt."

The amazing truth is that the answers often heal rather than hurt. And this is the truth of All Saints' theology and doctrine.

And so, in approaching this celebration where we sing "For all the saints, who from their labors rest..." and "I sing a song of the saints of God...," I asked the simple question, "What are the implications of this truth?" And the answers are five-fold, at least.

First, the doctrine of the communion of the saints establishes that we are not alone. The Epistle to the Hebrews assures us that we are "encompassed about by a great cloud of witnesses." We are surrounded by thousands of years of normal people who attempted by grace to be the people of God and who continue to exist. Julian of Norwich insightfully remembered, "If I look at myself I am nothing. If I look at us, I am hopeful." Chesterton assured us that, "Every heresy has been an effort to narrow the church." All Saints' theology expands the Body of Christ and assures us that we are not alone.

Phyllis McGinley in *Saint Watching* writes:

"The wonderful thing about saints is that they were *human*. They lost their tempers, got hungry, scolded God, were egotistical or testy or impatient in their turns, made mistakes and regretted them. Still they went on doggedly blundering toward heaven. And this is our heritage and hope. We are not alone."

A second truth of All Saints' doctrine is that it challenges us with reasonable success. There is no demand of perfection, no great commandments of super-humanity. "In that while we were yet sinners, Christ died for us," is a firm and clear statement of atonement theology. Rufus Jones summarizes this most poignantly: "Saints are not made for haloes, or for inward thrills; they are made to become the focus points of light and power...a good mother, a good neighbor, a good constructive force in society, a fragrance and a blessing." Someone aptly defined a saint this way: "Saint: a dead sinner revised and edited." Read the lives of real believers and we discover – "God helping, I'll be one too!"

The third doctrinal benefit of All Saints' theology is that it increases our numbers at worship. Each Sunday I speak with Perk as to our total attendance here at St. Gregory's. We must, for obvious reasons keep records. But we don't keep records to impress God – God alone counts those at worship.

In a few minutes, I will lead us in a Eucharistic prayer that says, "Therefore with angels and archangels and all the company of heaven, we laud and magnify your glorious name evermore praising you and say-ing…."

I spent nineteen years of my professional ministerial life in a denomination that emphasized church growth, and I am committed to the growth of the local parish. Every parish I have had the privilege of pastoring has grown significantly – it is an indicator of health and vitality, I believe. But to make this our only emphasis is to miss the fact that we cannot count the number of people at worship right now. There is the global com-munity of believers alive on earth at this moment, and there is the company of heaven – innumerable – wor-shipping at the throne of the Lamb of God. Therefore there is no such thing as a small church.

There is a fourth practical side of All Saints' doc-trine and that is that it instructs us that life continues. In the burial office are the most promising words, "life is changed – not ended!" The Christian promise is eter-nal life from the very words of Jesus himself, "For God loved the world so much that God gave the only begot-ten Son that whoever believes in Him should not per-ish but have everlasting life [John 3:16 – paraphrase].

The true story is related of a coach from a univer-sity in Ohio who had a player on his football team who was the most incapable player he had ever experienced. Whenever the coach allowed this player to play, the team lost the game. Needless to say the fellow sat on the sidelines most of the seasons.

Often the coach would see the student walking his father around the campus, explaining and describing the campus to him, for his father was totally blind and used a white cane to sense his way along. The happened several times each year through the boy's college career.

One day the team was doing particularly poorly, without the help of this lad. As the game neared the end, the boy said to the coach, "Coach, since we're going to lose this game anyway, would you please put me in and let me play?" The coach figured it could not hurt and acquiesced to the boy's request.

Immediately the game turned around, and to make a long story short, the fellow led his team to victory. They celebrated his efforts and carried him around on their shoulders and finally to the locker room. Once there, the coach asked, "What in the world has gotten into you? You played better than ever before. You won us the game.!"

The student relied, "Coach, my dad died this week, and, well, this is the first game he's ever been able to see me play."

While we cannot build a doctrine on this, it does, nonetheless, illustrate a Christian conviction that life is changed, not ended, and that we are surrounded by a great "cloud of witnesses."

Finally, the doctrine of All Saints' assures us of a glorious hope. We celebrate the lives of the saints who have gone on before, precisely because they have gone on before and we plan to join them.

Several years ago I was called on to preach the homily at my best friend's funeral. It was the most difficult work I have ever been called on to perform. Half way through working on the sermon, I knew Ray was with me, assuring me that the Scripture is reliable and trustworthy, that Jesus' words ring true: "In my Father's house are many rooms, if it were not so, I would have told you. I go to prepare a place for you, and if I go to prepare a place for you I will come again that where I am, there you may also be." Apostle Paul said that if we hope only in this world, we are of all people "most miserable."

And so, beloved friends in God:

"When engulfed by the terrors of tempestuous sea,
Unknown waves before you roll.
At the end of doubt and peril is eternity,
Though fear and conflict seize your soul.

"When surrounded by the blackness of the
darkest night,
O how lonely death can be.
At the end of this long tunnel is a shining light,
For death is swallowed up in victory.

"But just think of stepping on shore,
And finding it heaven.
Of touching a hand,
And finding it's God's.
Of breathing new air,
And finding it celestial.
Of waking up in glory,
And finding it home!"

L. E. Singer & Don Wyrtzen

"Therefore with angels and archangels and with all the company of heaven, we laud and magnify your glorious name, evermore praising you and saying, 'Holy, holy, holy.'" Amen!

CHAPTER 105
THE TWENTY-THIRD SUNDAY AFTER PENTECOST

St. Gregory's Episcopal Church, Woodstock, New York
Job 19:23-27a; Psalm 17; II Thessalonians 2:13-3:5
Luke 20:27-38

The account is told of the great athlete Mohammed Ali being in an airplane when the pilot announced that they were beginning to experience moderate turbulence and that all seat belts must be fastened. As the stewardess walked through the plane she saw that his was not fastened and said, "Sir, you must fasten your seat belt as we fly through this turbulence." To which Mr. Ali replied, "Superman don't need no seat belt." Without missing a beat, the stewardess retorted, "Superman don't need no airplane!"

Sometimes we think more highly of our bodies than we ought. Much of the erotomania and Playboy philosophy of the second half of the last century led us to believe that our bodies were all that there was. Secular psychology added to the conviction by showing us in Freudian terms that the mind is nothing but the brain at work and there is no essential difference between the two. That humanity is physical and nothing more was drummed into us over and over from myriad sources.

But for two-thousand years, the church has said much the opposite: that the body is evil and that spirit is good. Such a position, though officially condemned as heresy as in so many heterodox movements, has still reigned supreme in the church in the West (and I suspect in the East as well). Yet the texts of the morning seem to indicate something immensely different. And allow me to show you why I say this.

First, Job, the earliest human we encounter in Biblical history is confident that in the eternal state of things, it will be "in my body" that he shall see God. There is a confidence that the body has a place in eternity and in the infinite plan of God.

Second, Paul informs the believers at Thessalonica that they are to have their bodies doing "good works." That, not in the sense of earning anything in God's eyes but in the sense of working out their believer status, their bodies will show their loyalties.

And finally, in the Gospel record we are assured that God is the God of the living, and the dead are raised in the final and ultimate resurrection. There is a destiny for the body.

All of this together strongly indicates that the body figures completely into the scope of Christian faith and action. Things related to the body are wonderfully planned as well. The Rev'd Carroll M. Bates in *The Human Body: Good or Evil?* writes:

"We like to think that God's creatures are responsible for our sins! They are not! We like to blame the sins of the flesh on the human body instead of our selves, and so we call the body and its natural appetites evil! We like to blame drunkenness on wine or alcoholic drinks; and so heretics such as the Albigenses or Puritans, decided that these things (such as the human body and wine)—which God had created—were evil in themselves and had been created by the Devil! The heresy has effected all of Christendom! It gives us a feeling of righteousness to blame our sins on God's creation and creatures, instead of on ourselves—but this is *self-righteousness!*"

Bates says much more exciting things about the body, but we will leave the challenge there. The meaning is clear: the body is good.

The great St. Francis of Assisi once gathered all his brothers together with a challenge: "Go forth preaching the Gospel: if you must, use words." The implication is powerfully clear – their physical presence in the world was to be the Gospel presentation. And that could not come from an evil body.

The New Testament uses the Greek word *soma* for "body," meaning "the instrument of life." It is the aspect of the human person that makes us world conscious. The Greek word *sarx* is the word used for "flesh," often employed by Paul especially for a spiritual desire for that which is evil and anti-Christ. It does not necessarily refer to the physical flesh at all. It is rather "the weaker element in human nature."

So good is the body God created, that it is the repository for incarnate Deity – a celebration we will face in but six weeks. Incarnate, from the Latin *carne* meaning meat – "God in the meat!" I like my chili, but it must be "con carne," "with meat!" So must be my Savior!

Then the goodness of the body serves as a metaphor for the people of God, the "Body of Christ!" Would God employ an evil thing as the metaphor for the people who are under the redemptive provisions that God provides from His own being? Of course not! It is a powerful polemic for the goodness of the body itself.

Third, the body is the dwelling place of Holy Spirit. The Church has missed this truth for centuries, and it is the plainest possible teaching of the Apostle Paul. In I Corinthians 6:19, the words could not be more forcefully clear, "Do you not know that your body (soma) is the temple (the dwelling place) of the Holy Spirit?" [I often challenge my students who are sure that Holy Spirit lives in their spirit to read this and then the next morning, after their shower to stand naked in front of a full-length mirror and when the hilarious laughter ceases, to point to their body and say "that body is the temple of Holy Spirit who is in you!]. You may wish to do this exercise on Monday morning as well! It is quite health-giving!

Finally, the body is the means of the outworking of spiritual reality. All those things we are given to do as Christian acts are done in the body. Speaking kindness, gentleness, serving, loving, hospitality, peace – these are all actions of the body as well as mind-sets of the soul. All our acts, our *sacred acts,* our *sacrificial acts,* our *servant acts* are done in the body. And God calls that good!

And lest we err on the side of the hedonists or the Puritans, we must hear C. S. Lewis in his keenest statement on the physical frame:

"Man has held three views of his body. First there is that of the ascetic Pagans who called it the prison or the "tomb" of the soul, and of Christians like Fisher to whom it was a "sack of dung," food for worms, filthy, shameful, a source of nothing but temptation to bad men and humiliation to good men. Then there are the Neo-Pagans (they seldom know Greek), the nudists and the sufferers from Dark Gods, to whom the body is glorious. But thirdly we have the view which St. Francis expressed by calling his body "Brother Ass." All three may be—I am not sure—defensible; but give me St. Francis for my money. Ass is exquisitely right because no one in his senses can either revere or hate a donkey. It is a useful, sturdy, lazy, obstinate, patient, lovable, and infuriating beast; deserving now the stick and now the carrot; both pathetically and absurdidly beautiful. So the body. There's no living with it till we recognize that one of its functions in our lives is to play the part of buffoon."

Is it any wonder that St. Francis is called a fool for God? Let us, too, give ourselves, "our souls and bodies, to be a living sacrifice to God." Amen!

CHAPTER 106
THE TWENTY-FOURTH SUNDAY AFTER PENTECOST

St. Gregory's Episcopal Church, Woodstock, New York
Malachi 3:13-4:2a, 5-6; Psalm 98; II Thessalonians 3:6-13
Luke 21:5-19

As with most of Holy Scripture, we have interplays in today's lessons between God and humanity. This is the kernel of the Scriptures, and today is no different. We are told something of the Judeo-Christian God, something of the believer, and something of the relationship between the two. The omnipresence of the Scriptural God is a given in the Bible; and that the same God is involved in the affairs of humanity is often questioned; it is never a conclusion of honest reflection. The prophecy of the day is firm indication of this.

One of Britain's bishops once wrote:

"There was a young man who thought God
would find it exceedingly odd
when He sees that this tree continues to be
when there is no one about in the quad.
'Young man, your astonishment soars!

I'm always about in the quad,
and that's why this tree will continue to be,
since observed by yours faithfully, God."

So first we see that God is a God of conversation. As such, the Scriptural God hears complaints. I often tell my students, or those with whom I am counseling, to let God know when you have a beef with him. God has broad shoulders and can take your complaints. Years ago, David Wilkerson, of Teen Challenge fame [an organization that has literally saved thousands of young people from drugs and a life on the street] wrote a book titled, *I'm Not Mad at God.* I have often wanted to write the sequel, *I Am Mad at God.* This has been a time immemorial reaction of humanity to God who acts differently that we would predict.

But God is also a God who argues His cause. Called to think with the rationale of redemption, the Christian believer is challenged to know that God's ways vary from our ways at very definite points. Often God's way up is down; God's way in is out; God's way of deliverance is through rather than from; poverty is riches; and the first is to be the last. It is contrary to popular, secular philosophy; it is God's way.

The great Christian thinker and writer, C. S. Lewis captures this in a powerful way in his essay, "The Efficacy of Prayer," in the book, *The World's Last Night and Other Essays:*

"Our act, when we pray, must not, any more than all our other acts be separated from the continuous acts of God Himself, in which alone all finite causes operate.

"It would be even worse to think of those who get what they pray for as a sort of court favorites, people who have influence with the throne. The refused prayer of Christ in Gethsemane is answer enough to that! And I dare not leave out the hard saying which I once heard from an experienced Christian: 'I have seen many striking answers to prayer and more than one that I thought miraculous. But they usually come at the beginning: before conversion, or soon after it. As the Christian life proceeds, they tend to be rarer. The refusals, too, are not only more frequent; they become more unmistakable, more emphatic.'

"Does God then forsake just those who serve him best? Well, He who served Him best of all said, near His tortured death, 'Why hast Thou forsaken me?' When God becomes man, that Man, of all others, is least comforted by God, at His greatest need. There is a mystery here which, even if I had the power, I might not have the courage to explore. Meanwhile, little people like you and me, if our prayers are sometimes granted, beyond all hope and probability, had better not draw hasty conclusions to our own advantage. If we were stronger, we might be less tenderly treated. If we were braver, we might be sent, with far less help, to defend far more desperate posts in the great battle."

God is a God who argues His cause. God also is a God who reasons out our irrationalities. The preceding quote tells us that; the prophet posited it many years ago. When Job was thinking himself somebody, God rationally showed him otherwise. We can also conclude that God invites thinking and celebrates reflection.

The epistle reading turns our attention to our being a purposeful believer, a person of meaningful intent. "Be not weary in well-doing," says Apostle Paul, precisely because well doing makes one weary. The challenge is to succeed when that is not the easiest thing to do. And this leads us to the Gospel account which tells us that the God-human relationship is a relationship of endurance. By endurance, says Jesus "you will gain your life." Notice he doesn't intimate that we will gain our salvation by endurance, that is all of grace. But rather, endurance is the doorway to life! There is a bunch of living to do!

Ralph Cushman, the great Methodist divine writes this marvelous challenge:

I thank Thee just for life,
The chance to live,
To be alive! So great Thy gift,
If Thou dost nothing give.
Besides, it is enough,

To breathe Thy air,
To walk the mountain sod,
To feel the play of mighty winds,
To look Thee in the face,
And call Thee God!

The relationship is one of endurance. Therefore, live. So often the church has not freed us to live, but bound us to do, and Jesus would have none of that.

Mother Theresa in another moment of brilliant relationship with God said, "God I know that you will not give me more than I can handle. I just wish you didn't trust me so much." And in the difficulties, she still spoke to God.

I invite us to think of that relationship: us, to a God who keeps converse with those who believe. Amen.

CHAPTER 107
CHRIST THE KING

St. Gregory's Episcopal Church, Woodstock, New York
Jeremiah 23:1-6; Psalm 46; Colossians 1:11-20
Luke 23:35-43

The prevailing theology of 2,000 years of church history is that God is angry at humanity. It has kept many Roman Catholics, on the one hand, and many Protestant fundamentalists, on the other, in constant fear of judgment and punishment. Christ as King was always tempered with the Christ as judge motif in theology and preaching. Probably the quintessential representative of this was the hyper-Calvinist, Jonathan Edwards in early New England. When I was a student at Onteora High School, part of the New York State literature curriculum was the reading of *"Sinners in the Hands of An Angry God."* It was funny to a teenager and now I find it offensive and radically anti-Biblical and solidly anti-Christ in its teaching. Let's listen to a paragraph or two:

"The God that holds you over the pit of hell, much as one holds a spider, or some loathsome insect over the fire, abhors you, and is dreadfully provoked: his wrath towards you burns life fire; he looks upon you as worthy of nothing else but to be cast into the fire; he is of purer eyes than to bear to have you in his sight; you are ten thousand times more abominable in his sight, than the most hateful venomous serpent is in ours. You have offended him infinitely more than ever a stubborn rebel did his prince; and yet it is nothing but His hand that holds you from falling into the fire at this moment....

"O sinner! Consider the fearful danger you are in: it is a great furnace of wrath, a wide and bottomless pit, full of the fire of wrath, that you are held over in the hand of that God, whose wrath is provoked and incensed much against you, as against many of the damned in hell. You hang by a slender thread, with the flames of divine wrath flashing about it, and ready every moment to singe it, and burn it asunder...."

Now aren't you glad you came to church this morning? Good literature maybe; miserably lousy theology, however. It ignores the *agapao,* the love of God; and it deprecates the finished work of Christ, upon whom the wrath and judgment of God was completely and finally settled. King Jesus reigns today because God's wrath was satisfied totally, completely, and finally.

In light of this, let's take a keen little look at the pericopes of the morning. In Jeremiah, God tells Judah, that in spite of the situations and circumstances of failure, judgment, and loss that they find themselves, God will do a great thing for them. No less than five times does God, in a positive sense, full of promise, say, "I will...do...thus and so." This is a declaration of God's position toward humanity. God looks with favored eye, redeeming, saving, keeping, sanctifying. God has done this since the beginning, and continues to do so today. "I will," says God and so we trust.

The epistle reading challenges us with the words, "May you be strengthened with all power according to his (Jesus') glorious might..." Here we are granted the ability to become because of God's provision for humanity. Some saint of days gone by has rightly said, "God's will shall not lead you where God's providence cannot keep you." This is the keeping posture of King Jesus. And God does it repeatedly for ages upon ages and for person upon person. Over and over the provision is shown and applied.

And the Gospel is a power declaration that, "Today you will be with me in paradise." The "I will" of God in Jeremiah is echoed in Jesus' words here "you will." You and I are given the ability to become because God has so ordained. God is for you. God is, as a preacher friend of mine says, "quite fond of you." This is the reality of humanity in God. And God does this repeatedly, moment by moment, as the reigning Christ welcomes one after another into the prepared paradise of glory.

But lest we get too heavenly minded to be of any earthly good, let's move on.

Two insightful writers catch this intimacy and immanence of the reigning Christ in powerful ways. First, from *Orthodoxy* by G. K. Chesterton,

"Because Children have abounding vitality, because they are in spirit fierce and free, therefore they want things repeated and unchanged. They always say, "Do it again"; and the grown-up person does it again until he is nearly dead. For grown up people are not strong enough to exult in monotony. It is possible that God says every morning, "Do it again" to the sun; and every evening, 'Do it again' to the moon. It may not be automatic necessity that makes all daisies alike; it may be that God makes every daisy separately, but has never got tired of making them. It may be that He has the eternal appetite of infancy; for we have sinned and grown old, and our Father is younger than we. The repetition in Nature may not be a mere recurrence; it may be a theatrical encore."

Chesterton is at his best here. We are assured that God is for the world not against it! That God, somehow in the monotony of repetition, keeps on re-creating what was originally created, and that was very good! Quite the opposite of poor old Jonathan Edwards, I would say!

Then Father Robert Farrar Capon (you may have some of his cookbooks at home), an Episcopal priest from Long Island, writes:

"This world is *fundamentally* unnecessary. Nothing *has to* be. It needs a creator not only for its beginning but for every moment of its being....What happens is not that the Trinity manufactures the first duck and then the ducks take over the duck business as a kind of cottage industry. It is that every duck, down at the roots of its being, at the level where what is needed is not the ability to fertilize duck eggs but the moxie to stand outside of nothing—to *be* when there is no necessity of being—every duck at that level is a creative response to the creative act of God....It means that God the Father *thinks up* duck #47307 for the month of May, A.D. 1723, that God the Spirit rushes over to the edge of the formless void and, with unutterable groanings *broods* duck #47307, and the over his brooding, God the Son the eternal Word triumphantly *shouts* 'Duck #47307!' And presto! You have a duck. Not one, you will note tossed off in response to some mindless decree that there may as well be ducks as alligators, but one neatly fielded up in a game of delight by the eternal archetypes of Tinker, Evers, and Chance. The world isn't God's surplus inventory of artifacts, it is a whole barrelful of apples of his eye, constantly juggled, relished, and exchanged by the persons of the Trinity.

No wonder we love circuses, games, and magic. They prove we are in the image of God."

Now all of that to say this, if God delights in the monotonous repetition of morning, evening, and ducks, God must also delight in the monotonous repetition of those of us who awake each morning, sleep each evening, and hear the quack of ducks. There is nothing more satisfying than to have confirmed by the Scriptures that King Jesus isn't mad at us, but rather is positioned to will our success; set to provide for our continued spiritual life; and ready to invite us into a transcendent reality that relates us continually to him. We can either have sinners in the hands of an angry God, or we can be sinners in the hands of the reigning Jesus. The choice is that simple. Amen!

To order additional copies of

HIDDEN
MIRTH
THE GRACE BEHIND THE GOODNESS

Have your credit card ready and call:

1-877-421-READ (7323)

or please visit our web site at
www.pleasantword.com

Also available at:
www.amazon.com
and
www.barnesandnoble.com

Printed in the United States
73613LV00001B/1-21